Advances in Probabilistic and Other Parsing Technologies

Text, Speech and Language Technology

VOLUME 16

The titles published in this series are listed at the end of this volume.

Advances in Probabilistic and Other Parsing Technologies

Edited by

Harry Bunt
Tilburg University, The Netherlands

and

Anton Nijholt
University of Twente, Enschede, The Netherlands

KLUWER ACADEMIC PUBLISHERS
DORDRECHT / BOSTON / LONDON

A C.I.P. Catalogue record for this book is available from the Library of Congress.

ISBN 978-90-481-5579-8

Published by Kluwer Academic Publishers,
P.O. Box 17, 3300 AA Dordrecht, The Netherlands.

Sold and distributed in North, Central and South America
by Kluwer Academic Publishers,
101 Philip Drive, Norwell, MA 02061, U.S.A.

In all other countries, sold and distributed
by Kluwer Academic Publishers,
P.O. Box 322, 3300 AH Dordrecht, The Netherlands.

Printed on acid-free paper

Contents

List of Figures

ix

List of Tables

Acknowledgements

Previous versions of the papers in this book were presented at the Fifth International Workshop on Parsing Technologies (IWPT'97), that took place at MIT in Boston/Cambridge in September 1997. The workshop was organized by Bob Berwick (local arrangements chair), Harry Bunt (general chair), and Anton Nijholt (progamme chair). Of the 24 papers that were presented, 12 were selected for publication in book form. These papers were revised and extended by the authors in consultation with the editors, resulting in the chapters 2–13 of the present volume. These chapters show a strong orientation toward the development of new methods and techniques for probabilistic and approximative parsing. In the introductory chapter, the editors relate these chapters and their orientation to current issues and developments in the field of parsing technology.

We wish to acknowledge the important role of the IWPT'97 programme committee in reviewing submitted papers; these reviews have been the basis for selecting the material published in this book. The programme committee consisted of Bob Berwick, Harry Bunt, Bob Carpenter, Eva Hajičová, Mark Johnson, Aravind Joshi, Ron Kaplan, Martin Kay, Bernard Lang, Alon Lavie, Makoto Nagao, Anton Nijholt, Mark Steedman, Masaru Tomita, K. Vijay-Shanker, David Weir, Kent Wittenburg and Mats Wirén.

We would like to especially thank Hendri Hondorp for invaluable LaTeX support in the preparation of the final manuscript of this book.

Harry Bunt and Anton Nijholt

Chapter 1

NEW PARSING TECHNOLOGIES

BUNT Harry
*Computational Linguistics and Artificial Intelligence Unit, Tilburg University, 5000 LE Tilburg,
The Netherlands*
bunt@kub.nl

NIJHOLT Anton
*Department of Computer Science, University of Twente, P.O. Box 217, 7500 AE Enschede, The
Netherlands*
anijholt@cs.utwente.nl

1   WHY NEW PARSING TECHNOLOGIES?

Parsing technology is concerned with the automatic decomposition of complex structures into their constituent parts, a task that computers were applied to first, in their early days, in relation to the compilation and interpretation of computer programs. Since computer programs have in common with written text that they consist of symbol strings that can be decomposed into meaningful substrings, the idea soon came up to apply the techniques of programming language parsing to natural language expressions.

Parsing a natural language sentence is something altogether different from parsing a line in a computer program, however, as was soon recognized, for the following main reasons:

Ambiguity: Natural language sentences nearly always allow more than one decomposition into constituent parts, in contrast with formal languages, which are typically designed to be syntactically unambiguous. For parsing, the problem with ambiguity is that it occurs not only at sentence level but also locally, in smaller structures. In fact, it is the rule rather than the exception that a pair of adjacent words can enter into more than one syntactic relationship. This causes an explosion of the number of possible syntactic combinations that a parser has to consider at higher,

1

H. Bunt and A. Nijholt (eds.), Advances in Probabilistic and Other Parsing Technologies, 1–12.
© 2000 *Kluwer Academic Publishers.*

phrasal levels, and is the major source of inefficiency in natural language parsing.

Variability: In their grammatical details, natural languages exhibit a considerable amount of capriciousness. Natural language grammars are therefore inherently much more complex than formal language grammars, either in the rules that they use or in the grammatical units that the rules operate on (notably, the lexical structures). This is one of the reasons why, in spite of many years of linguistic research, we have no complete and accurate formal descriptions of any existing natural language, which is one of the reasons why *robustness* is an issue in natural language parsing: sooner or later a natural language parser is confronted with input structures that its grammar does not cover.

Equivocalness: The lack of complete and accurate descriptions of natural languages is caused not only by their complexity and variability, but also by the fact that it is not always clear whether something is grammatically correct in a given language or not. Grammatical correctness is often not a black and white matter, but rather a matter of degree. Natural languages have somewhat fuzzy boundaries. A grammar that aims at describing precisely how the sentences of the language may be built up from constituent parts, has to also make decisions in borderline cases. A practical natural language parser should probably be required to parse borderline case sentences, but should better not consider borderline case interpretations of sentence *parts* in a grammatically perfect sentence. This is witnessed by the well-known technique allowing a parser to handle grammatically imperfect sentences by relaxing certain syntactic conditions; this is known to degrade parsing efficiency a lot, since the parser now faces a greater amount of local ambiguity.

Opennes: Natural languages are 'open' communicative systems, continuously changing and incorporating elements from outside the language. For instance, numerical expressions, like '95.2', and expressions from physics, chemistry, computer science, medicine, and other disciplines, like 'kilobytes/second', 'minus 345 degrees Kelvin', 'you can ftp or telnet', '@', ':-)', 'H_2O', and 'surfactant phosphatidylcholine', mix freely with natural language expressions. The openness of natural languages in fact makes it questionable whether it is possible in principle to provide exhaustive, precise charaterizations of natural languages. Surely, attempts to produce exhaustive descriptions of all the *terms* that may occur in natural language sentences are doomed to failure. The open character of natural languages also suggests that sentence parsing can benefit from consulting and applying nonlinguistic knowledge, and that parsing should ideally be integrated with other processing, rather than form an isolated process.

Each of these characteristics of natural language and its parsing calls for developing other types of parsing techniques than for formal languages. In particular, probabilistic, approximative, and underspecification techniques have recently developed and appear to be promising.

1.1 PROBABILISTIC PARSING

Probabilistic parsing aims at finding the most probably parse of a given input (first or only), and is based on the observation that, when words or phrases can be combined in more than one way to form a larger constituent, some ways of combining them are more likely than others. Such observations are based on the relative frequencies of occurrence of the possible combinations in a representative corpus.

The study of natural language parsing is usually restricted to syntactic decomposition, taking only syntactic information into account. One might think that ambiguity is primarily a *semantic* phenomenon, that is less important in purely syntactic analysis. This is true to the extent that, when we look at the potential semantic interpretations of a given sentence, indeed the number is much higher than the number of possible syntactic interpretations.[1] Still, purely syntactic ambiguity is also a pervasive phenomenon in natural language; a rather conservative estimate is that an average 16-word sentence has in the order of 65.000 different syntactic analyses.[2]

Probabilistic parsing can be helpful for dealing with ambiguity, because a parser that is able to discard unlikely analyses on the fly can leave theoretically possible but unlikely combinations of words and phrases out of consideration, or at least postpone considering them until the need arises, for instance because using only likely combinations does not result in an analysis of the sentence as a whole. In an application domain where the relative frequencies of syntactic structures matches well with the probabilities used by the parser, this will on average save a lot of time.

The variable, capricious nature of natural languages, together with their equivocalness and their open character, have obstructed attempts to build generative grammars that would exhaustively and accurately describe the English language or any other natural language, even when its use is restricted to a certain domain of discourse or to a particular type of activity. One way to get around this is to use a corpus that records the language use in a particular domain to generate a grammar from the structures that are found in the corpus. When constructing such a corpus-induced grammar, it is natural to take the relative frequencies into account of the structures that are encountered. Structures with a very low frequency may for example be the accidental result of a printing error or some damage in a document, and should not be included in the grammar at all. Again, substantial differences in frequency may be attractive to record in the grammar for allowing a parser to find the most probable parse of a given sentence more efficiently.

A grammar that reflects the fact that natural languages have fuzzy boundaries seems bound to somehow attach weights to its syntactic structures, indicating that some constructions are more central to the language than others. One way to do this is, again, in terms of probabilities, assuming that borderline cases occur less frequently than perfectly correct uses of the language. This assumption is clearly not uncontroversial from a linguistic point of view, as frequency of occurrence is in general not a good measure of grammaticality, but seems adequate from a practical computational point of view: structures that occur rather frequently should, irrespective of their theoretical linguistic status, be expected by a parser and should be handled as well as linguistically perfect structures with a similar frequency. A probabilistic approach to parsing therefore seems appropriate also in view of the equivocalness of natural languages.

The open character of natural languages calls for an approach to constructing characterizations of natural language which are not, or at least not only, in terms of (theoretical) linguistic knowledge but also in terms of what is actually found in registrations of language use. It is in fact hard to imagine any other way to construct descriptively adequate grammars that do justice to the open character of natural language. Again, for the sake of parsing efficiency, once a corpus-based approach is followed it would only seem wise and natural to take the importance, in terms of relative frequency, of the various structures into account.

The ambiguity, the variability, the equivocalness, and the openness of natural languages have of course been realized long ago by computational linguists, and indeed the idea of probabilistic parsing is not new. However, the development of powerful probabilistic grammars and parsers depends critically on the availability of sufficiently large and rich corpora, in particular of corpora tagged with syntactic interpretations. One of the great developments in computational linguistics in recent years has been the development of such corpora, with the Penn Treebank (Marcus et al., 1994; Charniak, 1996) as a paramount example. As a result, the investigation of and experimentation with probabilistic and other corpus-based approaches to grammar and parser development have seen an impressive upsurge, which is reflected in this book.

1.2 APPROXIMATION, UNDERSPECIFICATION, AND OTHER TECHNIQUES

To increase parsing efficiency, an important class of techniques consists of the use of some form of approximation, either at the level of the grammar, at that of parsing control, or at that of the representations that the parser constructs.

Approximation at the level of grammar concerns the replacement of a given type of grammar by a simpler one that generates approximately the same language and that allows more efficient parsing. An example of this is the construction of a finite automaton from a context-free grammar, such that the regular language accepted by the automaton consists of the strings generated by the context-fee grammar plus an additional set of strings. The finite automaton can than be said to approximate the context-free grammar. This idea has been applied both to the error handling for programming language parsing (Heckert, 1994) and to the efficient parsing of natural language (Pereira and Wright, 1991). Similarly, context-free approximations have been proposed for unification-based grammars like HPSG and PATR-II (Kiefer and Krieger, 2000).

Approximation at the level of parser control consists of designing strategies that lead to the desired result in a number of steps each of which is closer to that result, for instance a process which aims at finding the 'best' analysis by filtering out invalid syntactic analyses in an efficient way. An approach of this kind is discussed in the chapter by Schmid in this volume.

Approximation may also be used in the representations that a parser constructs. A particular technique that has been proposed for dealing with syntactic ambiguity, and that could potentially also be of interest for dealing with the variability and the equivocalness as well as the open character of natural languages, is the use of *underspecification*. This was suggested originally by Marcus et al. (1983) in the context of designing a *deterministic* parser, that is a parser that would never have to retrace its steps unless in the case of garden path sentences. Marcus et al. (1983) suggested to conceive of a parser as having the task not to construct all the possible syntactic analysis trees of the substructures of the sentence that it tries to parse, but to construct a *description* of these trees. This approach, called '*D-Theory*', opens new possibilities to handle ambiguity because the description of a set of trees can be seen as a *partial* or *underspecified* representation of any of the trees that fit the description. A D-Theory parser does not necessarily worry about all the syntactic ambiguities that it encounters; rather than creating alternative analysis trees it constructs a description that fits both trees. The idea of D-Theory has in recent years been applied to (Lexicalized) Tree-Adjoining Grammar by K. Vijay-Shanker and colleagues (see Vijay-Shanker, 1992; Rambow, Vijay-Shanker and Weir, 1995; Rogers and Vijay-Shanker, 1996). D-Theory parsing seems very much in line with the approach in computational semantics of dealing with semantic ambiguity by means of *underspecified semantic representations*, i.e. representations that represent only the semantic information that a given sentence contains, leaving open those semantic aspects that the sentence does not unambiguously specify - in particular leaving semantic ambiguities like relative scopings underspecified.[3] The use of underspecified semantic representations has the computational advantage of allowing *monotonic interpretation*: as further semantic and/or pragmatic, contextual information becomes available, some or all of the underspecification can be resolved. Note that this is similar to the determinism in parsing that D-theory is after. The paper by Chen and Vijay-Shanker in this volume presents new developments in D-Theory parsing applied to Tree-Adjoining Grammar.

We mentioned above that the semantic ambiguity of a natural language sentence is much greater than its syntactic ambiguity; in that respect, purely syntactic analysis is simpler than when semantics is taken into consideration. On the other hand, one of the reasons why people are only rarely aware of syntactic ambiguity is because they use semantic (or, more generally, contextual) information to discard invalid analyses while parsing, so a purely syntactic parser can also be said to have an extra difficult task if it does not have access to semantic information. Well, why shouldn't it? Indeed, attempts at designing 'intelligent' integrated analysers that use semantic and (other) contextual information have occasionally been made (e.g. Winograd, 1983). A major problem for an integrated approach is that parsers are typically meant to be general-purpose, applicable to any domain of discourse, and consequentially such parsers should have access to semantic information about any domain of discourse.[4] An attractive possibility would seem to be a syntactic parser that allows domain-specific information to be 'plugged in' when the parser is applied to a particular domain of discourse. Steps in this direction have been taken in modular analysis systems, such as CARAMEL (Sabah and Briffault, 1993), but the analysers that have been developed in this category do not have a really sophisticated way of integrating the semantic information in the syntactic analysis. The chapters by Hektoen and by Hahn et al. in this volume suggest new ideas, partly in combination with probabilistic techniques, for applying semantic and contextual information during parsing.

2   ABOUT THIS BOOK

The first group of chapters in this book is concerned with probabilistic approaches to parsing, beginning with a set of five chapters where the focus is on the design of probabilistic grammars. The first and the second chapter both consider the use of frequency information in *lexicalized* grammars, i.e. grammars in which grammatical rules are specialized for some individual word.

Carroll and Weir in their chapter *Encoding frequency information in lexicalized grammars* address the issue of how to associate frequency information with lexicalized grammar formalisms, using Lexicalized Tree Adjoining Grammar as a representative formalism. They systematically consider a range of alternative possibilities of which they evaluate the theoretical adequacy and the empirical perspective using data from large treebanks. They also propose three orthogonal techniques for backing off probability estimates to cope with the large number of parameters involved.

Eisner in his chapter *Bilexical grammars and a cubic-time probabilistic parser* introduces weighted bilexical grammars, a formalism in which individual lexical items can have idiosyncratic selectional influences on each other. Such 'bilexicalism' is a theme in a considerable body of current work in parsing. Eisner's new formalism is derived from dependency grammars, but can also be used to model other bilexical approaches, including a variety of phrase-structure grammars and all link grammars. Its scoring approach is compatible with a wide variety of probability models. Eisner also presents a new parsing algorithm that has been implemented and used in large parsing experiments and which is $O(n^3)$, where the obvious parsing algorithm for bilexical grammars that most authors use is $O(n^5)$.

Goodman presents a new probabilistic grammar formalism in his chapter, *Probabilistic Feature Grammars*. A PFG combines most of the best properties of several other formalisms, and in experiments has a comparable or better performance. A PFG uses features with probabilities that are conditioned on other features in a local context. Because of the locality of the conditioning, efficient polynomial time parsing is possible for computing inside, outside, and Viterbi parses. Precision and recall are comparable to the state of the art with words, and the best reported without words. Probabilistic Feature Grammars can also be used for statistical language modelling to support applications like speech recognition. Furthermore, the dynamic programming used in the model is amenable to efficient rescoring of lattices output by speech recognizers.

In the chapter *Probabilistic GLR Parsing*, the authors **Inui, Sornlertlamvanich, Tanaka and Tokunaga** present a new formalization of probabilistic GLR language modeling for statistical parsing. This new formalization is a refinement of Briscoe and Carroll's generalized probabilistic LR model (Briscoe and Carroll, 1993), which assigns a probability to each LR parsing action according to its left and right context. Briscoe and Carroll's model is easily implemented and trained, but lacks a well-founded normalization of probabilities. The authors overcome this drawback while maintaining the advantages of the original model, and demonstrate through examples that the refined model is expected to improve parsing performance.

Manning and Carpenter in their chapter *Probabilistic parsing using left-corner language models* introduce another new probabilistic grammar model, which is based on left-corner parsing. Left-corner parsing has the attractive feature that it allows the probability of a grammar rule to be conditioned on both top-down and bottom-up derivations. The authors develop the underlying theory, and explain how a grammar can be induced from analyzed data. Using a probabilistic left-corner grammar induced from the Penn Treebank, they show that the left-corner approach provides an advantage over simple top-down probabilistic context-free grammars in parsing the Wall Street Journal. As a side result, they note that the Penn Treebank forms a fairly weak testbed due to the flatness of its trees and to the overgeneration and undergeneration of its induced grammar.

Following these chapters is a group of contributions concerned with the development of strategies for efficient probabilistic parsing.

Yoon, Kim and Song in their chapter *A new parsing method for Korean using a global association table* introduce a new parsing method developed especially for Korean, using statistical information extracted from a Korean corpus. Co-occurrence data are used to compute lexical associations which are stored in a table, the 'global association table'. These associations play a crucial role in determining the correct dependency relations between the words in Korean sentences. They develop a hybrid parsing method that uses the global association table to parse sentences semi-deterministically. They show that this parsing method is quite effective, and provide good test results concerning efficiency and precision; moreover, there are rather obvious ways in which the method could be refined and improved.

The chapter *Towards a reduced commitment, D-Theory style TAG parser* by **Chen and Vijay-Shanker** presents a new approach to parsing Tree-Adjoining Grammars based on the concepts of D-theory. As already mentioned above, D-theory parsing handles syntactic ambiguity by using underspecified descriptions of syntactic trees, as opposed to traditional TAG parsers that typically cope with ambiguity by considering all the possible choices as they unfold during parsing. The authors apply D-theoretic underspecification in particular to delay attachment decisions during TAG parsing (making 'reduced commitments'). The use of TAG on the other hand reveals the need for additional types of syntactic underspecification that have not been considered so far in the D-theoretic framework, including the combination of sets of trees into their underspecified equivalents as well as underspecifying combinations of trees. The chapter examines various issues that arise in this new approach to TAG parsing, presenting solutions to some of them, and discussing the possibilities for effective implementation of this parsing method.

Hektoen's chapter *Probabilistic parse selection based on semantic co-occurrences* presents a method for the addition of semantic information in probabilistic parsing, introducing probabilities that are based not just on the co-occurrence frequencies of linguistic elements, but (also) on co-occurrences in semantic forms (like quasi-logical forms, unscoped logical forms, or under-specified logical forms - see e.g. Bunt & Muskens, 1999). This method is specifically targeted at the differential distribution of such co-occurrences in correct and incorrect parses. It uses Bayesian estimation for the co-occurrence probabilities in order to achieve higher accuracy for sparse data than the more common maximum likelihood estimation would. The method is compatible with any parsing technique that is capable of supporting formal semantics, making it potentially much more useful in a wider, practical NLP system where any form of interpretation is required. It has been tested on the Wall Street Journal corpus in the Penn Treebank and shows encouraging results.

Hahn, Bröker and Neuhaus in their chapter *Let's ParseTalk – message-passing protocols for object oriented parsing* argue for a design of natural language grammars and their associated parsers in which declarative knowledge about linguistic structures and procedural knowledge about language use are equally balanced within a strictly object-oriented specification and implementation framework. In particular, they introduce fundamental message-passing protocols for object-oriented parsing, which include, besides one for dependency parsing, protocols for ambiguity handling, robustness, backtracking, preferential and predictive parsing, as well as textual reference resolution. The authors argue that this approach is better suited for real-world natural language processing tasks, which typically involve the need to deal with grammatically imperfect utterances and require an integration of syntax, semantics and discourse pragmatics, with massive ambiguity emerging at each of these levels, than traditional approaches that take grammatically perfect sentences as the object proper of linguistic study, and focus on purely syntactic description. Based on an empirical evaluation of their ParseTalk system, they also provide reasons for sacrificing parsing completeness in favour of gains in efficiency.

In the chapter *Performance evaluation of supertagging for partial parsing*, **Srinivas** presents a new application to parsing of supertagging, i.e. the assignment to each word of appropriate elementary trees in the sense of Lexicalized Tree-Adjoining Grammar. Such trees contain more information (such as sub-categorization and agreement information) than standard part-of-speech tags, and are thus appropriately called 'supertags'. As in standard art-of-speech disambiguation, supertagging can be done by a parser, but just as part-of-speech disambiguation prior to parsing makes parsing easier and faster, supertagging reduces the work of the parser even further. Srinivas shows that combining supertagging with a lightweight dependency analyzer leads to a robust and efficient partial parser. This work is significant for two reasons. First, it proves to be possible to achieve high-accuracy (92%) supertag disambiguation without parsing. Second, the partial parser gives excellent performance results, e.g. 93% recall and 92% precision in noun chunking.

The last two chapters of the book are both concerned with approximation techniques applied to grammars or parsers, with the aim of increasing parser efficiency.

Nederhof shows in his chapter *Regular approximation of context-fee languages: a grammatical view* that for every context-free grammar a new grammar can be constructed that generates a regular language. He first defines a condition on context-free grammars that is a sufficient condition for a grammar to generate a regular grammar, and subsequently gives a transformation that turns an arbitrary context-free grammar into one that satisfies this condition. This transformation has the effect of adding strings to the language generated by the original grammar in such a way that the language becomes regular. This construction differs from other existing methods of approximation in that the use of a pushdown automaton is altogether avoided This allows better insight into how the generated language is affected.

The chapter by **Schmid**, finally, *Parsing by successive approximation*, presents a parsing method for unification-based grammars with a context-free backbone which processes the input in three steps. The first step is context-free parsing. The second step evaluates syntactic feature constraints, and the third builds a semantic representation. It is argued that for each of these steps a different processing strategy is optimal. A novel iterative processing strategy for evaluating feature constraints is presented, which computes the feature structures in multiple passes through the parse forest and represents feature structures as trees rather than graphs. Experimental results are presented which indicate that the time complexity of this parser is close to cubic in the length of the input for a large English grammar. Finally, a compilation technique is presented which automatically compiles a set of finitely valued features into the context-free backbone.

Notes

1. Bunt and Muskens (1999) estimate that a 12-word sentence *without any syntactic ambiguity* has in the order of 90 million possible semantic interpretations, as a consequence of lexical semantic ambiguity, scoping ambiguities, and ambiguities in quantifier meanings.

2. If we assume that on average a natural language word has 2 syntactically different readings, and every pair of words or word groups can enter into 2 alternative possible syntactic combinations, which are both conservative estimates, then the number of possible parses of a 16-word sentence is $2^{16} = 65.536$. Moore (2000) reports that a grammar, extracted from the Penn Treebank and tested on a set of sentences ramdonly generated from a probabilistic version of the grammar, has on average 7.2×10^{27} parses per sentence.

3. See Bunt and Muskens (1999).

4. The availability nowadays of encyclopedia in electronic form and of large-scale internet information doesn't alleviate that problem, because this information is by and large only available in *textual form*, not in a formalized form that could be used in automated reasoning.

References

Briscoe, T. and J. Carroll (1993) Generalised probabilistic LR parsing of natural language (corpora) with unification-based grammars. *Computational Linguistics* 19 (1): 25–60.

Bunt, H. and R. Muskens (1999) Computational Semantics. In H. Bunt and R. Muskens (eds.) *Computing Meaning, vol. 1*, Dordrecht: Kluwer, pp. 1–32.

Charniak, E., (1996) Tree-bank grammars. Technical Report CS-96-02, Brown University, Providence, RI.

Charniak, E. (1997) Statistical parsing with a context-free grammar and word statistics. In *Proc. of the National Conference on Artificial Intelligence*, pp. 598–603.

Heckert, E. (1994) Behandlung von Syntaxfehlern für LR-SPrachen ohne Korrekturversuche. Ph.D. thesis, Ruhr-Universität, Bochum.

Kiefer, B. and H.-U. Krieger (2000) A Context-Free Approximation of Head-driven Phrase Structure Grammar. In *Proc. Sixth Intern. Workshop on Parsing Technologies*, pp. 135–146. Trento: ITC-IRST.

Marcus, M., D. Hindle and M. Fleck (1983) D-theory: Talking about talking about trees. In *Proc. 21st Annual Meeting of the ACL.* Cambridge (MA): Association for Computational Linguistics.

Marcus, M., G. Kim, M. Marcinkiewicz, R. MacIntyre, A. Bies, M. Ferguson, K. Katz and B. Schasberger (1994) The Penn Treebank: annotating predicate-argument structure. In *Proc. Human Language Technology Workshop, March 1994.* San Francisco: Morgan Kaufman.

Moore, R. (2000) Improved left-corner chart parsing for large context-free grammars. In *Proc. Sixth Intern. Workshop on Parsing Technologies*, pp. 171–182. Trento: ITC-IRST.

Pereira, F. and R. Wright (1991) Finite-state approximation of phrase structure grammars. In *Proc. 29th Annual Meeting of the ACL*, pp. 245–255. Cambridge (MA): Association for Computational Linguistics.

Rambow, O., K. Vijay-Shanker and D. Weir (1995) D-Tree Grammars. In *Proc. 33rd Annual Meeting of the ACL.* Cambridge (MA): Association for Computational Linguistics.

Rogers, J. and K. Vijay-Shanker (1996) Towards a formal understanding of the determinism hypothesis in D-theory. In H. Bunt and M. Tomita (eds.) *Recent Advances in Parsing Technology,* Kluwer, Dordrecht, pp. 59–78.

Sabah, G. and X. Briffault (1993) CARAMEL: a step towards reflection in natural language understanding systems. In *Proc. of IEEE Intern. Conference on Artificial Intelligence,* Boston, pp. 258–268.

Vijay-Shanker, K. (1992) Using Descriptions of Trees in a Tree-Adjoining Grammar. *Computational Linguistics* 18(4), 481–517.

Winograd, T. (1983) *Understanding Natural Language.* New York: Academic Press.

Chapter 2

ENCODING FREQUENCY INFORMATION IN LEXICALIZED GRAMMARS

John Carroll
David Weir
Cognitive and Computing Sciences, University of Sussex, Brighton BN1 9QH, UK
{ johnca,davidw } @cogs.susx.ac.uk

Abstract   We address the issue of how to associate frequency information with lexicalized grammar formalisms, using Lexicalized Tree Adjoining Grammar as a representative framework. We consider systematically a number of alternative probabilistic frameworks, evaluating their adequacy from both a theoretical and empirical perspective using data from existing large treebanks. We also propose three orthogonal approaches for backing off probability estimates to cope with the large number of parameters involved.

Keywords: Probabilistic parsing, lexicalized grammars

1   INTRODUCTION

When performing a derivation with a grammar it is usually the case that, at certain points in the derivation process, the grammar licenses several alternative ways of continuing with the derivation. In the case of context-free grammar (CFG) such nondeterminism arises when there are several productions for the nonterminal that is being rewritten. Frequency information associated with the grammar may be used to assign a probability to each of the alternatives. In general, it must always be the case that at every point where a choice is available the probabilities of all the alternatives sum to 1. This frequency information provides a parser with a way of dealing with the problem of ambiguity: the parser can use the information either to preferentially explore possibilities that are more likely, or to assign probabilities to the alternative parses.

There can be many ways of associating frequency information with the components making up a grammar formalism. For example, just two of the options in the case of CFG are: (1) associating a single probability with each

13

H. Bunt and A. Nijholt (eds.), Advances in Probabilistic and Other Parsing Technologies, 13–28.

production that determines the probability of its use wherever it is applicable (i.e. Stochastic CFG; SCFG Booth and Thompson, 1973); or (2) associating different probabilities with a production depending on the particular nonterminal occurrence (on the right-hand side of a production) that is being rewritten (Chitrao and Grishman, 1990). In the latter case probabilities depend on the context (within a production) of the nonterminal being rewritten. In general, while there may be alternative ways of associating frequency information with grammars, the aim is always to provide a way of associating probabilities with alternatives that arise during derivations.

This chapter is concerned with how the kind of frequency information that would be useful to a parser can be associated with lexicalized grammar formalisms. To properly ground the discussion we will use Lexicalized Tree Adjoining Grammar (LTAG as a representative framework, although our remarks can be applied to lexicalized grammar formalisms more generally. We begin by considering the derivation process, and, in particular, the nature of derivation steps. At the heart of a LTAG is a finite set of trees (the elementary trees of the grammar). In an LTAG these trees are 'anchored' with lexical items and the tree gives a possible context for its anchor by providing a structure into which its complements and modifiers can be attached. For example, Figure 2.1 shows four elementary trees – one *auxiliary* tree β and three *initial* trees α_1, α_2 and α_3. Nodes marked with asterisks, downward arrows and diamonds are foot, substitution and anchor nodes, respectively. In a derivation these trees are combined using the operations of substitution and adjunction to produce a derived tree for a complete sentence. Figure 2.2 shows a single derivation step in which α_2 and α_3 are substituted at frontier nodes (with addresses 1 and $2 \cdot 2$, respectively) of α_1, and β is adjoined at an internal node of α_1 (with address 2)[1].

When formalizing LTAG derivations, a distinction must be made between the (object-level) trees that are derived in a derivation and the (meta-level) trees that are used to fully encode what happens in derivations. These trees are referred to as derived and derivation trees, respectively. A scheme for encoding LTAG derivations was proposed by Vijay-Shanker (1987) and later modified by Schabes and Shieber (1994). Derivation trees show, in a very direct way, how the elementary trees are combined in derivations. Nodes of the derivation trees are labeled by the names of elementary trees, and edge labels identify tree addresses (i.e. node locations) in elementary trees. Figure 2.3 shows the derivation tree resulting from the derivation step in Figure 2.2.

The nodes identified in the derivation tree encode that when the elementary tree α_1 was used, the elementary trees $\beta, \alpha_2, \alpha_3$ were chosen to fit into the various complement and modifier positions. These positions are identified by the tree addresses i_1, i_2, i_3 labeling the respective edges, where[2] in this example $i_1 = 2, i_2 = 1$ and $i_3 = 2 \cdot 2$In other words, this derivation tree indicates which

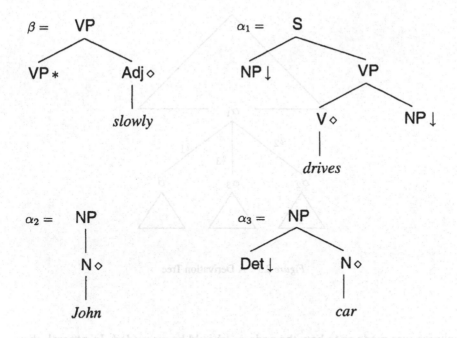

Figure 2.1 **An Example Grammar**

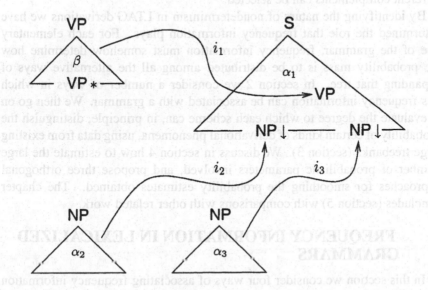

Figure 2.2 **A Derivation Step**

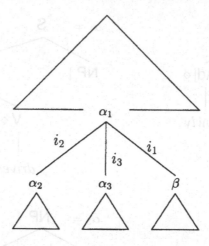

Figure 2.3   A Derivation Tree

choice was made as to how the node α_1 should be *expanded*. In general, there may have been many alternatives since modification is usually optional and different complements can be selected.

By identifying the nature of nondeterminism in LTAG derivations we have determined the role that frequency information plays. For each elementary tree of the grammar, frequency information must somehow determine how the probability mass is to be distributed among all the alternative ways of expanding that tree. In section 2 we consider a number of ways in which this frequency information can be associated with a grammar. We then go on to evaluate the degree to which each scheme can, in principle, distinguish the probability of certain kinds of derivational phenomena, using data from existing large treebanks (section 3). We discuss in section 4 how to estimate the large number of probabilistic parameters involved, and propose three orthogonal approaches for smoothing the probability estimates obtained. The chapter concludes (section 5) with comparisons with other related work.

2   FREQUENCY INFORMATION IN LEXICALIZED GRAMMARS

In this section we consider four ways of associating frequency information with lexicalized grammars. Using the LTAG framework outlined in section 1 as a basis we define four Stochastic Lexicalized Grammar formalisms which we will refer to as SLG(1), SLG(2), SLG(3) and SLG(4). The differences between them lie in how fine-grained the frequency information is, which in turn determines the extent to which the resulting probabilities can be dependent on derivational context.

2.1   CONTEXT-FREE FREQUENCIES

The first approach we consider is the simplest and will be referred to as **SLG(1)**. A single probability is associated with each elementary tree. This is the probability that that tree is used in a derivation in preference to another tree with the same nonterminal at its root. A grammar is therefore well-formed if, for each nonterminal symbol that can be at the root of a substitutable (adjoinable) tree, the sum of probabilities associated with all substitutable (adjoinable) trees with the same root nonterminal is 1. When nondeterminism arises in a derivation nothing about the derivational context can influence the way that a tree is expanded, since the probability that the various possible trees are adjoined or substituted at each node depends only on the identity of the nonterminal at that node. As a result we say the frequency information in an SLG(1) is *context-free*.

2.2   NODE-DEPENDENT FREQUENCIES

The second approach considered here, which we will call **SLG(2)**, has been described before by both Schabes (1992) and Resnik (1992). We describe the scheme of Schabes here, though the approach taken by Resnik is equivalent. In defining his scheme Schabes uses a stochastic version of a context-free-like grammar formalism called Linear Indexed Grammar (LIG). Based on the construction used to show the weak equivalence of LTAG and LIG (Vijay-Shanker and Weir, 1994), a LIG is constructed from a given LTAG such that derivation trees of the LIG encode the derived trees of the associated LTAG. Compiling LTAG to LIG involves decomposing the elementary trees into single-level trees and introducing additional productions explicitly encoding every possible adjunction and substitution possibility[3]. It is the LIG productions encoding adjunction and substitution possibilities that are assigned probabilities[4]. The probabilities associated with all the productions that encode possible adjunctions (substitutions) at a node must sum to 1. The key feature of these probability-bearing LIG productions, in the context of the current discussion, is that they encode the adjunction or substitution of a specific elementary tree at a specific place in another elementary tree. This means that the frequency information can to some extent be dependent on context. In particular, when faced with nondeterminism in the way that some elementary tree is expanded during a derivation, the probability distribution associated with the alternative adjunctions or substitutions at a given node can depend on which elementary tree that node comes from. As a result we call the frequency information in SLG(2) **node-dependent**. This makes SLG(2) more expressive than SLG(1).

As both Schabes and Resnik point out, by leveraging LTAG's extended domain of locality this approach allows probabilities to model both lexical and structural co-occurrence preferences.

The head automata of Alshawi (1996) also fit into the SLG(2) formalism since they involve a dependency parameter which gives the probability that a head has a given word as a particular dependent.

2.3   LOCALLY-DEPENDENT FREQUENCIES

The third approach is **SLG(3)** which falls out quite naturally from consideration of the LTAG derivation process. As we discussed in the introduction, LTAG derivations can be encoded with derivation trees in which nodes are labeled by the names of elementary trees and edges labeled by the addresses of substitution and adjunction nodes. The tree addresses can be omitted from derivation trees if a fixed linear order is established on *all* of the adjunction and substitution nodes in each elementary tree and this ordering is used to order siblings in the derivation tree. Given this possibility, Vijay-Shanker at al. (1987) have shown that the set of derivation trees associated with a LTAG forms a local set and can therefore be generated by a context-free grammar (CFG)[5]. The productions of this **meta-grammar** encode possible derivation steps of the grammar. In other words, each meta-production encodes one way of (fully) expanding an elementary tree[6]. In SLG(3) a probability is associated with each of these meta-productions. A SLG(3) is well-formed if for each elementary tree the sum of the probabilities associated with the meta-productions for that tree is 1.

In contrast to SLG(2) – which is limited to giving the probability that a tree anchored with a given lexical item is substituted or adjoined into a tree anchored with a second lexical item – SLG(3) specifies the probability that a particular *set* of lexical items is combined in a derivation step. It is the elementary trees of the underlying LTAG that determine the (extended local) domains over which these dependencies can be expressed since it is the structure of an elementary tree that determines the possible daughters in a meta-production. Although the types of elementary tree structures licensed are specific to a particular LTAG, it might be expected that a SLG(3) meta-grammar, for example, could encode the probability that a given verb takes a particular (type of) subject and combination of complements, including cases where the complements had been moved from their canonical positions, for example by extraction. A meta-grammar would also be likely to be able to differentiate the probabilities of particular co-occurrences of adverbial and prepositional phrase modifiers, and would moreover be able to distinguish between different orderings of the modifiers.

The approach described by Lafferty et al. (1992) of associating probabilities with Link Grammars – taken to its logical conclusion – corresponds to SLG(3), since in that approach separate probabilities are associated with each way of linking a word up with a combination of other words[7].

2.4   GLOBALLY-DEPENDENT FREQUENCIES

The fourth and final approach we consider is Bod's Data-Oriented Parsing(DOP) framework (Bod, 1998). In this chapter we call it **SLG(4)** for uniformity and ease of reference. Bod formalizes DOP in terms of a *stochastic tree-substitution grammar*, which consists of a finite set of elementary trees, each with an associated probability such that the probabilities of all the trees with the same non-terminal symbol sum to 1, with an operation of substitution to combine the trees. In DOP, or SLG(4), the elementary trees are arbitrarily large subtrees anchored at terminal nodes by words/part-of-speech labels, and acquired automatically from pre-parsed training data. This is in contrast to SLG(3), in which the size of individual meta-productions is bounded, since the structure of the meta-productions is wholly determined by the form of the elementary trees in the grammar.

3   EMPIRICAL EVALUATION

We have described four ways in which frequency information can be associated with a lexicalized grammar. Directly comparing the performance of the alternative schemes by training a wide-coverage grammar on an appropriate annotated corpus and then parsing further, unseen data using each scheme in turn would be a large undertaking outside the scope of this chapter. However, each scheme varies in terms of the degree to which it can, in principle, distinguish the probability of certain kinds of derivational phenomena. This can be tested without the need to develop and run a parsing system, since each scheme can be seen as making verifiable predictions about the absence of certain dependencies in derivations of sentences in corpus data.

SLG(1), with only context-free frequency information, predicts that the relative frequency of use of the trees for a given nonterminal is not sensitive to where the trees are used in a derivation. For example, there should be no significant difference between the likelihood that a given NP tree is chosen for substitution at the subject position and the likelihood that it is chosen for the object position. SLG(2) (using so-called node dependent frequency information) is able to cater fong so-called node-dependent frequency information) is able to cater for such differences but predicts that the likelihood of substituting or adjoining a tree at a given node in another tree is not dependent on what else is adjoined or substituted into that tree. With SLG(3) (which uses what we call locally-dependent frequency information) it is possible to encode such sensitivity, but more complex contextual dependencies cannot be expressed: for example, it is not possible for the probability associated with the substitution or adjunction of a tree γ into another tree γ' to be sensitive to where the tree γ' itself is adjoined or substituted. Only SLG(4) (in which frequency information can be globally-dependent) can do this.

In the remainder of this section we present a number of empirical phenomena that support or refute predictions made by each of the versions of SLG.

3.1   SLG(1) VS. SLG(2–4)

Magerman and Marcus (1991) report that, empirically, a noun phrase is more likely to be realized as a pronoun in subject position than elsewhere. To capture this fact it is necessary to have two different sets of probabilities associated with the different possible NP trees: one for substitution in subject position, and another for substitution in other positions. This cannot be done in SLG(1) since frequency information in SLG(1) is context-free. This phenomenon therefore violates the predictions of SLG(1), but it can be captured by the other SLG models.

Individual lexemes also exhibit these types of distributional irregularities. For example, in the Wall Street Journal (WSJ) portion of the Penn Treebank 2 (Marcus et al., 1994), around 38% of subjects of verbs used intransitively (i.e., without an object NP) in active, ungapped constructions are either pronouns or proper name phrases[8]. However, for the verbs *believe, agree,* and *understand,* there is a significantly higher proportion (in statistical terms) of proper name/pronoun subjects (in the case of *believe* 57%; χ^2, 40.53, 1 *df*, $p < 0.001$)[9]. This bias would, in semantic terms, be accounted for by a preference for subject types that can be coerced to *human*. SLG(2–4) can capture this distinction whereas SLG(1) cannot since it is not sensitive to where a given tree is used.

3.2   SLG(2) VS. SLG(3–4)

The Penn Treebank can also allow us to probe the differences between the predictions made by SLG(2) and SLG(3–4). From an analysis of verb phrases in active, ungapped constructions with only pronominal and/or proper name subjects and NP direct objects, it is the case that there is a (statistically) highly significant dependency between the type of the subject and the type of the object (χ^2, 29.79, 1 *df*, $p < 0.001$), the bias being towards the subject and direct object being either (a) both pronouns, or (b) both proper names. Thus the choice of which type of NP tree to fill subject position in a verbal tree can be dependent on the choice of NP type for object position. Assuming that the subject and object are substituted/adjoined into trees anchored by the verbs, this phenomenon violates the predictions of SLG(2) – hence also SLG(1) – but can still be modeled by SLG(3–4).

A similar sort of asymmetry occurs when considering the distribution of pronoun and proper name phrases against other NP types in subject and direct object positions. There is again a significant bias towards the subject and object either both being a pronoun/proper name phrase, or neither being of this type (x^2, 8.77, 1 df, $p = 0.3$). This again violates the predictions of SLG(2), but not SLG(3–4).

Moving on now to modifiers, specifically prepositional phrase (PP) modifiers in verb phrases, the Penn Treebank distinguishes several kinds including PPs expressing manner (PP-MNR), time (PP-TMP), and purpose (PP-PRP). Where these occur in combination there is a significant ordering effect: PP-MNR modifiers tend to precede PP-TMP (x^2, 4.12, 1 df, $p = 4.2$), and PP-TMP modifiers in their turn have a very strong tendency to precede PP-PRP ($p < 0.001$). Using Schabes and Shieber's (1994) formulation of the adjunction operation in LTAG, multiple PP modifier trees would be adjoined independently at the same node in the parent VP tree, their surface order being reflected by their ordering in the derivation tree. Therefore, in SLG(3) multiple modifying PPs would appear within a single meta-production in the order in which they occurred, and the particular ordering would be assigned an appropriate probability by virtue of this. In contrast, SLG(2) treats multiple adjunctions separately and so would not be able to model the ordering preference.

Significant effects involving multiple modification of particular lexical items are also evident in the treebank. For example, the verb *rise* occurs 83 times with a single PP-TMP modifier – e.g. (1a) – and 12 times with two (1b), accounting in total for 6% of all PPs annotated in this way as temporal.

(1) a Payouts on the S&P 500 stocks rose 10 % [PP-TMP in 1988] ,
       according to Standard & Poor's Corp. ...

    b It rose largely [PP-TMP throughout the session] [PP-TMP
       after posting an intraday low of 2141.7 in the first 40 minutes
       of trading].

The proportion of instances of two PP-TMP modifiers with *rise* is significantly more than would be exp-TMP modifiers with *rise* is significantly more than would be expected given the total number of instances occurring in the treebank (x^2, 25.99, 1 df, $p < 0.001$). The verb *jump* follows the same pattern ($p = 1.0$), but other synonyms and antonyms of *rise* (e.g. *fall*) do not. This idiosyncratic behavior of *rise* and *jump* cannot be captured by SLG(2), since each adjunction is effectively considered to be a separate independent event. In SLG(3), though, the two-adjunction case would appear in a single meta-production associated with *rise/jump* and be accorded a higher probability than similar meta-productions associated with other lexical items.

There is another, more direct but somewhat less extensive, source of evidence that we can use to investigate the differences between SLG(2) and (3–4). B. Srinivas at the University of Pennsylvania has recently created a substantial parsed corpus[10] by analyzing text from the Penn Treebank using the XTAG system (XTAG-Group, 1999). Some of the text has been manually disambiguated, although we focus here on the most substantial set – of some 9900 sentences from the WSJ portion – which has not been disambiguated, as yet. For each sentence we extracted the set of meta-level productions that would generate the XTAG derivation. To obtain reliable data from ambiguous sentences, we retained only the (approximately 37500) productions that were common across all derivations. In this set of productions we have found that with the elementary tree licensing subject–transitive-verb–object constructions, the likelihood that the object NP is expanded with a tree anchored in *shares* is much higher if the subject is expanded with with a tree anchored in *volume*, corresponding to sentences such as (2a) and (2b).

(2) a Volume totaled 14,890,000 shares.

    b Overall Nasdaq volume was 151,197,400 shares.

Indeed, in all 11 cases where *volume* is the anchor of the subject, an NP anchored in *shares* is analyzed as the object, whereas more generally *shares* is object in only 18 of the 1079 applications of the tree. This difference in proportions is statistically highly significant ($p < 0.001$). Correlation between each of *volume* and *shares* and the verbs that appear is much weaker. There is of course potential for bias in the frequencies since this data is based purely on unambiguous productions. We therefore computed the same proportions from productions derived from all sentences in the XTAG WSJ data; this also resulted in a highly significant difference. SLG(2) models the substitution of the subject and of the object as two independent events, whereas the data show that they can exhibit a strong inter-dependency.

3.3   SLG(3) VS. SLG(4)

Bod (1998) observes that there can be significant inter-dependencies between two or more linguistic units, for example words or phrases, that cut across the standard structural organization of a grammar. For example, in the Air Travel Information System (ATIS) corpus (Hemphill et al., 1990) the generic noun phrase (NP) *flights from X to Y* (as in sentences like *Show me flights from Dallas to Atlanta*) occurs very frequently. In this domain the dependencies between the words in the NP – but without X and Y filled in – are so strong that in ambiguity resolution it should arguably form a single statistical unit. Bod argues that Resnik and Schabes' schemes (i.e. SLG(2)) cannot model this; however it appears that SLG(3) can since the NP2)) cannot model this;

however it appears that SLG(3) can since the NP would give rise to a single meta-production (under the reasonable assumption that the *from* and *to* PPs would be adjoined into the NP tree anchored by *flights*).

An example given by Bod that does demonstrate the difference between SLG(3) and SLG(4) concerns sentences like *the emaciated man starved*. Bod argues that there is a strong (semantic) dependence between *emaciated* and *starved*, which would be captured in DOP – or SLG(4) – in the form of a single elementary tree in which *emaciated* and *starved* were the only lexical items. This dependence cannot be captured by SLG(3) since *emaciated* and *starved* would anchor separate elementary trees, and the associations made would merely be between (1) the S tree anchored by *starved* and the substitution of the NP anchored by *man* in subject position, and (2) the modification of *man* by *emaciated*.

3.4   DISCUSSION

The empirical phenomena discussed above mainly concern interdependencies within specific constructions between the types or heads of either complements or modifiers. The phenomena fall clearly into two groups:

- ones relating to distributional biases that are independent of particular lexical items, and
- others that are associated with specific open class vocabulary.

Token frequencies – with respect to treebank data – of phenomena in the former group are relatively high, partly because they are not keyed off the presence of a particular lexical item: for example in the case study into the complement distributions of pronoun/proper name phrases versus other NP types (section 3.2) there are 13800 data items (averaging one for every four treebank sentences). However, there appears to be a tendency for the phenomena in this group to exhibit smaller statistical biases than are evident in the latter, lexically-dependent group (although all biases reported here are significant at least to the 95% confidence level). In the latter group, although token frequencies for each lexical item are not large (for example, the forms of *rise* under consideration make up only 1% of comparable verbs in the treebank), the biases are in general very strong, in what are otherwise an unremarkable set of verbs and nouns (*believe*, *agree*, *understand*, *rise*, *jump*, *volume*, and *shares*). We might therefore infer that although individually token frequencies are not great, *type* frequencies are (i.e. there are a large number of lexical items that display idiosyncratic behavior of some form or other), and so lexicalized interdependencies are as widespread as non-lexical ones.

4   PARAMETER ESTIMATION
4.1   TRAINING REGIME

Schabes (1992) describes an iterative re-estimation procedure (based on the Inside-Outside Algorithm Baker, 1979) for refining the parameters of an SLG(2) grammar given a corpus of in-coverage sentences; the algorithm is also able to simultaneously acquire the grammar itself. The aim of the algorithm is to distribute the probability mass within the grammar in such a way that the *probability of the training corpus* is maximized, i.e. to model as closely as possible the language in that corpus. However, when the goal is to return as accurately as possible the *correct analysis* for each sentence using a pre-existing grammar, estimating grammar probabilities directly from normalized frequency counts derived from a pre-parsed training corpus can result in accuracy that is comparable or better to that obtained using re-estimation (Charniak, 1996). Direct estimation would mesh well with the SLG formalisms described in this chapter.

4.2   SMOOTHING

The huge number of parameters required for a wide-coverage SLG(2) (and even more so for SLG(3–4)) means that not only would the amount of frequency information be unmanageable, but data sparseness would make useful probabilities hard to obtain. We briefly present three (essentially orthogonal and independent) backing-off techniques that could be used to address this problem.

4.2.1   Unanchored Trees. It is the size of a wide-coverage lexicon that makes pure SLG(2–4) unmanageable. However, without lexical anchors a wide-coverage SLG would have only a few hundred trees (XTAG-Group, 1995). Backup frequency values could therefore be associated with unanchored trees and used when data for the anchored case was absent.

4.2.2   Lexical Rules. In a lexicalized grammar, elementary trees may be grouped into families which are related by lexical rules – such as *wh* extraction, and passivization. (For example, the XTAG grammar contains of the order of 500 rules grouped into around 20 families). In the absence of specific frequency values, approximate (backup) values could be obtained from a tree that was related by some lexical rule.

4.2.3   SLG(i) to SLG($i - 1$). Section 3 indicated informally how, when moving from SLG(1) through to SLG(4), the statistical model becomes successively more fine-grained, with each SLG(i) model subsuming the previous ones, in the sense that SLG(i) is able to differentiate probabilistically all structures that previous ones can. Thus, when there is insufficient training data, sub-parts of a finer-grained SLG model could be backed off to a model that is less detailed. For example, within a SLG(3) model, in cases where a particular set of meta-productions all with the same mother had a low collective probability, the set could be reduced to a single meta-production with unspecified daughters, i.e. giving the effect of SLG(1).

5   COMPARISON WITH OTHER WORK

The treatment of stochastic lexicalized grammar in this chapter has much in common with recent approaches to statistical language modeling outside the LTAG tradition. Firstly, SLG integrates statistical preferences acquired from training data with an underlying wide-coverage grammar, following an established line of research, for example Chitrao and Grishman, 1990; Charniak and Carroll, 1994; Briscoe and Carroll, 1995. The chapter discusses techniques for making preferences sensitive to context to avoid known shortcomings of the context-independent probabilities of SCFG (see e.g. Briscoe and Carroll, 1993),

Secondly, SLG is *lexical*, since elementary trees specify lexical anchors. Considering the anchor of each elementary tree as the head of the construction analyzed, successive daughters for example of a single SLG(3) meta-grammar production can in many cases correspond to a combination of Magerman's (1995) mother/daughter and daughter/daughter head statistics (although it would appear that Collins' (1996) head-modifier configuration statistics are equivalent only to SLG(2) in power). However, due to its extended domain of locality, SLG(3) is not limited to modeling local dependencies such as these, and it can express dependencies between heads separated by other, intervening material. For example, it can deal directly and naturally with dependencies between subject and any verbal complement without requiring mediation via the verb itself: c.f. the example of section 3.2.

Thirdly, the SLG family has the ability to model explicitly syntactic *structural* phenomena, in the sense that the atomic structures to which statistical measures are attached can span multiple levels of derived parse tree structure, thus relating constituents that are widely-separated – structurally as well as sequentially – in a sentence. Bod's DOP model (Bod, 1998) shares this characteristic, and indeed (as discussed in section 2.4) it fits naturally into this family, as what we have called SLG(4).

Srinivas et al. (1996) (see also Joshi and Srinivas, 1994) have described a novel approach to parsing with LTAG, in which each word in a sentence is first assigned the most probable elementary tree – or 'supertag' – given the context in which the word appears, according to a trigram model of supertags. The rest of the parsing process then reduces to finding of supertags. The rest of the parsing process then reduces to finding a way of combining the supertags to form a complete analysis. In this approach statistical information is associated simply with linear sub-sequences of elementary trees, rather than with trees within derivational contexts as in SLG(2–4). Although Srinivas' approach is in principle efficient, mistaggings mean that it is not guaranteed to return an analysis for every in-coverage sentence, in contrast to SLG. Also, its relatively impoverished probabilistic model would not be able to capture many of the phenomena reported in section 3.

Acknowledgments

This work was supported by UK EPSRC project GR/K97400 'Analysis of Naturally-occurring English Text with Stochastic Lexicalized Grammars' (<http://www.cogs.susx.ac.uk/lab/nlp/dtg/index.html>), and by an EPSRC Advanced Fellowship to tand Miles Osborne for useful comments on previous drafts.

Notes

1. The root of a tree has the address ϵ. The ith daughter (where siblings are ordered from left to right) of a node with address a has address $a \cdot i$

2. As Schabes and Shieber (1994) point out matters are somewhat more complex that this. What we describe here more closely follows the approach taken by Rambow et al. (1995) in connection with D-Tree Grammar.

3. This scheme has proved useful in the study of LTAG parsing (Schabes, 1990; Vijay-Shanker and Weir, 1993; Boullier, 1996) since this pre-compilation process alleviates the need to do what amounts to the same decomposition process during parsing.

4. The other productions (that decompose the tree structure) are assigned a probability of 1 since they are deterministic.

5. In such context-free grammars, the terminal and nonterminal alphabets are not necessarily disjoint, and only the trees generated by the grammar (not their frontier strings) are of any interest.

6. In the formulation of LTAG derivations given by Schabes and Shieber (1994) an arbitrary number of modifications can take place at a single node. This means that there are an infinite number of productions in the meta-grammar, i.e., an infinite number of ways of expanding trees. This means that a pure version of SLG(3) is not possible. See Section 4.2 for ways to deal with this issue.

7. Lafferty et al. (1992) appear to consider only cases where a word has at most one right and one left link, i.e., probabilities are associated with at most triples. However, the formalism as defined by Sleator and Temperley (1993) allows a more general case with multiple links in each direction, as would be required to deal with, for example, modifiers.

8. Subjects were identified as the NP-SBJ immediately preceding a VP bracketing introduced by a verb labeled VBD/VBP/VBZ; pronouns, words labeled PRP/PRP$; and proper noun phrases, sequences of words all labeled NNP/NNPS.

9. A value for p of 5 corresponds to statistical significance at the standard 95% confidence level; smaller values of p indicate higher confidence.

10. We wish to thank B. Srinivas for giving us access to this resource.

References

Alshawi, H. (1996). Head automata and bilingual tilings: Translation with minimal representations. In *Proceedings of the 34th Meeting of the Association for Computational Linguistics*, pp. 167–176.

Baker, J. (1979). Trainable grammars for speech recognition. In Klatt, D. and Wolf, J., ed., *Speech Communication Papers for the 97th Meeting of the Acoustical Society of America*, pp. 547–550. MIT, Cambridge, MA.

Bod, R. (1998). *Beyond Grammar: An Experience-Based Theory of Language*. CSLI Press, Stanford, CA.

Booth, T. and Thompson, R. Applying probability measures to abstract languages. *IEEE Transactions on Computers*, C-22(5).

Boullier, P. (1996). Another facet of LIG parsing. In *Proceedings of the 34th Meeting of the Association for Computational Linguistics*, pp. 87–94.

Briscoe, E. and Carroll, J. (1993). Generalised probabilistic LR parsing of natural language (corpora) with unification-based grammars. *Computational Linguistics*, 19(1):25–60.

Briscoe, E. and Carroll, J. (1995). Developing and evaluating a probabilistic LR parser of part-of-speech and punctuation labels. In *Proceedings of the Fourth International Workshop on Parsing Technologies, Prague.*, pp. 48–58.

Charniak, E. (1996). Tree-bank grammars. Technical Report CS-96-02, Brown University, Department of Computer Science.

Charniak, E. and Carroll, G. (1994). Context-sensitive statistics for improved grammatical language models. In *12th National Conference on Artificial Intelligence (AAAI'94)*, pp. 728–733.

Chitrao, M. and Grishman, R. (1990). Statistical parsing of messages. In *Proceedings of the Speech and Natural Language Workshop*, pp. 263–266, Hidden Valley, PA.

Collins, M. (1996). A new statistical parser based on bigram lexical dependencies. In *Proceedings of the 34th Meeting of the Association for Computational Linguistics*, pp. 184–191.

Hemphill, C., Godfrey, J., and Doddington, G. (1990). The ATIS spoken language systems pilot corpus. In *Proceedings of the Speech and Natural Language Workshop*, pp. 96–101, Hidden Valley, PA.

Joshi, A. and Srinivas, B. (1994). Disambiguation of super parts of speech (or supertags): almost parsing. In *Proceedings of the 15th International Conference on Computational Linguistics*, pp. 154–160.

Lafferty, J., Sleator, D., and Temperley, D. (1992). Grammatical trigrams: a probabilistic model of Link Grammar. In *AAAI Fall Symposium on Probabilistic Approaches to Natural Language*, pp. 89–97.

Magerman, D. (1995). Statistical decision-tree models for parsing. In *Proceedings of the 33rd Meeting of the Association for Computational Linguistics*, pp. 276–283.

Magerman, D. and Marcus, M. (1991). Pearl: a probabilistic chart parser. In *Proceedings of the Second International Workshop on Parsing Technologies*, pp. 193–199.

Marcus, M., Kim, G., Marcinkiewicz, M., MacIntyre, R., Bies, A., Ferguson, M., Katz, K., and Schasberger, B. (1994). The Penn Treebank: annotating predicate argument structure. In *Proceedings of the Human Language Technology Workshop, March 1994*. Morgan Kaufmann, San Francisco, CA.

Rambow, O., Vijay-Shanker, K., and Weir, D. (1995). D-Tree Grammars. In *Proceedings of the 33rd Meeting of the Association for Computational Linguistics*, pp. 151–158.

Resnik, P. (1992). Probabilistic tree-adjoining grammar as a framework for statistical natural language processing. In *Proceedings of the 14th International Conference on Computational Linguistics*, pp. 418–424.

Schabes, Y. (1990). *Mathematical and Computational Aspects of Lexicalized Grammars*. PhD thesis, Department of Computer and Information Science, University of Pennsylvania.

Schabes, Y. (1992). Stochastic lexicalized tree-adjoining grammars. In *Proceedings of the 14th International Conference on Computational Linguistics*, pp. 426–432.

Schabes, Y. and Shieber, S. (1994). An alternative conception of tree-adjoining derivation. *Computational Linguistics*, 20(1):91–124.

Sleator, D. and Temperley, D. (1993). Parsing English with a link grammar. In *Proceedings of the Third International Workshop on Parsing Technologies*, pp. 277–292.

Srinivas, B., Doran, C., Hockey, B., and Joshi, A. (1996). An approach to robust partial parsing and evaluation metrics. In Carroll, J., ed., *Proceedings of the Workshop on Robust Parsing*, pp. 70–82. 8th European Summer School in Logic, Language and Information.

Vijay-Shanker, K. (1987). *A Study of Tree Adjoining Grammars*. PhD thesis, Department of Computer and Information Science, University of Pennsylvania, Philadelphia, PA.

Vijay-Shanker, K. and Weir, D. (1993). Parsing some constrained grammar formalisms. *Computational Linguistics*, 19(4):591–636.

Vijay-Shanker, K. and Weir, D. (1994). The equivalence of four extensions of context-free grammars. *Mathematical Systems Theory*, 27:511–546.

Vijay-Shanker, K., Weir, D., and Joshi, A. (1987). Characterizing structural descriptions produced by various grammatical formalisms. In *Proceedings of the 25th Meeting of the Association for Computational Linguistics*, pp. 104–111.

XTAG-Group, T. (1995). A lexicalized Tree Adjoining Grammar for English. Technical Report IRCS Report 95-03, The Institute for Research in Cognitive Science, University of Pennsylvania.

XTAG-Group, T. (1999). A lexicalized Tree Adjoining Grammar for English. Technical Report http://www.cis.upenn.edu/~xtag/tech-report/tech-report.html, The Institute for Research in Cognitive Science, University of Pennsylvania.

Chapter 3

BILEXICAL GRAMMARS AND THEIR CUBIC-TIME PARSING ALGORITHMS

Jason Eisner

Dept. of Computer Science, University of Rochester, Rochester, NY 14627-0226, U.S.A.[*]

jason@cs.rochester.edu

Abstract   This chapter introduces weighted bilexical grammars, a formalism in which individual lexical items, such as verbs and their arguments, can have idiosyncratic selectional influences on each other. Such 'bilexicalism' has been a theme of much current work in parsing. The new formalism can be used to describe bilexical approaches to both dependency and phrase-structure grammars, and a slight modification yields link grammars. Its scoring approach is compatible with a wide variety of probability models.

The obvious parsing algorithm for bilexical grammars (used by most previous authors) takes time $O(n^5)$. A more efficient $O(n^3)$ method is exhibited. The new algorithm has been implemented and used in a large parsing experiment(Eisner, 1996b). We also give a useful extension to the case where the parser must undo a stochastic transduction that has altered the input.

1   INTRODUCTION

1.1   THE BILEXICAL IDEA

1.1.1   Lexicalized Grammars. Computational linguistics has a long tradition of *lexicalized* grammars, in which each grammatical rule is specialized for some individual word. The earliest lexicalized rules were word-specific subcategorization frames. It is now common to find fully lexicalized versions of many grammatical formalisms, such as context-free and tree-adjoining grammars (Schabes et al., 1988). Other formalisms, such as dependency grammar (Mel'čuk, 1988) and head-driven phrase-structure grammar (Pollard and Sag, 1994), are explicitly lexical from the start.

[*]This material is based on work supported by an NSF Graduate Research Fellowship and ARPA Grant N6600194-C-6043 'Human Language Technology' to the University of Pennsylvania.

H. Bunt and A. Nijholt (eds.), Advances in Probabilistic and Other Parsing Technologies, 29–61.
© *2000 Kluwer Academic Publishers.*

Lexicalized grammars have two well-known advantages. When syntactic acceptability is sensitive to the quirks of individual words, lexicalized rules are necessary for linguistic description. Lexicalized rules are also computationally cheap for parsing written text: a parser may ignore those rules that do not mention any input words.

1.1.2   Probabilities and the New Bilexicalism. More recently, a third advantage of lexicalized grammars has emerged. Even when syntactic *acceptability* is not sensitive to the particular words chosen, syntactic *distribution* may be Resnik (1993). Certain words may be able but highly unlikely to modify certain other words. Of course, only some such collocational facts are genuinely lexical (*the storm gathered/*convened*); others are presumably a weak reflex of semantics or world knowledge (*solve puzzles/??goats*). But both kinds can be captured by a *probabilistic* lexicalized grammar, where they may be used to resolve ambiguity in favor of the most probable analysis, and also to speed parsing by avoiding ('pruning') unlikely search paths. Accuracy and efficiency can therefore both benefit.

Work along these lines includes Charniak (1995); Collins (1996); Eisner (1996a); Charniak (1997); Collins (1997); Goodman (1997), who reported state-of-the-art parsing accuracy. Related models are proposed without evaluation in Lafferty et al., (1992); Alshawi, (1996).

This flurry of probabilistic lexicalized parsers has focused on what one might call **bilexical grammars**, in which each grammatical rule is specialized for not one but *two* individual words.[1] The central insight is that specific words subcategorize to some degree for other specific words: *tax* is a good object for the verb *raise*. These parsers accordingly estimate, for example, the probability that word w is modified by (a phrase headed by) word v, for each pair of words w, v in the vocabulary.

1.2   AVOIDING THE COST OF BILEXICALISM

1.2.1   Past Work. At first blush, bilexical grammars (whether probabilistic or not) appear to carry a substantial computational penalty. We will see that parsers derived directly from CKY or Earley's algorithm take time $O(n^3 \min(n, |V|)^2)$ for a sentence of length n and a vocabulary of $|V|$ terminal symbols. In practice $n \ll |V|$, so this amounts to $O(n^5)$. Such algorithms implicitly or explicitly regard the grammar as a context-free grammar in which a noun phrase headed by *tiger* bears the special nonterminal NP_{tiger}. These $O(n^5)$ algorithms are used by Charniak, (1995); Alshawi, (1996); Charniak, (1997); Collins, (1996); Collins, (1997) and subsequent authors.

1.2.2   Speeding Things Up. The present chapter formalizes a particular notion of bilexical grammars, and shows that a length-n sentence can be parsed in time only $O(n^3 g^3 t)$, where g and t are bounded by the grammar and are typically small. (g is the maximum number of senses per input word, while t measures the degree of interdependence that the grammar allows *among* the several lexical modifiers of a word.) The new algorithm also reduces space requirements to $O(n^2 g^2 t)$, from the cubic space required by CKY-style approaches to bilexical grammar. The parsing algorithm finds the highest-scoring analysis or analyses generated by the grammar, under a probabilistic or other measure.

The new $O(n^3)$-time algorithm has been implemented, and was used in the experimental work of Eisner (1996b); Eisner (1996a), which compared various bilexical probability models. The algorithm also applies to the Treebank Grammars of Charniak (1995). Furthermore, it applies to the head-automaton grammars (HAGs) of Alshawi (1996) and the phrase-structure models of Collins, (1996); Collins, (1997), allowing $O(n^3)$-time rather than $O(n^5)$-time parsing, granted the (linguistically sensible) restrictions that the number of distinct X-bar levels is bounded and that left and right adjuncts are independent of each other.

1.3   ORGANIZATION OF THE CHAPTER

This chapter is organized as follows. First we will develop the ideas discussed above. Section 2 presents a simple formalization of bilexical grammar, and then section 3 explains why the naive recognition algorithm is $O(n^5)$ and how to reduce it to $O(n^3)$.

Next, section 4 offers some extensions to the basic formalism. Section 4.1 extends it to weighted (probabilistic) grammars, and shows how to find the best parse of the input. Section 4.2 explains how to handle and disambiguate polysemous words. Section 4.3 shows how to exclude or penalize string-local configurations. Section 4.4 handles the more general case where the input is an arbitrary rational transduction of the 'underlying' string to be parsed.

Section 5 carefully connects the bilexical grammar formalism of this chapter to other bilexical formalisms such as dependency, context-free, head-automaton, and link grammars. In particular, we apply the fast parsing idea to these formalisms.

The conclusions in section 6 summarize the result and place it in the context of other work by the author, including a recent asymptotic improvement.

2   A SIMPLE BILEXICAL FORMALISM

The bilexical formalism developed in this chapter is modeled on dependency grammar (Gaifman, 1965; Mel'čuk, 1988). It is equivalent to the class of **split bilexical grammars** (including split bilexical CFGs and split HAGs) defined in Eisner and Satta, (1999). More powerful bilexical formalisms also exist, and improved parsing algorithms for these are cited in sections 5.6 and 5.8.

2.0.1   Form of the Grammar.   We begin with a simple version of the formalism, to be modified later in the chapter. A [split] unweighted bilexical grammar consists of the following elements:

- A set V of words, called the (terminal) **vocabulary**, which contains a distinguished symbol ROOT.

- For each word $w \in V$, a pair of deterministic finite-state automata ℓ_w and r_w. Each automaton accepts some regular subset of V^*.

t is defined to be an upper bound on the number of states in any single automaton. (g will be defined in section 4.2 as an upper bound on lexical ambiguity.)

The **dependents** of word w are the headwords of its arguments and adjuncts. Speaking intuitively, automaton ℓ_w specifies the possible sequences of left dependents for w. So these allowable sequences, which are word strings in V^*, form a regular set. Similarly r_w specifies the possible sequences of right dependents for w.

By convention, the first element in such a sequence is closest to w in the surface string. Thus, the possible dependent sequences (from left to right) are specified by $\mathcal{L}(\ell_w)^R$ and $\mathcal{L}(r_w)$ respectively. For example, if the tree shown in Figure 3.1a is grammatical, then we know that ℓ_{plan} accepts *the*, and r_{plan} accepts *of raise*.

To get fast parsing, it is reasonable to ask that the automata individually have few states (i.e., that t be small). However, we wish to avoid any penalty for having

- many (distinct) automata – two per word in V;

- many arcs leaving an automaton state – one per possible dependent in V.

That is, the vocabulary size $|V|$ should not affect performance at all.

We will use $Q(\ell_w)$ and $Q(r_w)$ to denote the state sets of ℓ_w and r_w respectively; $I(\ell_w)$ and $I(r_w)$ to denote their initial states; and predicate $F(q)$ to mean that q is a final state of its automaton. The transition functions may be notated as a single pair of functions ℓ and r, where $\ell(w, q, w')$ returns the state reached by ℓ_w when it leaves state q on an arc labeled w', and similarly $r(w, q, w')$.

Notice that as an implementation matter, if the automata are defined in any systematic way, it is not necessary to actually store them in order to represent the grammar. One only needs to choose an appropriate representation for states q and define the I, F, ℓ, and r functions.

2.0.2   Meaning of the Grammar.   We now formally define the language generated by such a grammar, and the structures that the grammar assigns to sentences of this language.

Let a **dependency tree** be a rooted tree whose nodes (both internal and external) are labeled with words from V, as illustrated in Figure 3.1a; the root is labeled with the special symbol ROOT $\in V$. The children ('dependents') of a node are ordered with respect to each other and the node itself, so that the node has both **left children** that precede it and **right children** that follow it.

A dependency tree is grammatical iff for every word token w that appears in the tree, ℓ_w accepts the (possibly empty) sequence of w's left children (from right to left), and r_w accepts the sequence of w's right children (from left to right).

A string $\omega \in V^*$ is generated by the grammar, with analysis T, if T is a grammatical dependency tree and listing the node labels of T in infix order yields the string ω followed by ROOT. ω is called the **yield** of T.

2.0.3   Bilexicalism.   The term *bilexical* refers to the fact that (i) each $w \in V$ may specify a wholly different choice of automata ℓ_w and r_w, and furthermore (ii) these automata ℓ_w and r_w may make distinctions among individual words that are appropriate to serve as *children* (dependents) of w. Thus the grammar is sensitive to specific *pairs* of lexical items.

For example, it is possible for one lexical verb to select for a completely idiosyncratic set of nouns as subject, and another lexical verb to select for an entirely different set of nouns. Since it never requires more than a two-state automaton (though with many arcs!) to specify the set of possible subjects for a verb, there is no penalty for such behavior in the parsing algorithm to be described here.

3 $O(n^5)$ AND $O(n^3)$ RECOGNITION

This section develops a basic $O(n^3)$ recognition method for simple bilexical grammars as defined above. We begin with a naive $O(n^5)$ method drawn from context-free 'dotted-rule' methods such as Earley (1970); Graham et al., (1980). Second, we will see why this method is inefficient. Finally, a more efficient $O(n^3)$ algorithm is presented.

Both methods are essentially chart parsers, in that they use dynamic programming to build up an analysis of the whole sentence from analyses of its substrings. However, the slow method combines traditional *constituents*, whose lexical heads may be in the middle, while the fast method combines what we will call *spans*, whose heads are guaranteed to be at the edge.

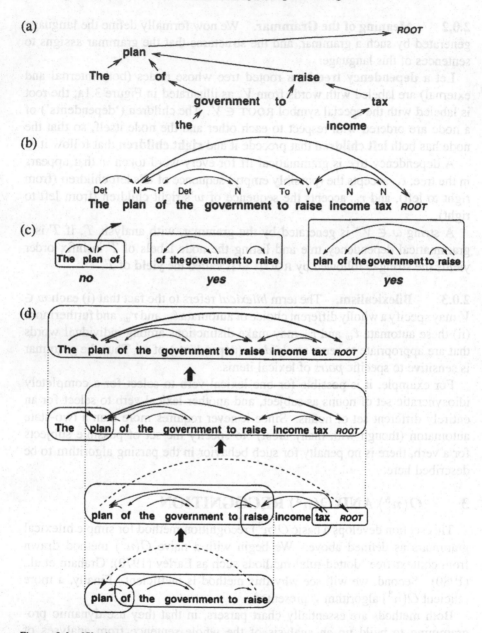

Figure 3.1 [Shading in this figure has no meaning.] (a) A dependency parse tree. (b) The same tree shown flattened out. (c) A span of the tree is any substring such that no interior word of the span links to any word outside the span. One non-span and two spans are shown. (d) A span may be decomposed into smaller spans as repeatedly shown; therefore, a span can be built from smaller spans by following the arrows upward. The parsing algorithm (Fig. 3.3–3.4) builds successively larger spans in a dynamic programming table (chart). The minimal spans, used to seed the chart, are linked or unlinked word bigrams, such as *The→plan* or *tax* ROOT, as shown.

3.1   NOTATION AND PRELIMINARIES

The input to the recognizer is a string of words, $\omega = w_1 w_2 \ldots w_n \in V^*$. We put $w_{n+1} = \text{ROOT}$, a special symbol that does not appear in ω. For $i \le j$, we write $w_{i,j}$ to denote the input substring $w_i w_{i+2} \ldots w_j$.

3.1.1   Generic Chart Parsing.
There may be many ways to analyze $w_{i,j}$. Each grammatical **analysis** has as its **signature** an **item**, or tuple, that concisely and completely describes its ability to combine with analyses of neighboring input substrings. Many analyses may have the same item as signature. This chapter will add some syntactic sugar and draw items as schematic pictures of analyses.

C (the **chart**) is an $(n+1) \times (n+1)$ array. The chart **cell** $C_{i,j}$ accumulates the set of signatures of all analyses of $w_{i,j}$. It must be possible to enumerate the set – or more generally, certain subsets defined by particular fixed properties – in time $O(1)$ per element.[2] In addition, it must be possible to perform an $O(1)$ duplicate check when adding a new item to a cell. A standard implementation is to maintain linked lists for enumerating the relevant subsets, together with a hash table (or array) for the duplicate check.

3.1.2   Analysis.
If S bounds the number of items per chart cell, then the space required by a recognizer is clearly $O(n^2 S)$. The time required by the algorithms we consider is $O(n^3 S^2)$, because for each of the $O(n^3)$ values of i, j, k such that $1 \le i \le j < k \le n+1$, they will test each of the $\le S$ items in $C_{i,j}$ against each of the $\le S$ items in $C_{j+1,k}$, to see whether analyses with those items as signatures could be grammatically combined into an analysis of $w_{i,k}$.

Efficiency therefore requires keeping S small. The key difference between the $O(n^5)$ method and the $O(n^3)$ method will be that S is $O(n)$ versus $O(1)$.

3.2   NAIVE BILEXICAL RECOGNITION

3.2.1   An Algorithm.
The obvious approach for bilexical grammars is for each analysis to represent a subtree, just as for an ordinary CFG. More precisely, each analysis of $w_{i,j}$ is a kind of **dotted subtree** that may not yet have acquired all its children.[3] The signature of such a dotted subtree is an item (w, q_1, q_2). This may be depicted more visually as

$$\overset{\displaystyle q_1 \; q_2}{\underset{i \;\; w \;\; j}{\triangle}}$$

where $w \in w_{i,j}$ is the **head word** at the root of the subtree, $q_1 \in Q(\ell_w)$, and $q_2 \in Q(r_w)$. If both q_1 and q_2 are final states, then the analysis is a complete constituent.

The resulting algorithm is specified declaratively using sequents in Figure 3.2a–b, which shows how the items combine.

3.2.2   Analysis.   It is easy to see from Figure 3.2a that each chart cell $C_{i,j}$ can contain $S = O(\min(n, |V|)t^2)$ possible items: there are $O(\min(n, |V|))$ choices for w, and $O(t)$ choices for each of q_1 and q_2 once w is known. It follows that the runtime is $O(n^3 S^2) = O(n^3 \min(n, |V|)^2 t^4)$.

More simply and generally, one can find the runtime by examining Figure 3.2b and seeing that there are $O(n^3 \min(n, |V|)^2 t^4)$ ways to instantiate the four rule templates. Each is instantiated at most once and in $O(1)$ time. McAllester (1999) proves that with appropriate indexing of items, this kind of runtime analysis is correct for a very general class of algorithms specified declaratively by inference rules.

3.2.3   An Improvement.   It is possible to reduce the t^4 factor to just t, since each attachment decision really depends only on one state (at the parent), not four states. This improved method is shown in Figure 3.2c. It groups complete constituents together under a single item even if they finished in different final states – a trick we will be using again.

Note that the revised method always attaches right children before left children, implying that a given dependency tree is only derived in one way. This property is important if one wishes to enhance the algorithm to compute the total number of distinct trees for a sentence, or their total probability, or related quantities needed for the Inside-Outside estimation algorithm.

3.2.4   Discussion.   Even with the improvement, parsing is still $O(n^5)$ (for $n < |V|$). Why so inefficient? Because there are too many distinct possible signatures. Whether LINK-L can make one tree a new child of another tree depends on the head words of both trees. Hence signatures must mention head words. Since the head word of a tree that analyzes $w_{i,j}$ could be any of the words $w_i, w_{i+1}, \ldots w_j$, and there may be n distinct such words in the worst case (assuming $n < |V|$), the number S of possible signatures for a tree is at least n.

In more concrete terms, the problem is that each chart cell may have to maintain many differently-headed analyses of the same string. Chomsky's noun phrase *visiting relatives* has two analyses: a kind of relatives vs. a kind of visiting. A bilexical grammar knows that only the first is appropriate in the context *hug visiting relatives*, and only the second is appropriate in the context *advocate visiting relatives*. So the two analyses must be kept separate in the chart: they will combine with context differently and therefore have different signatures.

(a) $q_1\ q_2$ $(1 \le i \le j \le n+1, w \in V, q_1 \in Q(\ell_w), q_2 \in Q(\ell_r))$
      $i\ \ w\ \ j$

(b)

SEED: ACCEPT: $q_1\ q_2$

$$\frac{}{\quad i\ w_i\ i\quad} \quad q_1 = I(\ell_{w_i}), q_2 = I(r_{w_i}) \qquad \frac{1\ \text{ROOT}\ n+1}{accept}\ F(q_1), F(q_2)$$

LINK-L: $q_1\ q_2$ $q_3\ q_4$

$$\frac{i\ w\ j\ \ j+1\ w'\ k}{i\ w\ k}\ F(q_3), F(q_4), q_2' = r(w, q_2, w')$$

(with $q_1\ q_2'$ in the conclusion triangle)

LINK-R: $q_1\ q_2$ $q_3\ q_4$

$$\frac{i\ w'\ j\ \ j+1\ w\ k}{i\ w\ k}\ F(q_1), F(q_2), q_3' = \ell(w, q_3, w')$$

(with $q_3'\ q_4$ in the conclusion triangle)

(c)

SEED: FLIP: q FINISH: $q\ F$

$$\frac{}{q}\ q = I(r_{w_i}) \qquad \frac{i\quad j}{q'\ F}\ F(q), q' = I(\ell_{w_i}) \qquad \frac{i\ w\ j}{F\ F}\ F(q)$$

LINK-L: q $F\ F$

$$\frac{i\quad j\ \ j+1\ w'\ k}{q'} \qquad q' = r(w_i, q, w')$$

$$\frac{}{i\quad k}$$

LINK-R: $F\ F$ $q\ F$ ACCEPT: $F\ F$

$$\frac{i\ w'\ j\ \ j+1\ w\ k}{q'\ F}\ q' = \ell(w, q, w') \qquad \frac{1\ \text{ROOT}\ n+1}{accept}$$

$$\frac{}{i\ w\ k}$$

Figure 3.2 Declarative specification of an $O(n^5)$ algorithm. (a) Form of items in the parse chart. (b) Inference rules. The algorithm can derive an analysis with the signature below ——— by combining analyses with the signatures above ———, provided that the input and grammar satisfy any properties listed to the right of ———. (c) A variant that reduces the grammar factor from t^4 to t. F is a literal that means 'an unspecified final state.'

3.3   EFFICIENT BILEXICAL RECOGNITION

3.3.1   Constituents vs. Spans.   To eliminate these two additional factors of n, we must reduce the number of possible signatures for an analysis. The solution is for analyses to represent some kind of contiguous string other than constituents. Each analysis in $C_{i,j}$ will be a new kind of object called a **span**, which consists of one or two 'half-constituents' in a sense to be described. The headword(s) of a span in $C_{i,j}$ are *guaranteed* to be at positions i and/or j in the sentence. This guarantee means that where $C_{i,j}$ in the previous section had up to n-fold uncertainty about the location of the headword of $w_{i,j}$, here it will have only 3-fold uncertainty. The three possibilities are that w_i is a headword, that w_j is, or that both are.

Given a dependency tree, we know what its constituents are: a constituent is any substring consisting of a word and all its descendants. The inefficient parsing algorithm of section 3.2 assembled the correct tree by finding and gluing together analyses of the tree's (dotted) constituents in an approved way. For something similar to be possible with spans, we must define what the spans of a given dependency tree are, and how to glue analyses of spans together into analyses of larger spans. Not every substring of the sentence is a constituent of this (or any) sentence's correct parse, and in the same way, not every substring is a span of this (or any) sentence's correct parse.

3.3.2   Definition of Spans.   Figure 3.1a–c illustrates what spans are. A span of the dependency tree in (a) and (b) is any substring $w_{i,j}$ of the input such that none of the interior words of the span communicate with any words outside the span. Formally: if $i < k < j$, and w_k is a child or parent of $w_{k'}$, then $i \leq k' \leq j$.

Thus, just as a constituent links to the rest of the sentence only through its head word, which may be located anywhere in the constituent, a span $w_{i,j}$ links to the rest of the sentence only through its **endwords** w_i and w_j, which are located at the edges of the span. We call $w_{i+1,j-1}$ the span's **interior**.

3.3.3   Assembling Spans.   Since we will build the parse by assembling possible spans, and the interiors of adjacent spans are insulated from each other, we crucially are allowed to forget the internal analysis of a span once we have built it. When we combine two adjacent such spans, we never add a link from or to the interior of either. For, by the definition of span, if such a link were necessary, then the spans being combined could not be spans of the true parse anyway. There is always some other way of decomposing the true parse (itself a span) into smaller spans so that no such links from or to interiors are necessary.

Figure 3.1d shows such a decomposition. Any span analysis of more than two words, say $w_{i,k}$, can be decomposed uniquely by the following deterministic procedure. Choose j such that w_j is the rightmost word in the interior of the span ($i < j < k$) that links to or from w_i; if there is no such word, put $j = i + 1$. Because crossing links are not allowed in a dependency tree – a property known as **projectivity**– the substrings $w_{i,j}$ and $w_{j,k}$ must also be spans. We can therefore assemble the original $w_{i,k}$ analysis by concatenating the $w_{i,j}$ and $w_{j,k}$ spans, and optionally adding a link between the endwords, w_i and w_k. By construction, there is never any need to add a link between any other pair of words. Notice that when the two narrower spans are concatenated, w_j gets its left children from one span and its right children from the other, and will never be able to acquire additional children since it is now span-internal.

By our choice of j, the left span in the concatenation, $w_{i,j}$, is always **simple** in the following sense: it has a direct link between w_i and w_j, or else has only two words. ($w_{i,k}$ is decomposed at the maximal j such that $i < j < k$ and $w_{i,j}$ is simple.) Requiring the left span to be simple assures a unique decomposition (see section 3.2 for motivation); the right span need not be simple.

3.3.4 Signatures of Spans.
A span's signature needs to record only a few pertinent facts about its internal analysis. It has the form shown in Figure 3.3a. i, j indicate that the span is an analysis of $w_{i,j}$. q_1 is the state of r_{w_i} after it has read the sequence of w_i's right children that appear in $w_{i+1,j}$, and q_2 is the state of ℓ_{w_j} after it has read the sequence of w_j's left children that appear in $w_{i,j-1}$. b_1 and b_2 are bits that indicate whether w_i and w_j, respectively, have parents within $w_{i,j}$. Finally, s is a bit indicating whether the span is simple in the sense described above.

The signature must record q_1 and q_2 so that the parser knows what additional dependents w_i or w_j can acquire. It must record b_1 and b_2 so that it can detect whether such a link would jeopardize the tree form of the dependency parse (by creating multiple parents, cycles, or a disconnected graph). Finally, it must record s to ensure that each distinct analysis is derived in at most one way.

It is useful to note the following four possible types of span:

- $b_1 = b_2 = 0$. Example: *of the government to raise* in Figure 3.1c. In this case, the endwords w_i and w_j are not yet connected to each other: that is, the path between them in the final parse tree will involve words outside the span. The span consists of two 'half-constituents' – w_i with all its right descendants, followed by w_j with all its left descendants.

- $b_1 = 0, b_2 = 1$. Example: *plan of the government to raise* in Figure 3.1c. In this case, w_j is a descendant of w_i via a chain of one or more leftward links within the span itself. The span consists of w_i and all its right descendants within $w_{i+1,j}$. (w_i or w_j or both may later acquire additional right children to the right of w_j.)

- $b_1 = 1, b_2 = 0$. Example: the whole sentence in Figure 3.1b. This is the mirror image of the previous case.

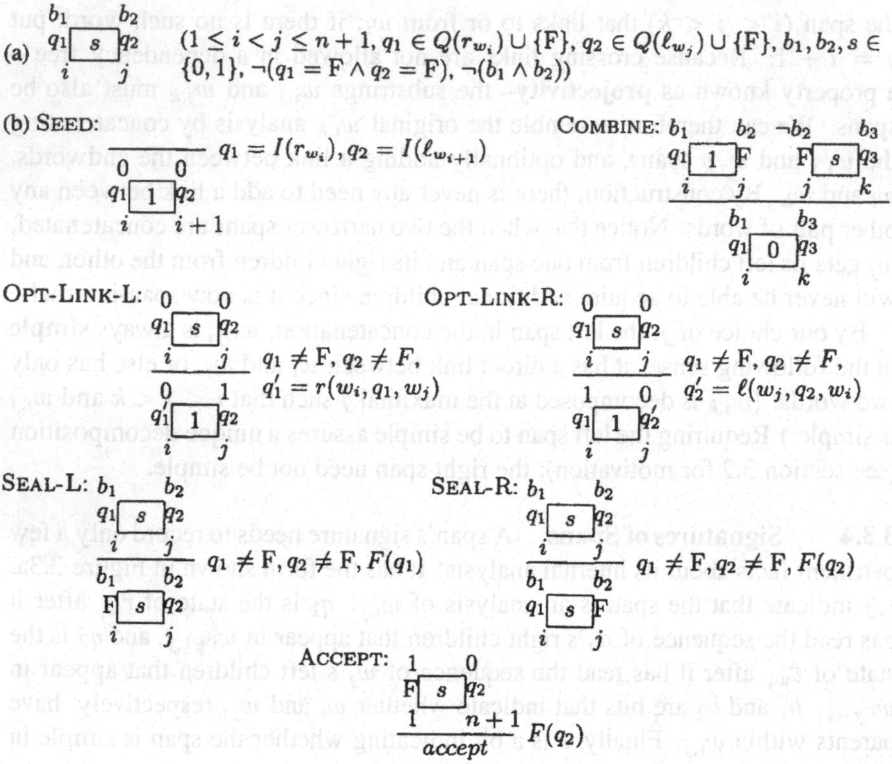

(a) $q_1 \boxed{\begin{array}{c} b_1 \quad b_2 \\ s \end{array}} q_2$ $(1 \le i < j \le n+1, q_1 \in Q(r_{w_i}) \cup \{F\}, q_2 \in Q(\ell_{w_j}) \cup \{F\}, b_1, b_2, s \in \{0, 1\}, \neg(q_1 = F \wedge q_2 = F), \neg(b_1 \wedge b_2))$

(b) SEED: $\cfrac{}{q_1 \boxed{\begin{array}{c} 0 \quad 0 \\ 1 \end{array}} q_2}$ $q_1 = I(r_{w_i}), q_2 = I(\ell_{w_{i+1}})$

COMBINE: $\cfrac{q_1 \boxed{\begin{array}{c} b_1 \quad b_2 \\ 1 \end{array}} F \quad F \boxed{\begin{array}{c} \neg b_2 \quad b_3 \\ s \end{array}} q_3}{q_1 \boxed{\begin{array}{c} b_1 \quad b_3 \\ 0 \end{array}} q_3}$

OPT-LINK-L: $\cfrac{q_1 \boxed{\begin{array}{c} 0 \quad 0 \\ s \end{array}} q_2}{q_1' \boxed{\begin{array}{c} 0 \quad 1 \\ 1 \end{array}} q_2}$ $q_1 \ne F, q_2 \ne F,$ $q_1' = r(w_i, q_1, w_j)$

OPT-LINK-R: $\cfrac{q_1 \boxed{\begin{array}{c} 0 \quad 0 \\ s \end{array}} q_2}{q_1 \boxed{\begin{array}{c} 1 \quad 0 \\ 1 \end{array}} q_2'}$ $q_1 \ne F, q_2 \ne F,$ $q_2' = \ell(w_j, q_2, w_i)$

SEAL-L: $\cfrac{q_1 \boxed{\begin{array}{c} b_1 \quad b_2 \\ s \end{array}} q_2}{F \boxed{\begin{array}{c} b_1 \quad b_2 \\ s \end{array}} q_2}$ $q_1 \ne F, q_2 \ne F, F(q_1)$

SEAL-R: $\cfrac{q_1 \boxed{\begin{array}{c} b_1 \quad b_2 \\ s \end{array}} q_2}{q_1 \boxed{\begin{array}{c} b_1 \quad b_2 \\ s \end{array}} F}$ $q_1 \ne F, q_2 \ne F, F(q_2)$

ACCEPT: $\cfrac{F \boxed{\begin{array}{c} 1 \quad 0 \\ s \end{array}} q_2}{accept}$ $F(q_2)$
(positions 1 and $n+1$)

Figure 3.3 Declarative specification of an $O(n^3)$ algorithm. (a) Form of items in the parse chart. (b) Inference rules. As in Fig. 3.2b, F is a literal that means 'an unspecified final state.'

- $b_1 = 1, b_2 = 1$. This case is impossible, for then some word interior to the span would need a parent outside it. We will never derive any analyses with this signature.

3.3.5   The Span-Based Algorithm.

A declarative specification of the algorithm is given in Figure 3.3, which shows how the items combine. The reader may choose to ignore s for simplicity, since the unique-derivation property may speed up recognition but does not affect its correctness. For concreteness, pseudocode is given in Figure 3.4.

The SEED rule seeds the chart with the minimal spans, which are two words wide. COMBINE is willing to combine two spans if they overlap in a word w_j that gets all its left children from the left span (hence 'F' appears in the rule), all its right children from the right span (again 'F'), and its parent in exactly one of the spans (hence '$b_2, \neg b_2$'). Whenever a new span is created by seeding or combining, the OPT-LINK rules can add an optional link between its endwords, provided that neither endword already has a parent.

```
1.   for i := 1 to n
2.        s := the item for w_{i,i+1} produced by SEED
3.        Discover(i, i + 1, s)
4.        Discover(i, i + 1, OPT-LINK-L(s))
5.        Discover(i, i + 1, OPT-LINK-R(s))
6.   for width := 2 to n
7.        for i := 1 to (n + 1) − width
8.             k := i + width
9.             for j := i + 1 to k − 1
10.                 foreach simple item s_1 in C^L_{i,j}
11.                      foreach item s_2 in C^R_{j,k} such that COMBINE(s_1, s_2) is defined
12.                           s := COMBINE(s_1, s_2)
13.                           Discover(i, k, s)
14.                           if OPT-LINK-L(s) and OPT-LINK-R(s) are defined
15.                                Discover(i, k, OPT-LINK-L(s))
16.                                Discover(i, k, OPT-LINK-R(s))
17.  foreach item s in C^R_{1,n+1}
18.       if ACCEPT(s) is defined
19.            return accept
20.  return reject
```

Figure 3.4 Pseudocode for an $O(n^3)$ recognizer. The functions in small caps refer to the (deterministic) inference rules of Figure 3.3. Discover(i, j, s) adds SEAL-L(s) (if defined) to $C^R_{i,j}$ and SEAL-R(s) (if defined) to $C^L_{i,j}$.

The SEAL rules check that an endword's automaton has reached a final (accepting) state. This is a precondition for COMBINE to trap the endword in the interior of a larger span, since the endword will then be unable to link to any more children. While COMBINE could check this itself, using SEAL is asymptotically more efficient because it conflates different final states into a single item – exactly as FINISH did in Figure 3.2c.

3.3.6   **Analysis.** The time requirements are $O(n^3 t^2)$, since that is the number of ways to instantiate the free variables in the rules of Figure 3.3b (McAllester, 1999). As t is typically small, this compares favorably with $O(n^5 t)$ for the naive algorithm of section 3.2. Even better, section 3.4 will obtain a speedup to $O(n^3 t)$.

The space requirements are naively $O(n^2 t^2)$, since that is the number of ways to instantiate the free variables in Figure 3.3a, i.e., the maximum number of items in the chart. The pseudocode in Figure 3.4 shows that this can be reduced to $O(n^2 t)$ by storing only items for which $q_1 = F$ or $q_2 = F$ (in separate charts C^R and C^L respectively). The other items need not be added to any chart, but can be fed to the OPT-LINK and SEAL rules immediately upon creation, and then destroyed.

3.4   AN ADDITIONAL $O(t)$ SPEEDUP

The above algorithm can optionally be sped up from $O(n^3t^2)$ to $O(n^3t)$, at the cost of making it perhaps slightly harder to understand.

Every item in Figure 3.3 has either 0 or 1 of the states q_1, q_2 instantiated as the special symbol F. We will now modify the algorithm so that either 1 or 2 of those states are always instantiated as F (except in items produced by SEED). This is possible because q_2 does not really matter in OPT-LINK-L, nor does q_1 in OPT-LINK-R. The payoff is that these rules, as well as COMBINE, will only need to consider one state at a time.

All that is necessary is to modify the applicability conditions of the inference rules. COMBINE gets the additional condition $q_1 = F \vee q_3 = F$. OPT-LINK-L and SEAL-L drop the condition that $q_2 \neq F$, while OPT-LINK-R and SEAL-R drop the condition that $q_1 \neq F$.

To preserve the property that derivations are unique, two additional modifications are now necessary. To eliminate the freedom to apply SEAL either before or after COMBINE, the SEAL rules should be restricted to apply only to simple spans (i.e., $s = 1$). And to eliminate the freedom to apply both SEAL-L and SEAL-R in either order to the output of SEED, the SEAL-L rule should require that $q_2 \neq F \vee b_2 = 1$.

4   VARIATIONS

In this section, we describe useful modifications that may be made to the formalism and/or the algorithm above.

4.1   WEIGHTED GRAMMARS

The ability of a verb to subcategorize for an idiosyncratic set of nouns, as above, can be used to implement black-and-white ('hard') selectional restrictions. Where bilexical grammars are really useful, however, is in capturing *gradient* ('soft') selectional restrictions. A **weighted bilexical grammar** can equip each verb with an idiosyncratic *probability distribution* over possible object nouns, or indeed possible dependents of any sort. We now formalize this notion.

4.1.1   Weighted Automata.   A **weighted DFA**, A, is a deterministic finite-state automaton that associates a real-valued **weight** with each arc and each final state (Mohri et al., 1996). Following heavily-weighted arcs is intuitively 'good,' 'probable,' or 'common'; so is stopping in a heavily-weighted final state. Each accepting path through A is automatically assigned a weight, namely, the sum of all arc weights on the path and the final-state weight of the last state on the path. Each string α accepted by A is assigned the weight of its accepting path.

4.1.2   Weighted Grammars.   Now, we may define a weighted bilexical grammar as a bilexical grammar in which all the automata ℓ_w and r_w are weighted DFAs. We define the weight of a dependency tree under the grammar as the sum, over all word tokens w in the tree, of the weight with which ℓ_w accepts w's sequence of left children plus the weight with which r_w accepts w's sequence of right children.

Given an input string ω, the **weighted parsing problem** is to find the highest-weighted grammatical dependency tree whose yield is ω.

4.1.3   From Recognition to Weighted Parsing.   One may turn the recognizer of section 3.3 into a parser in the usual way. Together with each item stored in a chart cell $C_{i,j}$, one must also maintain the highest-weighted known analysis with that item as signature, or a parse forest of all known analyses with that signature. In the implementation, items may be mapped to analyses via a hash table or array.

When we apply a rule from Figure 3.3b to derive a new item from old ones, we must also derive an associated analysis (or forest of analyses), and the weight of this analysis if the grammar is weighted.

When parsing, how should we *represent* an analysis of a span? (For comparison, an analysis of a constituent can be represented as a tree.) A general method is simply to store the span's derivation: we may represent any analysis as a copy of the rule that produced it together with pointers to the analyses that serve as inputs (i.e., antecedents) to that rule. Or similarly, one may follow the decomposition of section 3.3 and Figure 3.1d. Then an analysis of $w_{i,k}$ is a triple $(\alpha, \beta, linktype)$, where α points to an analysis of a simple span $w_{i,j}$, β points to an analysis of a span $w_{j,k}$, and $linktype \in \{\leftarrow, \rightarrow, \text{NONE}\}$ specifies the direction of the link (if any) between w_i and w_k. In the base case where $k = i + 1$, then α and β instead store w_i and w_k respectively.

We must also know how to compute the weight of an analysis. Any convenient definition will do, so long as the weight of a full parse comes out correctly. In all cases, we will define the weight of an analysis produced by a rule to be the total weight of the input(s) to that rule, plus another term derived from the conditions on the rule. For SEED and COMBINE, the additional term is 0; for OPT-LINK-L or OPT-LINK-R, it is the weight of the transition to q_1' or q_2' respectively; for SEAL-L, SEAL-R, or ACCEPT, it is the final-state weight of q_1, q_2, or q_2 respectively.

As usual, the strategy of maintaining only the highest-weighted analysis of each signature works because context-free parsing has the **optimal substructure property**. That is, any *optimal* analysis of a long string can be found by gluing together just *optimal* analyses of shorter substrings. For suppose that a and a' are analyses of the same substring, and have the same signature, but a has less weight than a'. Then suboptimal a cannot be part of any optimal analysis b in the chart – for if it were, the definition of signature ensures that we could substitute a' for a in b to get an analysis b' of greater total weight than b and the same signature as b, which contradicts b's optimality.

4.2 POLYSEMY

We now extend the formalism to deal with lexical selection. Regrettably, the input to a parser is typically not a string in V^*. Rather, it contains ambiguous tokens such as *bank*, whereas the 'words' in V are word senses such as $bank_1$, $bank_2$, and $bank_3$, or part-of-speech-tagged words such as *bank*/N and *bank*/V. If the input is produced by speech recognition or OCR, even more senses are possible.

One would like a parser to resolve these ambiguities simultaneously with the structural ambiguities. This is particularly true of a bilexical parser, where a word's dependents and parent provide clues to its sense and vice-versa.

4.2.1   Confusion Sets.   We may modify the formalism as follows. Consider the unweighted case first. Let Ω be the real input – a string not in V^* but rather in $\mathcal{P}(V)^*$, where $\mathcal{P}$ denotes powerset. Thus the ith symbol of Ω is a **confusion** set of possibilities for the ith word of the input, e.g., $\{bank_1, bank_2, bank_3\}$. Ω is generated by the grammar, with analysis T, if some string $\omega \in V^*$ is so generated, where ω is formed by replacing each set in Ω with one of its elements. Note that the yield of T is ω, not Ω.

For the weighted case, each confusion set in the input string Ω assigns a weight to each of its members. Again, intuitively, the heavily-weighted members are the ones that are commonly correct, so the noun *bank*/N would be weighted more highly than the verb *bank*/V. We score parses as before, except that now we also add to a dependency tree's score the weights of all the words that label its nodes, as selected from their respective confusion sets. Formally, we say that $\Omega = W_1 W_2 \ldots W_n \in \mathcal{P}(V)^*$ is generated by the grammar, with analysis T and weight $\mu_T \mu_1 + \cdots + \mu_n$, if some string $\omega = w_1 w_2 \ldots w_n \in V^*$ is generated with analysis T of weight μ_T, and for each $1 \le i \le n$, ω_i appears in the set W_i with weight μ_i.

4.2.2   Modifying the Algorithm.   Throughout the algorithm of Figure 3.3, we must replace each integer i (similarly j, k) with a pair of the form (i, w_i), where $w_i \in W_i$. That ensures that the signature of an analysis of $W_{i,j}$ will record the senses w_i and w_j of its endwords. The OPT-LINK rules refer to these senses when determining whether w_j can be a child of w_i or vice-versa. Moreover, COMBINE now requires its two input spans to agree not only on j but also on the sense w_j of their overlapping word W_j, so that this word's left children, right children, and parent are all appropriate to the same sense. The SEED rule nondeterministically chooses senses $w_i \in W_i$ and $w_{i+1} \in W_{i+1}$; to avoid double-counting, the weight of the resulting analysis is taken to be the weight with which w_i appears in W_i only.

If g is an upper bound on the size of a confusion set, then these modifications multiply the algorithm's space requirements by $O(g^2)$ and its time requirements by $O(g^3)$.

4.3   STRING-LOCAL CONSTRAINTS

When the parser is resolving polysemy as in section 4.2, it can be useful to implement string-local constraints. The SEED rule may be modified to disallow an arbitrary list of word-sense bigrams $w_i w_{i+1}$. More usefully, it may be made to favor some bigrams over others by giving them higher weights. Then the sense of one word will affect the preferred sense of adjacent words. (This is in addition to affecting the preferred sense of the words it links to).

For example, suppose each word is polysemous over several part-of-speech tags, which the parser must disambiguate. A useful hack is to define the weight of a parse as the log-probability of the parse, as usual, *plus* the log-probability of its tagged yield under the trigram tagging model of Church (1988). Then a highly-weighted parse will tend to be one whose tagged dependency structure and string-local structure are simultaneously plausible. This has been shown useful for probabilistic systems that simultaneously optimize tagging and parsing (Eisner, 1996a). (See Lafferty et al., 1992 for a different approach.)

To add in the trigram log-probability in this way, regard each input word as a confusion set W_i whose elements have the form $w_i = (v_i, t_i, t_{i+1})$. Here each v_i is an ordinary word (or sense) and t_i, t_{i+1} are hypothesized part-of-speech tags for v_i, v_{i+1} respectively. Now SEED should be restricted to produce only word-sense bigrams $(v_i, t_i, t_{i+1})(v_{i+1}, t_{i+1}, t_{i+2})$ that agree on t_{i+1}. The score of such a bigram is $\log \Pr(v_i \mid t_i) + \log \Pr(t_i \mid t_{i+1}, t_{i+2})$. (If $i = 1$, it is also necessary to add $\log \Pr(\text{STOP} \mid t_1, t_2)$.) Notice that (for notational convenience) we are treating the word sequence as generated from right to left, not vice-versa.

4.4   RATIONAL TRANSDUCTIONS

Polysemy (section 4.2) and string-local constraints (section 4.3) are both simple, local string phenomena that are inconvenient to model within the bilexical grammar. Many other such phenomena exist in language: they tend to be morphological in nature and easily modeled by finite-state techniques that apply to the yield of the dependency tree. This section conveniently extends the formalism and algorithm to accommodate such techniques. The previous two sections are special cases.

4.4.1   Underlying and Surface Strings. We distinguish the 'underlying' string $\omega = w_1 w_2 \ldots w_n \in V^*$ from the 'surface' string $\Omega = W_1 W_2 \ldots W_N \in X^*$. Thus V is a collection of morphemes (word senses), whereas X is typically a collection of graphemes (orthographic words). It is not necessary that $n = N$.

It is the underlying string ω that is described by the bilexical grammar. In general, ω is related to our input Ω by a possibly nondeterministic, possibly weighted finite-state transduction R (Mohri et al., 1996), as defined below.

We say that the surface string Ω is grammatical, with analysis (T, P), if T is a dependency parse tree whose fringe, ω ROOT, is transduced to Ω along an accepting path P in R. Notice that the analysis describes the tree, the underlying string, and the alignment between the underlying and surface strings.

The weighted parsing problem is now to reconstruct the best analysis (T, P) of Ω. The weight of an analysis is the weight of T plus the weight of P. For example, if weights are defined to be log-probabilities under a generative model, then the weight of T is the log-probability of stochastically generating the parse tree T and then stochastically transducing its fringe to the observed input.

4.4.2   Linguistic Uses. The transducer R may be used for many purposes. It can map different senses onto the same grapheme (polysemy) or vice-versa (spelling variation, contextual allomorphy). If the output alphabet X consists of letters rather than words, the transducer can apply morphological rules, such as the affixation and spelling rule in *try -ed* $\rightarrow$ *tried* (Koskenniemi, 1983; Kaplan and Kay, 1994). It can also perform more interesting kinds of local morphosyntactic processes (*PAST TRY* $\rightarrow$ *try -ed* (affix hopping), *NOT CAN* $\rightarrow$ {*can't, cannot*}, *PRO* $\rightarrow \epsilon$, ". " $\rightarrow$ '.').

In another vein, R may be an interestingly weighted version of the identity transducer. This can be used to favor or disfavor local patterns in the underlying string ω. A classic example is the 'that-trace' filter. Similarly, the trigram model of section 4.3 can be implemented easily with a transducer that merely removes the tags from tagged words, and whose weights are given by log-probabilities under a trigram model.

Finally, if R is used to describe a stochastic noisy channel that has corrupted or translated the input in some way, then the parser will automatically correct for the noise. Most ambitiously, R could be a generative acoustic model, and X an an alphabet of acoustic observations. In this case, the bilexical grammar would essentially be serving as the language model for a speech recognizer.

It is often convenient to define R as a composition of several simpler weighted transducers (Mohri et al., 1996), each of which handles just one of the above phenomena. For example, in order to map a sequence of abstract morphemes and punctuation tokens ($\in V*$) to a sequence of ASCII characters ($\in X*$), one could use the following transducer cascade: affix hopping, 'that-trace' penalization, followed by deletion of phonological nulls, then conventional processes such as capitalization marking and comma absorption, then realization of abstract morphemes as lemmas or null strings, then various morphological rules, and finally a stochastic model of typographical errors. Given some text Ω that is supposed to have emerged from this pipeline, the parser's job is to find a plausible way of renormalizing it that leads to a good parse.

4.4.3 Transducer Notation.

The **finite-state transducer** R has the same form as a (nondeterministic) finite-state automaton. However, the arcs are labeled not by symbols $w \in V$ but rather by pairs $\gamma : \Gamma$, where $\gamma \in V^*$ and $\Gamma \in X^*$.

The transducer R is said to **transduce** γ to Γ along path P if the arcs of P are consecutively labeled $\gamma_1 : \Gamma_1, \gamma_2 : \Gamma_2, \ldots \gamma_k : \Gamma_k$, and $\gamma_1\gamma_2 \cdots \gamma_k = \gamma$ and $\Gamma_1\Gamma_2 \cdots \Gamma_k = \Gamma$. We call this transduction **terminal** if $\gamma_k = \gamma$ (or $k = 0$).

One says simply that R transduces ω to Ω if it does so along an **accepting path**, i.e., a path from the initial state of R to a final state. The path's weight can be defined as in section 4.1, in terms of weights on the arcs and final states of R.

We may assume without loss of generality that the strings γ have length ≤ 1. That is, all arc labels have the form $\overline{w} : \Gamma$ where $\overline{w} \in V \cup \{\epsilon\}$ and $\Gamma \in X^*$.

We reuse the notation of section 2 as follows. $Q(R)$ and $I(R)$ denote the set of states and the initial state of R, and the predicate $F(r)$ means that state $r \in Q(R)$ is final. The transition predicate $R(r, r', \overline{w} : \Gamma)$ is true if there is an arc from r to r' with label $\overline{w} : \Gamma$. Its ϵ-left-closure $R^*(r, r', \overline{w} : \Gamma)$ is true iff R terminally transduces $\overline{w}$ to Γ along some path from r to r'.

4.4.4 Modifying the Inference Rules.

Recall that when modifying the algorithm to handle polysemy, we replaced each integer i in Figure 3.3 with a pair (i, w). For the more general case of transductions, we similarly replace i with a triple (i, w, r), where $w \in V, r \in Q(R)$. An item of the form

$$\underset{i,w,r \qquad\quad j,w',r'}{\cdots\boxed{\cdots}\cdots} \quad (0 \leq i \leq j \leq n;\ w, w' \in V;\ r, r' \in Q(R); \cdots)$$

represents the following hypothesis about the correct sentential analysis (T, P): that the tree T has a span $w\beta w'$ (for some string β) such that $\beta w'$ is terminally transduced to the surface substring $W_{i+1,j}$ along a subpath of P from state r to state r'.[4] Notice that if $i = j$ then $W_{i+1,j} = \epsilon$ by definition. Also notice that no claim is made about the relation of w to $W_{1,i}$ (but see below).

COMBINE must be modified along the same lines as for polysemy: it must require its two input spans to agree not only on j but on the entire triple (j, w', r'). As before, OPT-LINK should be defined in terms of the underlying words w, w'.

(a) SEED:
$$\frac{R^*(r,r',w':W_{i+1,j})}{\begin{array}{c} 0 \quad\;\; 0 \\ q_1 \boxed{1} q_2 \\ i,w,r \quad j,w',r' \end{array}} \quad q_1 = I(r_{w_i}), q_2 = I(\ell_{w_{i+1}})$$

ACCEPT:
$$\frac{R^*(I(R),r,w:W_{1,i}) \quad \begin{array}{c} 1 \quad\;\; 0 \\ \text{F}\boxed{s} q_2 \\ i,w,r \quad j,\text{ROOT},r' \end{array} \quad R^*(r',r'',\epsilon:W_{j+1,n})}{accept} \quad F(q_2), F(r'')$$

(b) FINAL-w:
$$\frac{R^*(r,r',w:W_{i+1,j})}{R(r,r',w:W_{i+1,j})}$$

FINAL-ϵ:
$$\frac{}{R^*(r,r,\epsilon:W_{i+1,i})}$$

EXT-LEFT:
$$\frac{R^*(r',r'',\overline{w}:W_{j+1,k})}{R^*(r,r'',\overline{w}:W_{i+1,k})} \quad R(r,r',\epsilon:W_{i+1,j})$$

(c)

START-PREFIX:
$$\frac{R^*(I(R),r,w:W_{1,i})}{\xrightarrow{i,w} r}$$

EXT-PREFIX:
$$\frac{\xrightarrow{i,w} r \quad R^*(r,r',w:W_{i+1,j})}{\xrightarrow{j,w'} r'}$$

START-SUFFIX:
$$\frac{R^*(r,r',\epsilon:W_{i+1,n})}{r \xrightarrow{i}} \quad F(r')$$

EXT-SUFFIX:
$$\frac{R^*(r,r',w':W_{i+1,j}) \quad r' \xrightarrow{j}}{r \xrightarrow{i}}$$

(d) SEED:
$$\frac{\xrightarrow{i,w} r \quad R^*(r,r',w':W_{i+1,j}) \quad r' \xrightarrow{j}}{\begin{array}{c} 0 \quad\;\; 0 \\ q_1 \boxed{1} q_2 \\ i,w,r \quad j,w',r' \end{array}} \quad q_1 = I(r_{w_i}), q_2 = I(\ell_{w_{i+1}})$$

(e)

1. $Agenda := \{\}$ (* priority queue of items by weight of their associated derivations *)
2. $Done := \{\}$ (* set of items indexed as discussed in section 3.1, section 3.2 *)
3. **foreach** x that can be produced by a rule with no inputs
4.   AddAgenda(x, $Agenda$) (* if duplicate, then also removes copy with the lighter derivation *)
5. **while** $Agenda \neq \{\}$
6. $x := $ Pop($Agenda$) (* highest-weighted item *)
7.   **if** $x = accept$ **then return** $accept$ (* also return associated derivation *)
8.   **if** $x \notin Done$
9.   AddDone(x, $Done$) (* updates indices appropriately *)
10.   **foreach** rule r
11.   **if** $r(x)$ is defined **then** AddAgenda($r(x)$, $Agenda$) (* as above *)
12.   **foreach** $z \in \bigcup_{y \in Done}\{(x,y),(y,x)\}$ with $r(z)$ defined (* use indices *)
13.   AddAgenda($r(z)$, $Agenda$) (* as above *)
14. **return** $reject$

Figure 3.5 All non-trivial changes to Figure 3.3 needed for handling transductions of the input. (a) The minimal modification to ensure correctness. The predicate $R^*(r,r',w':W_{i+1,j})$ is used here as syntactic sugar for an item $[r,r',w',i+1,j]$ (where $i \leq j$) that will be derived iff the predicate is true. (b) Rules for deriving those items during preprocessing of the input. (c) Deriving 'forward-backward' items during preprocessing. (d) Adding 'forward-backward' antecedents to parsing to rule out items that are impossible in context. (e) Generic pseudocode for agenda-based parsing from inference rules. Line 12 uses indices on y to enumerate z efficiently.

It is only the SEED and ACCEPT rules that actually need to examine the transducer R. Modified versions are shown in Figure 3.5a. These rules make reference to the ϵ-left-closed transition relation $R^*(\cdots)$, which Figure 3.5b shows how to precompute on substrings of the input Ω.

4.4.5   From Recognition to Parsing. This modified recognition algorithm yields a parsing algorithm just as in section 4.1. An analysis with the signature shown above has two parts: an analysis of the span $w\beta w'$, and the r-to-r' subpath that terminally transduces $\beta w'$ to $W_{i+1,j}$. Its weight is the sum of the weights of these two parts. To compute this weight, each rule in Figure 3.5a–b should define the weight of its output to be the total weight of its inputs, plus the arc or final-state weight associated with any $R(r, r', \ldots)$ or $F(\cdots)$ that it tests.

4.4.6   Cyclic Derivations. If R can transduce non-empty underlying substrings to ϵ, we must now use chart cells $C_{i,i}$, for spans that correspond to the surface substring $W_{i+1,i} = \epsilon$. In the general case where R can do so along cyclic paths, so that such spans may be unbounded, items can no longer be combined in a fixed order as in Figure 3.4 (lines 10–16).[5] This is because combining items from $C_{i,i}$ and $C_{i,j}$ ($i \leq j$) may result in adding new items back into $C_{i,j}$, which must be allowed to combine with their progenitors in $C_{i,i}$ again. The usual duplicate check ensures that we will terminate with the same time bounds as before, but managing this incestuous computation requires a more general agenda-based control mechanism (Kay, 1986), whose weighted case is shown in Figure 3.5e.[6]

4.4.7   Analysis. The analysis is essentially the same as for polysemy (section 4.2), i.e., $O(n^3 g^3 t^2)$ time, or $O(n^3 g^3 t)$ if we use the speedup of section 3.4. The priority queue in Figure 3.5e introduces an extra factor of $\log |Agenda| = O(\log ngt)$. An ordinary FIFO or LIFO queue can be substituted in the unweighted case or if there are no cycles of the form discussed.[7]

However, g now bounds the number of possible *triples* (i, w, r) compatible with a position i in the input Ω. Notice that as with ℓ_w and r_w, there is no penalty for the number of arcs in R, i.e. the sizes of the vocabularies V, X.

Is g small? The intuition is that most transductions of interest give a small bound g, since they are locally 'almost' invertible: they are constrained by the surface string Ω to only consider a few possible underlying words and states at each position i. For example, a transducer to handle polysemy (map senses onto words) allows only a few underlying senses w per surface word W_i, and it needs only one state r.

But alas, the algorithm so far does not respect these constraints. Consider the SEED rule in Figure 3.5a: w (though not w') is allowed to take any value in

V regardless of the input, and r, r' are barely more constrained. So the parser would allow many unnecessary triples and run very slowly. We now fix it to reclaim the intuition above.

4.4.8   Restoring Efficiency. We wish to constrain the (i, w, r) triples actually considered by the parser, by considering W_i and more generally the broader context provided by the entire input Ω. A triple (i, w, r) should never be considered unless it is consistent with some transduction that could have produced Ω.

We introduce two new kinds of items that let us check this consistency. The rules in Figure 3.5 derive the 'forward item' $\xrightarrow{i,w} r$ iff R can terminally transduce αw (for some α) to $W_{1,i}$ on a subpath from $I(R)$ to r. They derive the 'backward item' $r \xrightarrow{i}$ iff R can transduce some β to $W_{i+1,n}$ on a subpath from r to a final state. Figure 3.5d modifies the SEED rule to require such items as antecedents, which is all we need.

4.4.9   Remark. The new antecedents are used only as a filter. In parsing, they contribute no weight or detail to the analyses produced by the revised rule SEED. However, their weights might be used to improve parsing efficiency. Work by Caraballo and Charniak (1998) on best-first parsing suggests that the total weight of the three items

$$\xrightarrow{i,w} r \qquad \boxed{} \qquad r' \xrightarrow{j}$$
$$i, w, r \qquad j, w', r'$$

may be a good heuristic measure of the viability of the middle item (representing a type of span) in the context of the rest of the sentence. (Notice that the middle item cannot be derived at all unless the other two also can.)

5   RELATION TO OTHER FORMALISMS

The bilexical grammar formalism presented here is flexible enough to capture a variety of grammar formalisms and probability models. On the other hand, as discussed in section 5.6, it does not achieve the (possibly unwarranted) power of certain other bilexical formalisms.

5.1   MONOLEXICAL DEPENDENCY GRAMMAR

5.1.1   Lexicalized Dependency Grammar. It is straightforward to encode dependency grammars such as those of Gaifman (1965). We focus here on the case that Milward, 1994 calls Lexicalized Dependency Grammar (LDG). Milward demonstrates a parser for this case that requires $O(n^3 g^3 t^3)$ time and $O(n^2 g^2 t^2)$ space, using a left-to-right algorithm that maintains its state as an acyclic directed graph. Here t is taken to be the maximum number of dependents on a word.

LDG is defined to be only *monolexical*. Each word sense entry in the lexicon is for a word tagged with the type of phrase it projects. An entry for *helped*/S, which appears as head of the sentence *Nurses helped John wash*, may specify that it wants a left dependent sequence of the form w_1/N and a right dependent sequence of the form w_2/N, w_3/V. However, under LDG it cannot constrain the lexical content of w_1, w_2, or w_3, either discretely or probabilistically.[8]

By encoding a monolexical LDG as a bilexical grammar, and applying the algorithm of this chapter, we can reduce parsing time and space by factors of t^2 and t, respectively. The encoding is straightforward. To capture the preferences for *helped*/S as above, we define $\ell_{helped/S}$ to be a two-state automaton that accepts exactly the set of nouns, and $r_{helped/S}$ to be a three-state automaton that accepts exactly those word sequences of the form (noun, verb).

Obviously, $\ell_{helped/S}$ includes a great many arcs – one arc for every noun in V. This does not however affect parsing performance, which depends only on the number of *states* in the automaton.

5.1.2 Optional and Iterated Dependents.

The use of automata to specify dependents is similar to the idea of allowing regular expressions in CFG rules, e.g., NP → (Det) Adj* N (Woods, 1969). It makes the bilexical grammar above considerably more flexible than the LDG that it encodes. In the example above, $r_{helped/S}$ can be trivially modified so that the dependent verb is optional (*Nurses helped John*). LDG can accomplish this only by adding a new lexical sense of *helped*/S, increasing the polysemy term g.

Similarly, under a bilexical grammar, $\ell_{nurses/N}$ can be specified to accept dependent sequences of the form (adj, adj, adj, ... adj, (det)). Then *nurses* may be expanded into *weary Belgian nurses*. Unbounded iteration of this sort is not possible in LDG, where each word sense has a fixed number of dependents. In LDG, as in categorial grammars, *weary Belgian nurses* would have to be headed by the adjunct *weary*. Thus, even if LDG were sensitive to bilexicalized dependencies, it would not recognize *nurses→helped* as such a dependency in *weary Belgian nurses helped John*. (It would see *weary→helped* instead.)

5.2 BILEXICAL DEPENDENCY GRAMMAR

In the example of section 5.1, we may arbitrarily weight the individual noun arcs of the ℓ_{helped} automaton, according to how appropriate those nouns are as subjects of *helped*. (In the unweighted case, we might choose to rule out inanimate subjects altogether, by removing their arcs or assigning them the weight $-\infty$.) This turns the grammar from monolexical to bilexical, without affecting the cubic-time cost of the parsing algorithm of section 3.3.

5.3   TEMPLATE MATCHING

Becker (1975) argues that much naturally-occurring language is generated by stringing together fixed phrases and templates. To the bilexical construction of section 5.2, one may add handling for special phrases. Consider the idioms (a) *run scared*, (b) *run circles [around NP]*, and (c) *run NP [into the ground]*. (a), like most idioms, is only bilexical, so it may be captured 'for free': simply increase the weight of the *scared* arc in $r_{run/V}$. But because (b) and (c) are trilexical, they require augmentation to the grammar, possibly increasing t and g. (b) requires a special state to be added to $r_{run/V}$, so that the dependent sequence (*circles, around*) may be recognized and weighted heavily. (c) requires a specialized lexical entry for *into*; this sense is a preferred dependent of *run* and has *ground* as a preferred dependent.

5.4   PROBABILISTIC BILEXICAL MODELS

Eisner (1996a) compares several distinct probability models for dependency grammar. Each model simultaneously evaluates the part-of-speech tags and the dependencies in a given dependency parse tree. Given an untagged input sentence, the goal is to find the tagged dependency parse tree with highest probability under the model.

Each of these models can be accommodated to the bilexical parsing framework, allowing a cubic-time solution. In each case, V is a set of part-of-speech-tagged words. Each weighted automaton ℓ_w or r_w is defined so that it accepts any dependent sequence in V^* – but the automaton has 8 states, arranged so that the weight of a given dependent w' (or the probability of halting) depends on the major part-of-speech category of the previous dependent.[9] Thus, any arc that reads a noun (say) terminates in the Noun state. The w'-reading arc *leaving* the Noun state may be weighted differently from the w'-reading arcs from other states; so the word w' may be more or less likely as a child of w according to whether its preceding sister was a noun.

As sketched in Eisner (1996b), each of Eisner's probability models is implemented as a particular scheme for weighting these automaton. For example, model C regards ℓ_w and r_w as Markov processes, where each state specifies a probability distribution over its exit options, namely, its outgoing arcs and the option of halting. The weight of an arc or a final state is then the log of its probability. Thus if $r_{helped/V}$ includes an arc labeled with $bathe/V$ and this arc is leaving the Noun state, then the arc weight is (an estimate of)

$$\log \Pr(\text{next right dependent is } bathe/V \mid \text{parent is } helped/V \text{ and previous} \\ \text{right dependent was a noun} \qquad)$$

The weight of a dependency parse tree under this probability model is a sum of such factors, which means that it estimates $\log \Pr(\text{dependency links \& input}$

words) according to a generative model. By contrast, model D estimates $\log \Pr(\text{dependency links} \mid \text{input words})$, using arc weights that are roughly of the form

$$\log \Pr(bathe/V \text{ is a right dep. of } helped/V \mid \text{both words appear in sentence and prev. right dep. was a) noun}$$

which is similar to the probability model of Collins (1996). Thus, different probability models are simply different weighting schemes within our framework. Some of the models use the trigram weighting approach of section 4.3.

5.5   BILEXICAL PHRASE-STRUCTURE GRAMMAR

5.5.1   Nonterminal Categories as Sense Distinctions. In some situations, conventional phrase-structure trees appear preferable to dependency trees. Collins (1997) observes that since VP and S are both verb-headed, the dependency grammars of section 5.4 would falsely expect them to appear in the same environments. (The expectation is false because *continue* subcategorizes for VP only.) Phrase-structure trees address the problem by subcategorizing for phrases that are labeled with nonterminals like VP and S.

Within the present formalism, the solution is to distinguish multiple senses (section 4.2) for each word, one for each of its possible maximal projections. Then *help*/VP$_{\text{inf}}$ and *help*/S are separate senses: they take different dependents (yielding *to help John* vs. *nurses help John*), and only the former is an appropriate dependent of *continue*.

5.5.2   Unflattening the Dependency Structure. A second potential advantage of phrase-structure trees is that they are more articulated than dependency trees. In a (headed) phrase-structure tree, a word's dependents may attach to it at different levels (with different nonterminal labels), providing an obliqueness order on the dependents. Obliqueness is of semantic interest; it is also exploited by Wu (1995), whose statistical translation model preserves the topology (ID but not LP) of binary-branching parses.

For the most part, it is possible to recover this kind of structure under the present formalism. A scheme can be defined for converting dependency parse trees to labeled, binary branching phrase-structure trees. Then one can use the fast bilexical parsing algorithm of section 3.3 to generate the highest-weighted dependency tree, and then convert that tree to a phrase-structure tree, as shown in Figure 3.6.

For concreteness, we sketch how such a scheme might be defined. First label the states of all automata ℓ_w, r_w with appropriate nonterminals. For example, $r_{help/S}$ might start in state V; it transitions to state VP after reading its object,

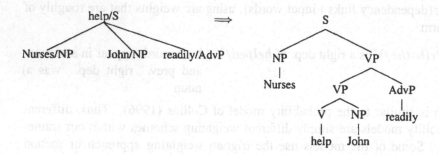

Figure 3.6 Unflattening a dependency tree when the word senses and automaton states bear nonterminal labels.

John/NP; and it loops back to VP when reading an adjunct such as *readily/AdvP*. Now, given a dependency tree for *Nurses help John readily*, we can reconstruct the sequence V, VP, VP of states encountered by $r_{help/S}$ as it reads *help*'s right children, and thereby associate a nonterminal attachment level with each child.

To produce the full phrase-structure tree, we must also decide on an obliqueness order for the children. Since this amounts to an order for the nodes at which the children attach, one approach is to derive it from a preferred total ordering on node types, according to which, say, right-branching VP nodes should always be lower than left-branching S nodes. We attach the children one at a time, referring to the ordering whenever we have a choice between attaching the next left child and the next right child.

This kind of scheme is adequate for most linguistic purposes. (For example, together with polysemy (section 4.2) it can be used to encode the Treebank grammars of Charniak, 1995.) It is interesting to compare it to Collins (1996), who maps phrase-structure trees to dependency trees whose edges are labeled with triples of nonterminals. In that paper Collins defines the probability of a phrase-structure tree to be the probability of its corresponding dependency tree. However, since his map is neither 'into' nor 'onto,' this does not quite yield a probability distribution over phrase-structure trees; nor can he simply find the best dependency tree and convert it to a phrase-structure tree as we do here, since the best dependency tree may correspond to 0 or 2 phrase-structure trees.

Neither the present scheme nor that of Collins (1996) can produce arbitrary phrase-structure trees. In particular, they cannot produce trees in which several adverbs alternately left-adjoin and right-adjoin to a given VP. We now consider the more powerful class of head-automaton grammars and bilexical context-free grammars, which *can* describe such trees.

5.6 HEAD AUTOMATA

Weighted bilexical grammars are essentially a special case of head-automaton grammars (Alshawi, 1996). As noted in the introduction, HAGs are bilexical in spirit. However, the left and right dependents of a word w are accepted not separately, by automata ℓ_w and r_w, but in interleaved fashion by a single weighted automaton, d_w. d_w assigns weight to strings over the alphabet $V \times \{\leftarrow, \rightarrow\}$; each such string is an interleaving of lists of left and right dependents from V.

Head automata, as well as Collins (1997), can model the case that section 5.5 cannot: where left and right dependents are arbitrarily interleaved. Alshawi (1996) points out that this makes head automata fairly powerful. A head automaton corresponding to the regular expression $((a, \leftarrow)(b, \rightarrow))^*$ requires its word to have an equal number of left and right dependents, i.e,. $a^n w b^n$. (Bilexical or dependency grammars are context-free in power, so they can also generate $\{a^n w b^n : n \geq 0\}$ – but only with a structure where the a's and b's depend bilexically on each other, not on w. Thus, they allow only the usual linguistic analysis of the doubly-center-embedded sentence *Rats cats children frequently mistreat chase squeak.*)

For syntactic description, the added generative power of head automata is probably unnecessary. (Linguistically plausible interactions among left and right subcat frames, such as fronting, can be captured in bilexical grammars simply via multiple word senses.)

Head automaton grammars and an equivalent bilexical CFG-style formalism are discussed further in Eisner and Satta (1999), where it is shown that they can be parsed in time $O(n^4 g^2 t^2)$.

5.7 LINK GRAMMARS

There is a strong connection between the algorithm of this chapter and the $O(n^3)$ link grammar parser of Sleator and Temperley (1993). As Alon Lavie (p.c.) has pointed out, both algorithms use essentially the same decomposition into what are here called spans. Sleator and Temperley's presentation (as a top-down memoizing algorithm) is rather different, as is the parse scoring model introduced by Lafferty et al. (1992). (Link grammars were unknown to this author when he developed and implemented the present algorithm in 1994.)

This section makes the connection explicit. It gives a brief (and attractive) definition of link grammars and shows how a minimal variant of the present algorithm suffices to parse them. As before, our algorithm allows an arbitrary weighting model (section 4.1) and can be extended to parse the composition of a link grammar and a finite-state transducer (section 4.4).

5.7.1 Formalism. A link grammar may be specified exactly as the bilexical grammars of section 2 are. A link grammar parse of $\Omega = W_1 W_2 \ldots W_n$, called a **linkage**, is a connected undirected graph whose vertices $\{1, 2, \ldots n{+}1\}$ are respectively labeled with $w_1 \in W_1, w_2 \in W_2, \ldots w_n \in W_n, w_{n+1} = $ ROOT, and whose edges do not 'cross,' i.e., edges $i{-}k$ and $j{-}\ell$ do not both exist for any $i < j < k < \ell$. The linkage is grammatical iff for each vertex i, ℓ_{w_i} accepts the sequence of words $\langle w_j : j < i, i{-}j$ is an edge$\rangle$ (ordered by decreasing j), and r_{w_i} accepts the sequence of words $\langle w_j : j > i, i{-}j$ is an edge$\rangle$ (ordered by increasing j).

Traditionally, the edges of a linkage are labeled with named grammatical relations. In this case, ℓ_{w_i} should accept the sequence of pairs $\langle (w_j, R) : j < i, i{-}j$ is an edge labeled by $R\rangle$, and similarly for r_{w_i}.

5.7.2   Discussion.   The above formalism improves slightly on Sleator and Temperley (1993) by allowing arbitrary DFAs rather than just straight-line automata (cf. section 5.1). This makes the formalism more expressive, so that it is typically possible to write grammars with a lower polysemy factor g. In addition, any weights or probabilities are sensitive to the underlying word senses w_i (known in link grammar as **disjuncts**), not merely the surface graphemes W_i.

Allowing finite-state post-processing as in section 4.4 also makes the formalism more expressive. It allows a modular approach to writing grammars: the link grammar handles dependencies (topology-local phenemona) while the transducer handles string-local phenomena.

5.7.3   Modifying the Algorithm.   Linkages have a less restricted form than dependency trees. Both are connected graphs without crossing edges, but only dependency trees disallow cycles or distinguish parents from children. The algorithm of Figure 3.3 therefore had to take extra pains to ensure that each word has a unique directed path to ROOT. It can be simplified for the link grammar case, where we only need to ensure connectedness. In place of the bits b_1 and b_2, the signature of an analysis of $w_{i,j}$ should include a single bit indicating whether the analysis is a connected graph; if not, it has two connected components. The input to ACCEPT and at least one input to COMBINE must be connected. (As for output, obviously SEED's output is not connected, OPT-LINK's is, and COMBINE or SEAL's output is connected iff all its inputs are.) To prevent linkages from becoming multigraphs, each item needs an extra bit indicating whether it is the output of OPT-LINK; if so, it may not be input to OPT-LINK again.

Figure 3.3 (or Figure 3.5) needs one more change to become an algorithm for link grammars. There should be only one OPT-LINK rule, which should advance the state q_1 of r_{w_i} to some state q_1' by reading w_j (like OPT-LINK-L), and *simultaneously* advance the state q_2 of ℓ_{w_j} to some state q_2' by reading w_i (like OPT-LINK-R). (Or if edges are labeled, there must be a named relation

R such that r_{w_i} reads (w_j, R) and ℓ_{w_j} reads (w_i, R).) This is because link grammar's links are not directional: the linked words w_i and w_j stand in a symmetric relation wherein they must accept each other.

5.7.4   Analysis. The resulting link grammar parser runs in time $O(n^3 g^3 t^2)$; so does the obvious generalization of Sleator and Temperley (1993) to our automaton-based formalism. A minor point is that t is measured differently in the two algorithms, since the automata ℓ_w, r_w used in the Sleator-Temperley-style top-down algorithm must be the reverse of those used in the above bottom-up algorithm. (The minimal DFAs accepting a language L and its reversal L^R may have exponentially different sizes t.)

The improvement of section 3.4 to $O(n^3 g^3 t)$ is not available for link grammars. Nor is the improvement of Eisner and Satta (1999) to $O(n^3 g^2 t)$, which uses a different decomposition that relies on acyclicity of the dependency graph.

5.8   LEXICALIZED TREE-ADJOINING GRAMMARS

The formalisms discussed in this chapter have been essentially context-free. The kind of $O(n^3)$ or $O(n^4)$ algorithms we have seen here cannot be expected for the more powerful class of mildly context-sensitive grammars (Joshi et al., 1991), where the best known parsing algorithms are $O(n^6)$ even for *non-lexicalized* cases. However, it is worth remarking that similar problems and solutions apply when bilexical preferences are added. In particular, Lexicalized Tree-Adjoining Grammar (Schabes et al., 1988) is actually bilexical, since each tree contains a lexical item and may select for other trees that substitute or adjoin into it. Eisner and Satta (2000) show that standard TAG parsing essentially takes $O(n^8)$ in this case, but can be sped up to $O(n^7)$.

6   CONCLUSIONS

Following recent trends in probabilistic parsing, this chapter has introduced a new grammar formalism, weighted bilexical grammars, in which individual lexical items can have idiosyncratic selectional influences on each other.

The new formalism is derived from dependency grammar. It can also be used to model other bilexical approaches, including a variety of phrase-structure grammars and (with minor modifications) all link grammars. Its scoring approach is compatible with a wide variety of probability models.

The obvious parsing algorithm for bilexical grammars (used by most authors) takes time $O(n^5 g^2 t)$. A new method is exhibited that takes time $O(n^3 g^3 t)$. An extension parses sentences that have been 'corrupted' by a rational transduction.

The simplified $O(n^3 g^3 t^2)$ variant of section 3.3 was originally sketched in Eisner (1996b) and presented (though without benefit of Figure 3.3) in Eisner

(1997). It has been used successfully in a large parsing experiment (Eisner, 1996a).

The reader may wish to know that more recently, Eisner and Satta (1999) found an alternative algorithm that combines half-constituents rather than spans. It has the same space requirements, and the asymptotically faster runtime of $O(n^3 g^2 t)$ – achieving the same cubic time on the input length but with a grammar factor as low as that of the naive n^5 algorithm.

While the algorithm presented in this chapter is not as fast asymptotically as that one, there are nonetheless a few reasons to consider using it:

- It is perhaps simpler to implement, as the chart contains not four types of subparse but only one.[10]

- With minor modifications (section 5.7), the same implementation can be used for link grammar parsing. This does not seem to be true of the faster algorithm.

- In some circumstances, it may run faster despite the increased grammar constant. This depends on the grammar (i.e., the values of g and t) and other constants in the implementation.

- Using probabilities or a hard grammar to prune the chart can significantly affect average-case behavior. For example, in one unpublished experiment on Penn Treebank/*Wall Street Journal* text (reported by the author at ACL '99), probabilistic pruning closed the gap between the $O(n^3 g^3 t^2)$ and $O(n^3 g^2 t)$ algorithms. (Both still substantially outperformed the pruned $O(n^5)$ algorithm.)

- With the improvement presented in section 3.4, the asymptotic penalty of the span-based approach presented here is reduced to only $O(g)$.

Thus, while Eisner and Satta (1999) is the safer choice overall, the relative performance of the two algorithms in practice may depend on various factors.

One might also speculate on algorithms for related problems. For example, the g^3 factor in the present algorithm (compared to Eisner and Satta's g^2) reflects the fact that the parser sometimes considers three words at once. In principle this could be exploited. The probability of a dependency link could be conditioned on all three words or their senses, yielding a 'trilexical' grammar. Lafferty et al. (1992) use precisely such a probability model in their related $O(n^3)$ algorithm for parsing link grammars, although it is not clear how relevant their third word is to the probability of the link (Eisner, 1996b).

Acknowledgments

I am grateful to Michael Collins, Joshua Goodman, and Alon Lavie for useful discussion of this work.

Notes

1. Actually, Lafferty et al. (1992) is formulated as a *trilexical* model, though the influence of the third word could be ignored: see section 6.

2. Having unified an item with the left input of an inference rule, such as COMBINE in Figure 3.3, the parser must enumerate all items that can then be unified with the right input.

3. In the sense of the dotted rules of Earley (1970).

4. Notice that our assumption about the form of arc labels, above, guarantees that any span of T will be transduced to some substring of Ω by an an exact subpath of P. Without that assumption, the span might begin in the middle of some arc of P.

5. Cycles that transduce ϵ to ϵ would create a similar problem for the rules of Figure 3.5b, but R can always be transformed so as to eliminate such cycles.

6. We assume that the output of a rule is no heavier than any of its inputs, so that additional trips around a derivational cycle cannot increase weight unboundedly. (E.g., all rule weights are log-probabilities and hence ≤ 0.) In this case the code can be shown correct: it pops items from the agenda only after their highest-weighted (Viterbi) derivations are found, and never puts them back on the agenda.

The algorithm is actually a generalization to hypergraphs of the single-source shortest-paths algorithm of Dijkstra (1959). In a hypergraph such as the parse forest, each parent of a vertex (item) is a *set* of vertices (antecedents). Our single source is taken to be the empty antecedent set. Note that finding the *total* weight of all derivations would be much harder than finding the maximum, in the presence of cycles (Stolcke, 1995; Goodman, 1998).

7. The time required for the agenda-based algorithm is proportional to the number of rule instances used in the derivation forest. The space is proportional to the number of items derived.

8. What would happen if we tried to represent bilexical dependencies in such a grammar? In order to restrict w_2 to appropriate objects of *helped*/S, the grammar would need a new nonterminal symbol, $N_{helpable}$. All nouns in this class would then need additional lexical entries to indicate that they are possible heads of $N_{helpable}$. The proliferation of such entries would drive g up to $|V|$ in Milward's algorithm, resulting in $O(n^3|V|^3t^3)$ time (or by ignoring rules that do not refer to lexical items in the input sentence, $O(n^6t^3)$).

9. The eight states are START, Noun, Verb, Noun Modifier, Adverb, Prep, Wh-word, and Punctuation.

10. On the other hand, for indexing purposes it is helpful to partition this type into at least two subtypes: see the two charts of Figure 3.4.

References

Alshawi, H. (1996). Head automata and bilingual tiling: Translation with minimal representations. In *Proceedings of the 34th ACL*, pp. 167–176, Santa Cruz, CA.

Becker, J. D. (1975). The phrasal lexicon. Report 3081 (AI Report No. 28), Bolt, Beranek, and Newman.

Caraballo, S. A. and Charniak, E. (1998). New figures of merit for best-first probabilistic chart parsing. *Computational Linguistics.*

Charniak, E. (1995). Parsing with context-free grammars and word statistics. Technical Report CS-95-28, Department of Computer Science, Brown University, Providence, RI.

Charniak, E. (1997). Statistical parsing with a context-free grammar and word statistics. In *Proceedings of the Fourteenth National Conference on Artificial Intelligence*, pp. 598–603, Menlo Park. AAAI Press/MIT Press.

Church, K. W. (1988). A stochastic parts program and noun phrase parser for unrestricted text. In *Proceedings of the 2nd Conf. on Applied NLP*, pp. 136–148, Austin, TX.

Collins, M. J. (1996). A new statistical parser based on bigram lexical dependencies. In *Proceedings of the 34th ACL*, pp. 184–191, Santa Cruz, July.

Collins, M. J. (1997). Three generative, lexicalised models for statistical parsing. In *Proceedings of the 35th ACL and 8th European ACL*, pp. 16–23, Madrid, July.

Dijkstra, E. W. (1959). A note on two problems in connexion with graphs. *Numerische Mathematik*, 1:269–271.

Earley, J. (1970). An efficient context-free parsing algorithm. *Communications of the ACM*, 13(2):94–102.

Eisner, J. (1996a). An empirical comparison of probability models for dependency grammar. Technical Report IRCS-96-11, Institute for Research in Cognitive Science, Univ. of Pennsylvania.

Eisner, J. (1996b). Three new probabilistic models for dependency parsing: An exploration. In *Proceedings of the 16th International Conference on Computational Linguistics (COLING-96)*, pp. 340–345, Copenhagen.

Eisner, J. (1997). Bilexical grammars and a cubic-time probabilistic parser. In *Proceedings of the Fifth International Workshop on Parsing Technologies*, pp. 54–65, MIT, Cambridge, MA.

Eisner, J. and Satta, G. (1999). Efficient parsing for bilexical context-free grammars and head-automaton grammars. In *Proceedings of the 37th ACL*, pp. 457–464, University of Maryland.

Eisner, J. and Satta, G. (2000). A faster parsing algorithm for lexicalized tree-adjoining grammars. In *Proceedings of the 5th Workshop on Tree-Adjoining Grammars and Related Formalisms (TAG+5)*, Paris.

Gaifman, H. (1965). Dependency systems and phrase structure systems. *Information and Control*, 8:304–337.

Goodman, J. (1997). Probabilistic feature grammars. In *Proceedings of the 1997 International Workshop on Parsing Technologies*, pp. 89–100, MIT, Cambridge, MA.

Goodman, J. (1998). *Parsing Inside-Out*. PhD thesis, Harvard University.

Graham, S. L., Harrison, M. A., and Ruzzo, W. L. (1980). An improved context-free recognizer. *ACM Transactions on Programming Languages and Systems*, 2(3):415–463.

Joshi, A. K., Vijay-Shanker, K., and Weir, D. (1991). The convergence of mildly context-sensitive grammar formalisms. In Sells, P., Shieber, S. M., and Wasow, T., editors, *Foundational Issues in Naural Language Processing*, chapter 2, pp. 31–81. MIT Press.

Kaplan, R. M. and Kay, M. (1994). Regular models of phonological rule systems. *Computational Linguistics*, 20(3):331–378.

Kay, M. (1986). Algorithm schemata and data structures in syntactic processing. In Grosz, B. J., Sparck Jones, K., and Webber, B. L., editors, *Natural Language Processing*, pp. 35–70. Kaufmann, Los Altos, CA.

Koskenniemi, K. (1983). Two-level morphology: A general computational model for word-form recognition and production. Publication 11, Department of General Linguistics, University of Helsinki.

Lafferty, J., Sleator, D., and Temperley, D. (1992). Grammatical trigrams: A probabilistic model of link grammar. In *Proceedings of the AAAI Fall Symposium on Probabilistic Approaches to Natural Language*, pp. 89–97, Cambridge, MA.

McAllester, D. (1999). On the complexity analysis of static analyses. In *Proceedings of the 6th International Static Analysis Symposium*, Venezia, Italy.

Mel'čuk, I. (1988). *Dependency Syntax: Theory and Practice*. State University of New York Press.

Milward, D. (1994). Dynamic dependency grammar. *Linguistics and Philosophy*, 17:561–605.

Mohri, M., Pereira, F., and Riley, M. (1996). Weighted automata in text and speech processing. In *Workshop on Extended Finite-State Models of Language (ECAI-96)*, pp. 46–50, Budapest.

Pollard, C. and Sag, I. A. (1994). *Head-Driven Phrase Structure Grammar*. University of Chicago Press and Stanford: CSLI Publications, Chicago.

Resnik, P. (1993). *Selection and Information: A Class-Based Approach to Lexical Relationships*. PhD thesis, University of Pennsylvania. Technical Report IRCS-93-42, November.

Schabes, Y., Abeillé, A., and Joshi, A. (1988). Parsing strategies with 'lexicalized' grammars: Application to Tree Adjoining Grammars. In *Proceedings of COLING-88*, pp. 578–583, Budapest.

Sleator, D. and Temperley, D. (1993). Parsing English with a link grammar. In *Proceedings of the 3rd International Workshop on Parsing Technologies*, pp. 277–291.

Stolcke, A. (1995). An efficient probabilistic context-free parsing algorithm that computes prefix probabilities. *Computational Linguistics*, 21(2):165–201.

Woods, W. A. (1969). Augmented transition networks for natural language analysis. Report CS-1, Harvard Computation Laboratory, Harvard University, Cambridge, MA.

Wu, D. (1995). An algorithm for simultaneously bracketing parallel texts by aligning words. In *Proceedings of the 33rd ACL*, pp. 244–251, MIT.

Chapter 4

PROBABILISTIC FEATURE GRAMMARS

Joshua Goodman

Harvard University, 40 Oxford St., Cambridge, MA 02138

goodman@eecs.harvard.edu

Abstract   We present a new formalism, *probabilistic feature grammar* (PFG). PFGs combine most of the best properties of several other formalisms, including those of
Collins, Magerman, and Charniak, and in experiments have comparable or better
performance. PFGs generate features one at a time, probabilistically, conditioning the probabilities of each feature on other features in a local context. Because
the conditioning is local, efficient polynomial time parsing algorithms exist for
computing inside, outside, and Viterbi parses. PFGs can produce probabilities
of strings, making them potentially useful for language modeling. Precision
and recall results are comparable to the state of the art with words, and the best
reported without words.

1   INTRODUCTION

Recently, many researchers have worked on statistical parsing techniques
which try to capture additional context beyond that of simple probabilistic context-free grammars (PCFGs), including Magerman (1995), Charniak
(1996), Collins (1996, 1997), Black et al. (1992b), Eisele (1994), and Brew
(1995). Each researcher has tried to capture the hierarchical nature of language, as typified by context-free grammars, and to then augment this with
additional context sensitivity based on various *features* of the input. However,
none of these works combines the most important benefits of all the others,
and most lack a certain elegance. We have therefore tried to synthesize these
works into a new formalism, *probabilistic feature grammar* (PFG). PFGs have
several important properties. First, PFGs can condition on features beyond
the nonterminal of each node, including features such as the head word or
grammatical number of a constituent. Also, PFGs can be parsed using efficient
polynomial-time dynamic programming algorithms, and learned quickly from
a treebank. Finally, unlike most other formalisms, PFGs are potentially useful

63

H. Bunt and A. Nijholt (eds.), Advances in Probabilistic and Other Parsing Technologies, 63–84.
© *2000 Kluwer Academic Publishers.*

for language modeling or as one part of an integrated statistical system (e.g. Miller et al., 1996) or for use with algorithms requiring outside probabilities. Empirical results are encouraging: our best parser is comparable to those of Magerman (1995) and Collins (1996) when run on the same data. When we run using part-of-speech (POS) tags alone as input, we perform significantly better than comparable parsers.

2   MOTIVATION

PFG can be regarded in several different ways: as a way to make history-based grammars (Magerman, 1995) more context free, and thus amenable to dynamic programming; as a way to generalize the work of Black et al. (1992a); as a way to turn Collins' parser (Collins, 1996) into a generative probabilistic language model; or as an extension of language-modeling techniques to stochastic grammars. The resulting formalism is relatively simple and elegant. In Section 4, we will compare PFGs to each of the systems from which it derives, and show how it integrates their best properties.

Consider the following simple parse tree for the sentence *The man dies*:

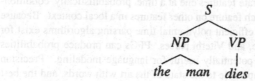

While this tree captures the simple fact that sentences are composed of noun phrases and verb phrases, it fails to capture other important restrictions. For instance, the NP and VP must have the same number, both singular, or both plural. Also, a man is far more likely to die than spaghetti, and this constrains the head words of the corresponding phrases. This additional information can be captured in a parse tree that has been augmented with features, such as the category, number, and head word of each constituent, as is traditionally done in many feature-based formalisms, such as HPSG, LFG, etc.

While a normal PCFG has productions such as

$$S \rightarrow NP\ VP$$

we will write these augmented productions as, for instance,

$$(S, singular, dies) \rightarrow (NP, singular, man)(VP, singular, dies)$$

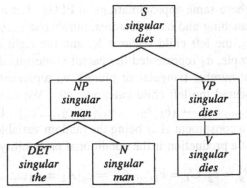

In a traditional probabilistic context-free grammar, we could augment the first tree with probabilities in a simple fashion. We estimate the probability of $S \rightarrow NP\ VP$ using a tree bank to determine $\dfrac{C(S \rightarrow NP\ VP)}{C(S)}$, the number of occurrences of $S \rightarrow NP\ VP$ divided by the number of occurrences of S. For a reasonably large treebank, probabilities estimated in this way would be reliable enough to be useful (Charniak, 1996). On the other hand, it is not unlikely that we would never have seen any counts at all of

$$\frac{C((S, singular, dies) \rightarrow (NP, singular, man)(VP, singular, dies))}{C((S, singular, dies))}$$

which is the estimated probability of the corresponding production in our grammar augmented with features.

The introduction of features for number and head word has created a data sparsity problem. Fortunately, the data-sparsity problem is well known in the language-modeling community, and we can use their techniques, n-gram models and smoothing, to help us. Consider the probability of a five word sentence, $w_1 ... w_5$:

$$P(w_1 w_2 w_3 w_4 w_5) =$$

$$P(w_1) \times P(w_2|w_1) \times P(w_3|w_1 w_2) \times P(w_4|w_1 w_2 w_3) \times P(w_5|w_1 w_2 w_3 w_4)$$

While exactly computing $P(w_5|w_1 w_2 w_3 w_4)$ is difficult, a good approximation is $P(w_5|w_1 w_2 w_3 w_4) \approx P(w_5|w_3 w_4)$.

Let $C(w_3 w_4 w_5)$ represent the number of occurrences of the sequence $w_3 w_4 w_5$ in a corpus. We can then empirically approximate $P(w_5|w_3 w_4)$ with $\frac{C(w_3 w_4 w_5)}{C(w_4 w_5)}$. Unfortunately, this approximation alone is not enough; there may still be many three word combinations that do not occur in the corpus, but that should not be assigned zero probabilities. So we *smooth* this approximation, for instance by using

$$P(w_5|w_3 w_4) \approx \lambda_1 \frac{C(w_3 w_4 w_5)}{C(w_3 w_4)} + (1 - \lambda_1) \left(\lambda_2 \frac{C(w_4 w_5)}{C(w_4)} + (1 - \lambda_2) \frac{C(w_5)}{\sum_w C(w)} \right)$$

Now, we can use these same approximations in PFGs. Let us assume that our PFG is binary branching and has g features, numbered $1...g$; we will call the parent features a_i, the left child features b_i, and the right child features c_i. In our earlier example, a_1 represented the parent nonterminal category; a_2 represented the parent number (singular or plural); a_3 represented the parent head word; b_1 represented the left child category; etc. We can write a PFG production as $(a_1, a_2, ..., a_g) \rightarrow (b_1, b_2, ..., b_g)(c_1, c_2, ..., c_g)$. If we think of the set of features for a constituent A as being the random variables $A_1, ..., A_g$, then the probability of a production is the conditional probability

$$P(B_1 = b_1, ..., B_g = b_g, C_1 = c_1, ..., C_g = c_g | A_1 = a_1, ..., A_g = a_g)$$

We write a_1^k to represent $A_1 = a_1, ..., A_k = a_k$, and sometimes write a_i as shorthand for $A_i = a_i$. We can then write this conditional probability as

$$P(b_1^g, c_1^g | a_1^g)$$

This joint probability can be factored as the product of a set of conditional probabilities in many ways. One simple way is to arbitrarily order the features as $b_1, ..., b_g, c_1, ..., c_g$. We then condition each feature on the parent features and all features earlier in the sequence.

$$P(b_1^g, c_1^g | a_1^g) = P(b_1 | a_1^g) \times P(b_2 | a_1^g, b_1^1) \times P(b_3 | a_1^g, b_1^2) \times \cdots \times P(c_g | a_1^g, b_1^g, c_1^{g-1})$$

We can now approximate the various terms in the factorization by making independence assumptions. For instance, returning to the concrete example above, consider feature c_1, the right child nonterminal or terminal category. The following approximation should work fairly well in practice:

$$P(c_1 | a_1^g b_1^g) \approx P(c_1 | a_1, b_1)$$

That is, the category of the right child is well determined by the category of the parent and the category of the left child. Just as n-gram models approximate conditional lexical probabilities by assuming independence of words that are sufficiently distant, here we approximate conditional feature probabilities by assuming independence of features that are sufficiently unrelated. Furthermore, we can use the same kinds of backing-off techniques that are used in smoothing traditional language models to allow us to condition on relatively large contexts. In practice, a grammarian determines which features should be considered independent, and the optimal order of backoff, possibly using experiments on development test data for feedback. It might be possible to determine the factorization order, the best independence assumptions, and the optimal order of backoff automatically, a subject of future research.

Intuitively, in a PFG, features are produced one at a time. This order corresponds to the order of the factorization. The probability of a feature

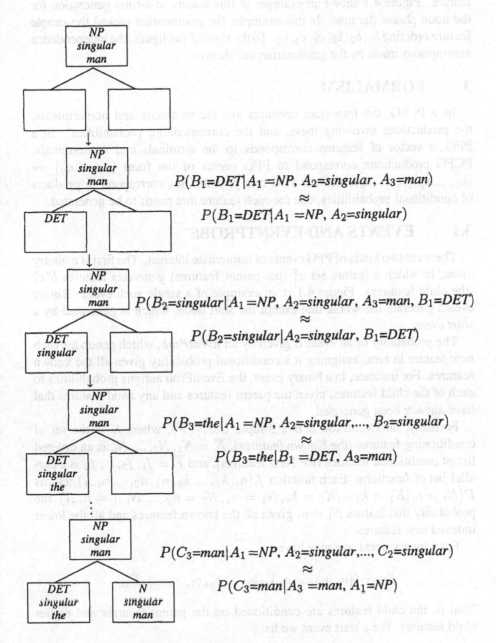

$$P(B_1=DET|A_1=NP, A_2=singular, A_3=man)$$
$$\approx$$
$$P(B_1=DET|A_1=NP, A_2=singular)$$

$$P(B_2=singular|A_1=NP, A_2=singular, A_3=man, B_1=DET)$$
$$\approx$$
$$P(B_2=singular|A_2=singular, B_1=DET)$$

$$P(B_3=the|A_1=NP, A_2=singular,..., B_2=singular)$$
$$\approx$$
$$P(B_3=the|B_1=DET, A_3=man)$$

$$P(C_3=man|A_1=NP, A_2=singular,..., C_2=singular)$$
$$\approx$$
$$P(C_3=man|A_3=man, A_1=NP)$$

Figure 4.1 Producing *the man*, one feature at a time

being produced depends on a subset of the features in a local context of that feature. Figure 4.1 shows an example of this feature-at-a-time generation for the noun phrase *the man*. In this example, the grammarian picked the simple feature ordering $b_1, b_2, b_3, c_1, c_2, c_3$. To the right of the figure, the independence assumptions made by the grammarian are shown.

3   FORMALISM

In a PCFG, the important concepts are the terminals and nonterminals, the productions involving these, and the corresponding probabilities. In a PFG, a vector of features corresponds to the terminals and nonterminals. PCFG productions correspond to PFG *events* of the form $(a_1, ..., a_g) \rightarrow (b_1, ..., b_g)(c_1, ..., c_g)$, and our PFG rule probabilities correspond to products of conditional probabilities, one for each feature that needs to be generated.

3.1   EVENTS AND EVENTPROBS

There are two kinds of PFG events of immediate interest. The first is a *binary event*, in which a feature set a_1^g (the parent features) generates features $b_1^g c_1^g$ (the child features). Figure 4.1 is an example of a single such event. Binary events generate the whole tree except the start node, which is generated by a *start event*.

The probability of an event is given by an *EventProb*, which generates each new feature in turn, assigning it a conditional probability given all the known features. For instance, in a binary event, the EventProb assigns probabilities to each of the child features, given the parent features and any child features that have already been generated.

Formally, an EventProb $\mathcal{E}$ is a 3-tuple $\langle \mathcal{K}, \overline{N}, \overline{F} \rangle$, where $\mathcal{K}$ is the set of conditioning features (the Known features), $\overline{N} = N_1, N_2, ..., N_n$ is an ordered list of conditioned features (the New features), and $\overline{F} = f_1, f_2, ..., f_n$ is a parallel list of functions. Each function $f_i(n_i, k_1, ..., k_k, n_1, n_2, ..., n_{i-1})$ returns $P(N_i = n_i | K_1 = k_1, ... K_k = k_k, N_1 = n_1, N_2 = n_2, ..., N_{i-1} = n_{i-1})$, the probability that feature $N_i = n_i$ given all the known features and all the lower indexed new features.

For a binary event, we may have

$$\mathcal{E}_B = \langle \{a_1, a_2, ..., a_g\}, \langle b_1, ..., b_g, c_1, ..., c_g \rangle, \overline{F}_B \rangle$$

That is, the child features are conditioned on the parent features and earlier child features. For a start event we have

$$\mathcal{E}_S = \langle \{\}, \langle a_1, a_2, ..., a_g \rangle, \overline{F}_S \rangle$$

Here, the parent features are conditioned only on each other.

3.2   TERMINAL FUNCTION, BINARY PFG, ALTERNATING PFG

We need one last element: a function T from a set of g features to $\{T, N\}$ which tells us whether a part of an event is terminal or nonterminal: the *terminal function*. A Binary PFG is then a quadruple $\langle g, \mathcal{E}_B, \mathcal{E}_S, T \rangle$: a number of features, a binary EventProb, a start EventProb, and a terminal function.

Of course, using binary events allows us to model n-ary branching grammars for any fixed n: we simply add additional features for terminals to be generated in the future, as well as a feature for whether or not this intermediate node is a 'dummy' node (the continuation feature). We demonstrate how to do this in detail in Section 6.1.

On the other hand, it does not allow us to handle unary branching productions. In general, probabilistic grammars that allow an unbounded number of unary branches are very difficult to deal with (Stolcke, 1993). There are a number of ways we could have handled unary branches. The one we chose was to enforce an alternation between unary and binary branches, marking most unary branches as 'dummies' with the continuation feature, and removing them before printing the output of the parser.

To handle these unary branches, we add one more EventProb, $\mathcal{E}_U$. Thus, an *Alternating PFG* is a quintuple of $\{g, \mathcal{E}_B, \mathcal{E}_S, \mathcal{E}_U, T\}$.

It is important that we allow only a limited number of unary branches. In probabilistic frameworks, unlimited unary branches lead to infinite sums. For conventional PCFG-style grammar formalisms, these infinite sums can be computed using matrix inversion, which is still fairly time-consuming. For a formalism such as ours, or a similar formalism, the effective number of nonterminals needed in the matrix inversion is potentially huge, making such computations impractical. Thus, instead we simply limit the number of unary branches, meaning that the sum is finite, for computing both the inside and the outside values. Two competing formalisms, those of Collins (1997) and Charniak (1997) allow unlimited unary branches, but because of this, can only compute Viterbi probabilities, not inside and outside probabilities.

4   COMPARISON TO PREVIOUS WORK

PFG bears much in common with previous work, but in each case has at least some advantages over previous formalisms.

Some other models (Charniak, 1996; Brew, 1995; Collins, 1996; Black et al., 1992b) use probability approximations that do not sum to 1, meaning that they should not be used either for language modeling, e.g. in a speech recognition system, or as part of an integrated model such as that of Miller et al. (1996). Some models (Magerman, 1995; Collins, 1996) assign probabilities to parse trees conditioned on the strings, so that an unlikely sentence with a single parse might get probability 1, making these systems unusable for language modeling. PFGs use joint probabilities, so can be used both for language modeling and as part of an integrated model.

Furthermore, unlike all but one of the comparable systems, PFGs can compute outside probabilities, which are useful for grammar induction, some parsing algorithms (Goodman, 1996), and, as we will show, pruning (Goodman, 1997).

Bigram Lexical Dependency Parsing. Collins (1996) introduced a parser with extremely good performance. From this parser, we take many of the particular conditioning features that we will use in PFGs. As noted, this model cannot be used for language modeling. There are also some inelegancies in the need for a separate model for Base-NPs, and the treatment of punctuation as inherently different from words. The model also contains a non-statistical rule about the placement of commas. Finally, Collins' model uses memory proportional to the sum of the squares of each training sentence's length. PFGs in general use memory which is only linear.

Generative Lexicalized Parsing. Collins (1997) worked independently from us to construct a model that is very similar to ours. In particular, Collins wished to adapt his previous parser (Collins, 1996) to a generative model. In this he succeeded. However, while we present a fairly simple and elegant formalism, which captures all information as features, Collins uses a variety of different techniques. First, he uses variables, which are analogous to our features. Next, both our models need a way to determine when to stop generating child nodes; like everything else, we encode this in a feature, but Collins creates a special STOP nonterminal. For some information, Collins modifies the names of nonterminals, rather than encoding the information as additional features. Finally, all information in our model is generated top-down. In Collins' model, most information is generated top-down, but distance information is propagated bottom-up. Thus, while PFGs encode all information as top-down features, Collins' model uses several different techniques. This lack of homogeneity fails to show the underlying structure of the model, and the ways it could be expanded. While Collins' model could not be encoded exactly as a PFG, a PFG that was extremely similar could be created.

Furthermore, our model of generation is very general. While our implementation captures head words through the particular choice of features, Collins' model explicitly generates first the head phrase, then the right children, and finally the left children. Thus, our model can be used to capture a wider variety of grammatical theories, simply by changing the choice of features.

Simple PCFGs. Charniak (1996) showed that a simple PCFG formalism in which the rules are simply 'read off' of a treebank can perform very competitively. Furthermore, he showed that a simple modification, in which productions at the right side of the sentence have their probability boosted to encourage right branching structures, can improve performance even further. PFGs are a superset of PCFGs, so we can easily model the basic PCFG grammar used by Charniak, although the boosting cannot be exactly duplicated. However, we can use more principled techniques, such as a feature that captures whether a particular constituent is at the end of the sentence, and a feature for the length of the constituent. Charniak's boosting strategy means that the scores of constituents are no longer probabilities, meaning that they cannot be used with the inside-outside algorithm. Furthermore, the PFG feature-based technique is not extra-grammatical, meaning that no additional machinery needs to be added for parsing or grammar induction.

PCFG with Word Statistics. Charniak (1997) uses a grammar formalism which is in many ways similar to the PFG model, with several minor differences, and one important one. The main difference is that while we binarize trees, and encode rules as features about which nonterminal should be generated next, Charniak explicitly uses rules, in the style of traditional PCFG parsing, in combination with other features. This difference is discussed in more detail in Section 6.1.

Stochastic HPSG. Brew (1995) introduced a stochastic version of HPSG. In his formalism, in some cases even if two features have been constrained to the same value by unification, the probabilities of their productions are assumed independent. The resulting probability distribution is then normalized so that probabilities sum to one. This leads to problems with grammar induction pointed out by Abney (1996). Our formalism, in contrast, explicitly models dependencies to the extent possible given data sparsity constraints.

IBM Language Modeling Group. Researchers in the IBM Language Modeling Group developed a series of successively more complicated models to integrate statistics with features.

The first model (Black et al., 1993; Black et al., 1992b) essentially tries to convert a unification grammar to a PCFG, by instantiating the values of the features. Due to data sparsity, however, not all features can be instantiated. Instead, they create a grammar where many features have been instantiated, and many have not; they call these partially instantiated features sets *mnemonics*. They then create a PCFG using the mnemonics as terminals and nonterminals. Features instantiated in a particular mnemonic are generated probabilistically, while the rest are generated through unification. Because no smoothing is done, and because features are grouped, data sparsity limits the number of features that can be generated probabilistically, whereas because we generate features one at a time and smooth, we are far less limited in the number of features we can use. Their technique of generating some features probabilistically, and the rest by unification, is somewhat inelegant; also, for the probabilities to sum to one, it requires an additional step of normalization, which they appear not to have implemented.

In their next model (Black et al., 1992a; Magerman, 1994, pp. 46–56), which strongly influenced our model, five attributes are associated with each nonterminal: a syntactic category, a semantic category, a rule, and two lexical heads. The rules in this grammar are the same as the mnemonic rules used in the previous work, developed by a grammarian. These five attributes are generated one at a time, with backoff smoothing, conditioned on the parent attributes and earlier attributes. Our generation model is essentially the same as this. Notice that in this model, unlike ours, there are two kinds of features: those features captured in the mnemonics, and the five categories; the categories and mnemonic features are modeled very differently. Also, notice that a great deal of work is required by a grammarian, to develop the rules and mnemonics.

The third model (Magerman, 1994), extends the second model to capture more dependencies, and to remove the use of a grammarian. Each decision in this model can in principal depend on any previous decision and on any word in the sentence. Because of these potentially unbounded dependencies, there is no dynamic programming algorithm: without pruning, the time complexity of the model is exponential. One motivation for PFG was to capture similar information to this third model, while allowing dynamic programming. This third model uses a more complicated probability model: all probabilities are determined using decision trees; it is an area for future research to determine whether we can improve our performance by using decision trees.

Probabilistic LR Parsing with Unification Grammars. Briscoe and Carroll describe a formalism (Briscoe and Carroll, 1993; Carroll and Briscoe, 1992) similar in many ways to the first IBM model. In particular, a context-free covering grammar of a unification grammar is constructed. Some features are captured by the covering grammar, while others are modeled only through unifications. Only simple plus-one-style smoothing is done, so data sparsity is still significant. The most important difference between the work of Briscoe (1993) and that of Black (1993) is that Briscoe et. al. associate probabilities with the (augmented) transition matrix of an LR Parse table; this gives them more context sensitivity than Black et. al. However, the basic problems of the two approaches are the same: data sparsity; difficulty normalizing probabilities; and lack of elegance due to the union of two very different approaches.

5   PARSING

The parsing algorithm we use is a simple variation on probabilistic versions of the CKY algorithm for PCFGs, using feature vectors instead of nonterminals (Baker, 1979; Lari and Young, 1990). The parser computes inside probabilities (the sum of probabilities of all parses, i.e. the probability of the sentence) and Viterbi probabilities (the probability of the best parse), and, optionally, outside probabilities. In Figure 4.2 we give the inside algorithm for PFGs. Notice

for each length l, shortest to longest
    for each start s
        for each split length t
            for each b_1^g s.t. $chart[s, s + t, b_1^g] \neq 0$
                for each c_1^g s.t. $chart[s + t, s + l, c_1^g] \neq 0$
                    for each a_1 consistent with $b_1^g c_1^g$

$$\vdots$$

                    for each a_g consistent with $b_1^g c_1^g a_1^{g-1}$
$$chart[s, s + l, a_1^g] + = \mathcal{E}_B(a_1^g \rightarrow b_1^g c_1^g)$$
return $\sum_{a_1^g} \mathcal{E}_S(a_1^g) \times chart[1, n + 1, a_1^g])$

Figure 4.2 PFG inside algorithm

that the algorithm requires time $O(n^3)$ in sentence length, but is potentially exponential in the number of children, since there is one loop for each parent feature, a_1 through a_g.

When parsing a PCFG, it is a simple matter to find for every right and left child what the possible parents are. On the other hand, for a PFG, there are some subtleties. We must loop over every possible value for each feature. At first, this sounds overwhelming, since it requires guessing a huge number of feature sets, leading to a run time exponential in the number of features; in practice, most values of most features will have zero probabilities, and we can avoid considering these. For instance, features such as the length of a constituent take a single value per cell. Many other features take on very few values, given the children. For example, we arrange our parse trees so that the head word of each constituent is dominated by one of its two children. This means that we need consider only two values for this feature for each pair of children. The single most time consuming feature is the Name feature, which corresponds to the terminals and non-terminals of a PCFG. For efficiency, we keep a list of the parent/left-child/right-child name triples which have non-zero probabilities, allowing us to hypothesize only the possible values for this feature given the children. Careful choice of features helps keep parse times reasonable.

5.1 PRUNING

We use two pruning methods to speed parsing. The first is a simple beam-search method, inspired by techniques used by Collins (1996) and Charniak (1996), and described in detail by Goodman (1997). Within each cell in the parse chart, we multiply each entry's inside probability by the prior probability of the parent features of that entry, using a special EventProb, $\mathcal{E}_P$. We then remove those entries whose combined probability is too much lower than the best entry of the cell.

In speech recognition, multiple-pass recognizers (Zavaliagkos et al., 1994) have been very successful. We can use an analogous technique, multiple-pass parsing (Goodman, 1997) with either PCFGs or PFGs. We use a simple, fast grammar for the first pass, which approximates the later pass. We then remove any events whose combined inside-outside product is too low: essentially those events that are unlikely given the complete sentence. The first pass is fast, and does not slow things down much, but allows us to speed up the second pass significantly. The technique is particularly natural for PFGs, since for the first pass, we can simply use a grammar with a superset of the features from the previous pass. Actually, the features we used in our first pass were Name, Continuation, and two new features especially suitable for a fast first pass, the length of the constituent and the terminal symbol following the constituent. Since these two features are uniquely determined by the chart cell of the constituent, they are especially suitable for use in a first pass, since they provide useful information without increasing the number of elements in the chart. However, when used in our second pass, these features did not help performance, presumably because they captured information similar to that captured by other features. Multiple-pass techniques have dramatically sped up PFG parsing.

6   EXPERIMENTAL RESULTS

The PFG formalism is an extremely general one that has the capability to model a wide variety of phenomena, and there are very many possible sets of features that could be used in a given implementation. We will, on an example set of features, show that the formalism can be used to achieve a high level of accuracy.

6.1   FEATURES

In this section, we will describe the actual features used by our parser. The most interesting and most complicated features are those used to encode the rules of the grammar, the child features. We will first show how to encode a PCFG as a PFG. The PCFG has some maximum length right hand side, say four symbols. We would then create a PFG with five features. The first feature would be N, the nonterminal symbol. Since PFGs are binarized, while PCFGs are n-ary branching, we will need a feature that allows us to recover the n-ary branching structure from a binary branching tree. This feature, which we call the continuation feature, C, will be 0 for constituents that are the top of a rule, and 1 for constituents that are used internally. The next 4 features describe the future children of the nonterminal. We will use the symbol $\star$ to denote an empty child. To encode a PCFG rule such as $A \rightarrow BCDE$, we would assign the following probabilities to the feature sets:

$$\mathcal{E}_B((A, 0, B, C, D, E) \rightarrow (B, 0, X_1, ..., X_4)(A, 1, C, D, E, \star)) = P(B \rightarrow X_1...X_4)$$
$$\mathcal{E}_B((A, 1, C, D, E, \star) \rightarrow (C, 0, X_1, ..., X_4)(A, 1, D, E, \star, \star)) = P(C \rightarrow X_1...X_4)$$
$$\mathcal{E}_B((A, 1, D, E, \star, \star) \rightarrow (D, 0, X_1, ..., X_4) \ (E, 0, Y_1, ..., Y_4)) = P(D \rightarrow X_1...X_4)$$
$$\times P(E \rightarrow Y_1...Y_4)$$

It should be clear that we can define probabilities of individual features in such a way as to get the desired probabilities for the events. We also need to define a distribution over the start symbols:

$$\mathcal{E}_S((S, 0, A, B, C, D, E)) = P(S \rightarrow ABCDE)$$

A quick inspection will show that this assignment of probabilities to events leads to the same probabilities being assigned to analogous trees in the PFG as in the original PCFG.

Now, imagine if rather than using the raw probability estimates from the PCFG, we were to smooth the probabilities in the same way we smooth all of our feature probabilities. This will lead to a kind of smoothed 4-gram model on right hand sides. Presumably, there is some assignment of smoothing parameters that will lead to performance which is at least as good, if not better, than unsmoothed probabilities. Furthermore, what if we had many other features in our PFG, such as head words and distance features. With more features, we might have too much data sparsity to make it really worthwhile to keep all four of the children as features. Instead, we could keep, say, the first two children as features. After each child is generated as a left nonterminal, we could generate the next child (the third, fourth, fifth, etc.) as the Child2 feature of the right child. Our new grammar probabilities might look like:

$$\mathcal{E}_B((A, 0, B, C) \rightarrow (B, 0, X_1, X_2)(A, 1, C, D)) =$$
$$P(A \rightarrow BCD...|A \rightarrow BC...) \times P(B \rightarrow X_1 X_2...)$$
$$\mathcal{E}_B((A, 1, C, D) \rightarrow (C, 0, X_1, X_2)(A, 1, D, E)) =$$
$$P(A \rightarrow ...CDE...|A \rightarrow ...CD...) \times P(C \rightarrow X_1 X_2...)$$
$$\mathcal{E}_B((A, 1, D, E) \rightarrow (D, 0, X_1, X_2)(E, 0, Y_1, Y_2)) =$$
$$P(A \rightarrow ...DE|A \rightarrow ...DE...) \times P(D \rightarrow X_1 X_2...) \times P(E \rightarrow Y_1 Y_2...)$$

where $P(B \rightarrow X_1 X_2...) = \sum_\alpha P(B \rightarrow X_1 X_2 \alpha)$. This assignment will produce a good approximation to the original PCFG, using a kind of trigram model on right hand sides, with fewer parameters and fewer features than the exact PFG. Fewer child features will be very helpful when we add other features to the model. We will show in Section 6.4 that with the set of features we use, 2 children is optimal.

N   Name Corresponds to the terminals and nonterminals of a PCFG.

C   Continuation Tells whether we are generating modifiers to the right or the left, and whether it is time to generate the head node.

1   Child1 Name of first child to be generated.

2   Child2 Name of second child to be generated. In combination with Child1, this allows us to simulate a second order Markov process on nonterminal sequences.

H   Head name Name of the head category.

P   Head pos Part of speech of head word.

W   Head word Actual head word. Not used in POS only model.

D^L Δ left Count of punctuation, verbs, words to left of head.

D^R Δ right Counts to right of head.

D^B Δ between Counts between parent's and child's heads.

Table 4.1 Features used in experiments

We can now describe the features actually used in our experiments. We used two PFGs, one that used the head word feature, and one otherwise identical grammar with no word based features, only POS tags. The grammars had the features shown in Table 4.1. A sample parse tree with these features is given in Figure 4.3.

Recall that in Section 5 we mentioned that in order to get good performance, we made our parse trees binary branching in such a way that every constituent dominates its head word. To achieve this, rather than generating children strictly left to right, we first generate all children to the left of the head word, left to right, then we generate all children to the right of the head word, right to left, and finally we generate the child containing the head word. It is because of this that the root node of the example tree in Figure 4.3 has *NP* as its first child, and *VP* as its second, rather than the other way around.

The feature D^L is a 3-tuple, indicating the number of punctuation characters, verbs, and words to the left of a constituent's head word. To avoid data sparsity, we do not count higher than 2 punctuation characters, 1 verb, or 4 words. So, a value of $D^L = 014$ indicates that a constituent has no punctuation, at least one verb, and 4 or more words to the left of its head word. D^R is a similar feature for the right side. Finally, D^B gives the numbers between the constituent's head word, and the head word of its other child. Words, verbs, and punctuation are counted as being to the left of themselves: that is, a terminal verb has one verb and one word on its left.

Notice that the continuation of the lower *NP* in Figure 4.3 is R1, indicating that it inherits its child from the right, with the 1 indicating that it is a 'dummy' node to be left out of the final tree.

6.2   EXPERIMENTAL DETAILS

The probability functions we used were similar to those of Section 2, but with three important differences. The first is that in some cases, we can compute a probability exactly. For instance, if we know that the head word of a parent is 'man' and that the parent got its head word from its right child, then we know that with probability 1, the head word of the right child is 'man.' In cases where we can compute a probability exactly, we do so. Second, we smoothed slightly differently. In particular, when smoothing a probability estimate of the form

$$p(a|bc) \approx \lambda \frac{C(abc)}{C(bc)} + (1 - \lambda)p(a|b)$$

we set $\lambda = \frac{C(bc)}{k + C(bc)}$, using a separate k for each probability distribution. Finally, we did additional smoothing for words, adding counts for the unknown word.

The actual tables that show for each feature the order of backoff for that feature are given by Goodman (1998). In this section, we simply discuss a single example, the order of backoff for the 2_R feature, the category of the second child of the right feature set. The most relevant features are first: $N_R, C_R, H_R, 1_R, N_P, C_P, N_L, C_L, P_R, W_R$. We back off from the head word feature first, because, although relevant, this feature creates significant data sparsity. Notice that in general, features from the same feature set, in this case the right features, are kept longest; parent features are next most relevant; and sibling features are considered least relevant. We leave out entirely features that are unlikely to be relevant and that would cause data sparsity, such as W_L, the head word of the left sibling.

6.3   RESULTS

We used the same machine-labeled data as Collins (1996, 1997): TreeBank II sections 2-21 for training, section 23 for test, section 00 for development, using all sentences of 40 words or less.[1] We also used the same scoring method (replicating even a minor bug for the sake of comparison).

Table 4.2 gives the results. Our results are the best we know of from POS tags alone, and, with the head word feature, fall between the results of Collins and Magerman, as given by Collins (1997). To take one measure as an example, we got 1.47 crossing brackets per sentence with POS tags alone, versus Collins'

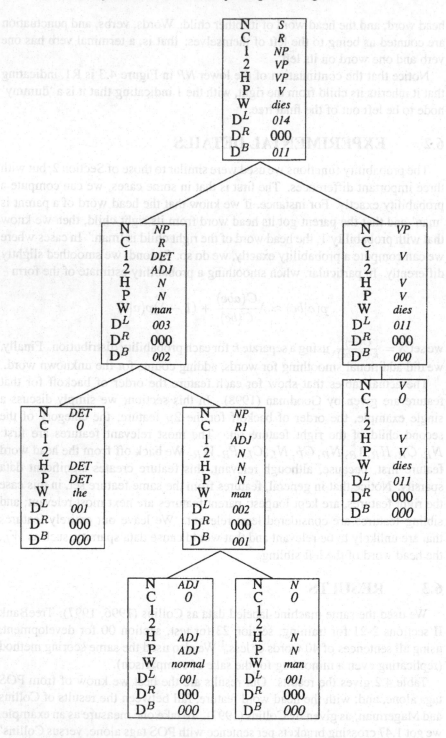

Figure 4.3 Example tree with features: *The normal man dies*

Model	Labeled Recall	Labeled Prec	Cross Brack	0 Cross Brack	≤ 2 Cross Brack
PFG Words	84.8%	85.3%	1.21	57.6%	81.4%
PFG POS only	81.0%	82.2%	1.47	49.8%	77.7%
Collins 97 best	88.1%	88.6%	0.91	66.5%	86.9%
Collins 96 best	85.8%	86.3%	1.14	59.9%	83.6%
Collins 96 POS only	76.1%	76.6%	2.26		
Magerman	84.6%	84.9%	1.26	56.6%	81.4%

Table 4.2 PFG experimental results

results of 2.26 in similar conditions. With the head word feature, we got 1.21 crossing brackets, which is between Collins' .91 and Magerman's 1.26. The results are similar for other measures of performance.

6.4   CONTRIBUTION OF INDIVIDUAL FEATURES

In this subsection we analyze the contribution of features, by running experiments using the full set of features minus some individual feature. The difference in performance between the full set and the full set minus some individual feature gives us an estimate of the feature's contribution. Note that the contribution of a feature is relative to the other features in the full set. For instance, if we had features for both head word and a morphologically stemmed head word, their individual contributions as measured in this manner would be nearly negligible, because both are so highly correlated. The same effect will hold to lesser degrees for other features, depending on how correlated they are. Some features are not meaningful without other features. For instance, the child2 feature is not particularly meaningful without the child1 feature. Thus, we cannot simply remove just child1 to compute its contribution; instead we first remove child2, compute its contribution, and then remove child1, as well.

When performing these experiments, we used the same dependencies and same order of backoff for all experiments. This probably causes us to overestimate the value of some features, since when we delete a feature, we could add additional dependencies to other features that depended on it. We kept the thresholding parameters constant, but adjusted the parameters of the backoff algorithm.

In the original work on PFGs, we did not perform this feature contribution experiment, and thus included the head name (H) feature in all of our original experiments. When we performed these experiments, we discovered that the

Name	Features	Label Recall	Label Prec	Cross Brack	0 Cross Brack	Time
Base	HNCWPD^{B}D^{L}D^{R}12	86.4%	87.2%	1.06	60.8%	40619
NoW	HNC PD^{B}D^{L}D^{R}12	82.7%	84.1%	1.36	52.2%	39142
NoP	HNCW D^{B}D^{L}D^{R}12	85.8%	86.5%	1.18	57.5%	46226
NoD^B	HNCWP D^{L}D^{R}12	86.0%	84.9%	1.24	56.6%	49834
NoD	HNCWP 12	85.9%	85.9%	1.23	59.4%	45375
No2	HNCWPD^{B}D^{L}D^{R}1	85.2%	86.5%	1.17	58.7%	47977
No12	HNCWPD^{B}D^{L}D^R	76.6%	79.3%	1.65	45.8%	37912
BaseH	NCWPD^{B}D^{L}D^{R}12	86.7%	87.7%	1.01	61.6%	52785
NoWH	NC PD^{B}D^{L}D^{R}12	82.7%	84.0%	1.38	51.9%	40080
NoPH	NCW D^{B}D^{L}D^{R}12	86.1%	87.2%	1.08	59.5%	38502
NoD^{B}H	NCWP D^{L}D^{R}12	86.2%	85.2%	1.19	57.2%	41415
NoDH	NCWP 12	86.4%	86.4%	1.17	59.9%	39387
No2H	NCWPD^{B}D^{L}D^{R}1	82.4%	86.7%	1.11	56.8%	37854
No12H	NCWPD^{B}D^{L}D^R	65.1%	80.0%	1.69	41.5%	36790
NoNames	CWPD^{B}D^{L}D^R			2.41	41.9%	55862
NoHPlus3	NCWPD^{B}D^{L}D^{R}123	86.9%	87.3%	1.07	61.7%	41676

Table 4.3 Contribution of individual features

head name feature had a negative contribution. We thus removed the head name feature, and repeated the feature contribution experiment without this feature. Both sets of results are given here. In order to minimize the number of runs on the final test data, all of these experiments were run on the development test section (section 00) of the data.

Table 4.3 shows the results of 16 experiments removing various features. Our first test was the baseline. We then removed the head word feature, leading to a fairly significant but not overwhelming drop in performance (6.8% combined precision and recall). Our results without the head word are perhaps the best reported. The other features – head pos, distance between, all distance features, and second child – all lead to modest drops in performance (1.3%, 2.7%, 1.8%, 1.9%, respectively, on combined precision and recall). On the other hand, when we removed both child1 and child2, we got a 17.7% drop. When we removed the head name feature, we achieved a 0.8% improvement. We repeated these experiments without the head name feature. Without the head name feature, the contributions of the other features are very similar: the head word feature contributed 7.7%. Other features – head pos, distance between, all distance features, and second child – contributed 1.1%, 3.0%, 1.6%, 5.3%. Without child1 and child2, performance dropped 29.3%. This is presumably because there were now almost no name features remaining, except for name itself. When the name feature was also removed, performance dropped even further (to about 2.41 crossing brackets per sentence, versus 1.01 for the no head name baseline – there are no labels here, so we cannot compute labelled precision or labelled recall for this case.) Finally, we tried adding in the child3 feature, to see if we had examined enough child features. Performance dropped negligibly: 0.2%.

These results are significant regarding child1 and child2. While the other features we used are very common, the child1 and child2 features are much less used. Both Magerman (1995) and Ratnaparkhi (1997) make use of essentially these features, but in a history-based formalism. One generative formalism which comes close to using these features is that of Charniak (1997), which uses a feature for the complete rule. This captures the child1, child2, and other child features. However, it does so in a crude way, with two drawbacks. First, it does not allow any smoothing; and second, it probably captures too many child features. As we have shown, the contribution of child features plateaus at about two children; with three children there is a slight negative impact, and more children probably lead to larger negative contributions. On the other hand, Collins (1996, 1997) does not use these features at all, although he does use a feature for the head name. (Comparing No12 to No12H, in Table 4.3, we see that without Child1 and Child2, the head name makes a significant positive contribution.) Extrapolating from these results, integrating the Child1 and Child2 features (and perhaps removing the head name feature) in a state-of-the-art model such as that of Collins (1997) would probably lead to improvements.

The last column of Table 4.3, the Time column, is especially interesting. Notice that the runtimes are fairly constrained, ranging from a low of about 36,000 seconds to a high of about 55,000 seconds. Furthermore, the longest runtime comes with the worst performance, and the fewest features. Better models often allow better thresholding and faster performance. Features such as child1 and child2 that we might expect to significantly slow down parsing, because of the large number of features sets they allow, in some cases (Base to No2) actually speed performance. Of course, to fully substantiate these claims would require a more detailed exploration into the tradeoff between speed and performance for each set of features, which would be beyond the scope of this chapter.

We reran our experiment on section 23, the final test data, this time without the head name feature. The results are given here, with the original results with the head name repeated for comparison. The results are disappointing, leading to only a slight improvement. The smaller than expected improvement might be attributable to random variation, either in the development test data, or in the final test data, or to some systematic difference between the two sets. Analyzing the two sets directly would invalidate any further experiments on the final test data, so we cannot determine which of these is the case.

Model	Labeled Recall	Labeled Prec	Cross Brack	0 Cross Brack	≤ 2 Cross Brack
Words, head name	84.8%	85.3%	1.21	57.6%	81.4%
Words, no head name	84.9%	85.3%	1.19	58.0%	82.0%

7   CONCLUSIONS AND FUTURE WORK

While the empirical performance of probabilistic feature grammars is very encouraging, we think there is far more potential. First, for grammarians wishing to integrate statistics into more conventional models, the features of PFG are a very useful tool, corresponding to the features of DCG, LFG, HPSG, and similar formalisms. TreeBank II is annotated with many semantic features, currently unused in all but the simplest way by all systems; it should be easy to integrate these features into a PFG.

PFG has other benefits worth exploring, including the possibility of its use as a language model, for applications such as speech recognition. Furthermore, the dynamic programming used in the model is amenable to efficient rescoring of lattices output by speech recognizers.

Another benefit of PFG is that both inside and outside probabilities can be computed, making it possible to reestimate PFG parameters. It would be interesting to try experiments using PFGs and the inside/outside algorithm to estimate parameters from unannotated text.

Because the PFG model is so general, it is amenable to many further improvements: we would like to try a wide variety of them. PFG would benefit from more sophisticated smoothing techniques, as well as more sophisticated probability models, such as decision trees. Many other features could be used, including classes of words and nonterminals, and morphologically stemmed words, and integrating the most useful features from recent work, such as that of Collins (1997) . Finally, it would be interesting to perform much more detailed research into the optimal order for backoff than the few pilot experiments used here.

While the generality and elegance of the PFG model makes these and many other experiments possible, we are also encouraged by the very good experimental results. Wordless model performance is excellent, and the more recent models with words are comparable to the state of the art.

Notes

1. We are grateful to Michael Collins and Adwait Ratnaparkhi for supplying us with the part-of-speech tags.

References

Abney, S. (1996). Stochastic attribute-value grammars. Available as cmp-lg/9610003.

Baker, J. K. (1979). Trainable grammars for speech recognition. In *Proceedings of the Spring Conference of the Acoustical Society of America*, pp. 547–550, Boston, MA.

Black, E., Garside, G., and Leech, G. (1993). *Statistically-Driven Computer Grammars of English: the IBM/Lancaster Approach*, volume 8 of *Language and Computers: Studies in Practical Linguistics*. Rodopi, Amsterdam.

Black, E., Jelinek, F., Lafferty, J., Magerman, D. M., Mercer, R., and Roukos, S. (1992a). Towards history-based grammars: Using richer models for probabilistic parsing. In *Proceedings of the February 1992 DARPA Speech and Natural Language Workshop*.

Black, E., Lafferty, J., and Roukos, S. (1992b). Development and evaluation of a broad-coverage probabilistic grammar of English-language computer manuals. In *Proceedings of the 30th Annual Meeting of the ACL*, pp. 185–192.

Brew, C. (1995). Stochastic HPSG. In *Proceedings of the Seventh Conference of the European Chapter of the ACL*, pp. 83–89, Dublin, Ireland.

Briscoe, T. and Carroll, J. (1993). Generalized probabilistic LR parsing of natural language (corpora) with unification-based grammars. *Computational Linguistics*, 19:25–59.

Carroll, J. and Briscoe, T. (1992). Probabilistic normalisation and unpacking of packed parse forests for unification-based grammars. In *Proceedings of the AAAI Fall Symposium on Probabilistic Approaches to Natural Language*, pp. 33–38, Cambridge, MA.

Charniak, E. (1996). Tree–bank grammars. Technical Report CS-96-02, Department of Computer Science, Brown University. Available from ftp://ftp.cs.brown.edu/pub/techreports/96/cs96-02.ps.Z.

Charniak, E. (1997). Statistical parsing with a context-free grammar and word statistics. In *Proceedings of the AAAI*, pp. 598–603, Providence, RI. AAAI Press/MIT Press.

Collins, M. (1996). A new statistical parser based on bigram lexical dependencies. In *Proceedings of the 34th Annual Meeting of the ACL*, pp. 184–191, Santa Cruz, CA. Available as cmp-lg/9605012.

Collins, M. (1997). Three generative, lexicalised models for statistical parsing. In *Proceedings of the 35th Annual Meeting of the ACL*, pp. 16–23, Madrid, Spain. Available as cmp-lg/9706022.

Eisele, A. (1994). Towards probabilistic extensions of constraint-based grammars. DYANA-2 Deliverable R1.2.B. Available from ftp://ftp.ims.uni-stuttgart.de/papers/DYANA2/R1.2.B.

Goodman, J. (1996). Parsing algorithms and metrics. In *Proceedings of the 34th Annual Meeting of the ACL*, pp. 177–183, Santa Cruz, CA. Available as cmp-lg/9605036.

Goodman, J. (1997). Global thresholding and multiple-pass parsing. In *Proceedings of the Second Conference on Empirical Methods in Natural Language Processing*, pp. 11–25.

Goodman, J. (1998). *Parsing Inside-Out*. PhD thesis, Harvard University. Available as cmp-lg/9805007 and from *http://www.research.microsoft.com/~joshuago/thesis.ps*.

Lari, K. and Young, S. (1990). The estimation of stochastic context-free grammars using the inside-outside algorithm. *Computer Speech and Language*, 4:35–56.

Magerman, D. (1994). *Natural Language Parsing as Statistical Pattern Recognition*. PhD thesis, Stanford University University. Available as cmp-lg/9405009.

Magerman, D. (1995). Statistical decision–models for parsing. In *Proceedings of the 33rd Annual Meeting of the ACL*, pp. 276–283, Cambridge, MA.

Miller, S., Stallard, D., Bobrow, R., and Schwartz, R. (1996). A fully statistical approach to natural language interfaces. In *Proceedings of the 34th Annual Meeting of the ACL*, pp. 55–61, Santa Cruz, CA.

Ratnaparkhi, A. (1997). A linear observed time statistical parser based on maximum entropy models. In *Proceedings of the Second Conference on Empirical Methods in Natural Language Processing*, pp. 1–10.

Stolcke, A. (1993). An efficient probabilistic context-free parsing algorithm that computes prefix probabilities. Technical Report TR-93-065, International Computer Science Institute, Berkeley, CA. Available as cmp-lg/9411029.

Zavaliagkos, G., Anastasakos, T., Chou, G., Lapre, C., Kubala, F., Makhoul, J., Nguyen, L., Schwartz, R., and Zhao, Y. (1994). Improved search, acoustic and language modeling in the BBN Byblos large vocabulary CSR system. In *Proceedings of the ARPA Workshop on Spoken Language Technology*, pp. 81–88, Plainsboro, New Jersey.

Chapter 5

PROBABILISTIC GLR PARSING

INUI Kentaro
Department of Artificial Intelligence, Kyushu Institute of Technology
inui@ai.kyutech.ac.jp

Virach SORNLERTLAMVANICH
Software and Language Engineering Laboratory
National Electronics and Computer Technology Center, Bangkok
virach@links.nectec.or.th

TANAKA Hozumi
Graduate School of Information Science and Engineering
Tokyo Institute of Technology
tanaka@cl.cs.titech.ac.jp

TOKUNAGA Takenobu
Graduate School of Information Science and Engineering
Tokyo Institute of Technology
take@cl.cs.titech.ac.jp

Abstract   This chapter presents a new formalization of probabilistic GLR language modeling for statistical parsing. Our model inherits its essential features from Briscoe
and Carroll's generalized probabilistic LR model (Briscoe and Carroll 1993),
which takes context of parse derivation into account by assigning a probability
to each LR parsing action according to its left and right context. Briscoe and
Carroll's model, however, has a drawback in that it is not formalized in any probabilistically well-founded way, which may degrade its parsing performance. Our
formulation overcomes this drawback with a few significant refinements, while
maintaining all the advantages of Briscoe and Carroll's modeling. We discuss
the formal and qualitative aspects of our model, illustrating the qualitative dif-

H. Bunt and A. Nijholt (eds.), Advances in Probabilistic and Other Parsing Technologies, 85–104.
© 2000 *Kluwer Academic Publishers.*

ferences between Briscoe and Carroll's model and our model, and their expected impact on parsing performance.

1   INTRODUCTION

The increasing availability of text corpora has encouraged researchers to explore statistical approaches for various tasks in natural language processing. Statistical parsing is one of these approaches. In statistical parsing, one of the most straightforward methodologies is to generalize context-free grammars by associating a probability with each rule in producing probabilistic context-free grammars (PCFGs). However, as many researchers have already pointed out, PCFGs are not quite adequate for statistical parsing due to their inability to encapsulate the context of parse derivation. Probabilistic GLR parsing is one existing statistical parsing methodology which takes context into account to a greater degree than PCFG-based parsing.

Several attempts have been made to incorporate probability into generalized LR (GLR) parsing (Tomita 1986). For example, Wright and Wrigley proposed an algorithm to distribute probabilities originally associated with CFG rules to LR parsing actions, in such a way that the resulting model is equivalent to the original PCFG (Wright and Wrigley 1991). Perhaps the most naive way of coupling a PCFG model with the GLR parsing framework would be to assign the probability associated with each CFG rule to the reduce actions for that rule. Wright and Wrigley expanded on this general methodology by distributing probabilities to shift actions as well as reduce actions, so that the parser can prune improbable parse derivations after shift actions as well as reduce actions. This can be advantageous particularly when one considers applying a GLR parser to, for example, continuous speech recognition. However, since their principal concern was in compiling PCFGs into the GLR parsing framework, their language model still failed to capture context-sensitivity of languages.

Su et al. proposed a way of introducing probabilistic distribution into the shift-reduce parsing framework (Su et al. 1991). Unlike Wright and Wrigley's work, the goal of this research was the construction of a model that captures context. Their model assigns probabilities to stack transitions between two shift actions, and associates a probability with each parse derivation, given by the product of the probability of each change included in the derivation. Further, they also described an algorithm to handle this model within the GLR parsing framework, gaining parse efficiency. However, since their probabilistic model in itself is not intimately coupled with the GLR parsing algorithm, their model needs an additional complex algorithm for training.

On the other hand, Briscoe and Carroll proposed the assignment of probabilities directly to each action in an LR table (Briscoe and Carroll 1993). Their model overcomes the derivational context-insensitivity of PCFGs by estimating the probability of each LR parsing action according to its left (i.e. LR parse state) and right context (i.e. next input symbol). The probability of each parse derivation is computed as the product of the probability assigned to each action included in the derivation. Unlike the approach of Su et al., this makes it easy to implement context-sensitive probabilistic parsing by slightly extending GLR parsers, and the probabilistic parameters can be easily trained simply by counting the frequency of application of each action in parsing the training sentences. Furthermore, their model is expected to be able to allow the parser to prune improbable parse derivations at an equivalently fine-grained level as that of Wright and Wrigley's statistical parser, since it assigns probabilities to both shift and reduce actions. However, in as far as we have tested the performance of Briscoe and Carroll's model (B&C model, hereafter) in our preliminary experiments, it seems that, in many cases, it does not significantly improve on the performance of the PCFG model, and furthermore, in the worst case it can be even less effective than the PCFG model (Sornlertlamvanich et al. 1997). According to our analysis, these seem to be the results, principally, of the method used for normalizing probabilities in their model, which may not be probabilistically well-founded. In fact, Briscoe and Carroll have not explicitly presented any formalization of their model.

This line of reasoning led us to consider a new formalization of probabilistic GLR (PGLR) parsing. In this chapter we propose a newly formalized PGLR language model for statistical parsing, which has the following advantages:

- It provides probabilistically well-founded distributions.

- It captures the context of a parse derivation.

- It can be trained simply by counting the frequency of each LR parsing action.

- It allows the parser to prune improbable parse derivations, even after shift actions.

The focus of this chapter is on the formal and qualitative aspects of our PGLR model rather than on the empirical quantitative evaluation of the model. Large-scale experiments for the empirical evaluation are under way; in preliminary experiments, we have so far been achieving promising results, some of which have been reported elsewhere (Sornlertlamvanich et al. 1997; Sornlertlam-vanich et al. 1999). In what follows, we first present our new formalization of PGLR parsing (Section 2). We then review the B&C model according to our formalization, demonstrating that the B&C model may not be probabilistically well-founded, through the use of simple examples (Section 3). We finally discuss how our refinement is expected to influence parsing performance through a further example (Section 4).

2   A PGLR LANGUAGE MODEL

Suppose we have a CFG and its corresponding LR table. Let V_n and V_t be the nonterminal and terminal alphabets, respectively, of the CFG. Further, let S and A be the sets of LR parse states and parsing actions appearing in the LR table, respectively. For each state $s \in S$, the LR table specifies a set $La(s) \subseteq V_t$ of possible next input symbols. Further, for each coupling of a state s and input symbol $l \in La(s)$, the table specifies a set of possible parsing actions: $Act(s, l) \subseteq A$. Each action $a \in A$ is either a shift action or a reduce action. Let A_s and A_r be the sets of shift and reduce actions, respectively, such that $A = A_s \cup A_r \cup \{accept\}$ (*accept* is a special action denoting the completion of parsing).

As with most statistical parsing frameworks, given an input sentence, we rank the parse tree candidates according to the probabilities of the parse derivations that generate those trees. In LR parsing, each parse derivation can be regarded as a complete sequence of transitions between LR parse stacks, which we describe in detail below. Thus, in the following, we use the terms parse tree, parse derivation, and complete stack transition sequence interchangeably.

Given an input word sequence $W = w_1 \ldots w_n$, we estimate the distribution over the parse tree candidates T as follows:

$$P(T|W) = \alpha \cdot P(T) \cdot P(W|T) \tag{5.1}$$

The scaling factor α is a constant that is independent of T, and thus does not need to be considered in ranking parse trees. The second factor $P(T)$ is the distribution over all the possible trees, i.e. complete stack transition sequences, that can be derived from a given grammar, such that, for T being the infinite set of all possible complete stack transition sequences:

$$\sum_{T \in \mathcal{T}} P(T) = 1 \tag{5.2}$$

We estimate this syntactic distribution $P(T)$ using a PGLR model. The third factor $P(W|T)$ is the distribution of lexical derivations from T, where each terminal symbol of T is assumed to be a part of speech symbol. Most statistical parsing frameworks estimate this distribution by assuming that the probability of the i-th word w_i of W depends only on its corresponding terminal symbol (i.e. part of speech) l_i. Since l_i is uniquely specified by T for each i, we obtain equation (5.3):

$$P(W|T) = \prod_{i=1}^{n} P(w_i|l_i) \tag{5.3}$$

where n is the length of W. One could take richer context in estimating the lexical distribution $P(W|T)$. For example, we propose to incorporate the statistics of word collocations into this lexical derivation model elsewhere (Inui et al., 1997a; Shirai et al. 1998). However, this issue is beyond the scope of this chapter.

A stack transition sequence T can be described as in (5.4):

$$\sigma_0 \overset{l_1,a_1}{\Longrightarrow} \sigma_1 \overset{l_2,a_2}{\Longrightarrow} \cdots \overset{l_{n-1},a_{n-1}}{\Longrightarrow} \sigma_{n-1} \overset{l_n,a_n}{\Longrightarrow} \sigma_n \qquad (5.4)$$

where σ_i is the i-th stack, whose stack-top state is denoted by $top(\sigma_i)$, and where $l_i \in La(top(\sigma_{i-1}))$ and $a_i \in Act(top(\sigma_{i-1}), l_i)$ are, respectively, an input symbol and a parsing action chosen at σ_{i-1}. A parse derivation completes if $l_n = \$$ and $a_n = accept$. We say stack transition sequence T is complete if $l_n = \$$, $a_n = accept$, and $\sigma_n = final$, where $final$ is a dummy symbol denoting the stack when parsing is completed. Hereafter, we consistently refer to an LR parse state as a *state* and an LR parse stack as a *stack*. And, unless defined explicitly, s_i denotes the stack-top state of the i-th stack σ_i, i.e. $s_i = top(\sigma_i)$.

The probability of a complete stack transition sequence T can be decomposed as in (5.6):

$$P(T) = P(\sigma_0, l_1, a_1, \sigma_1, \ldots, \sigma_{n-1}, l_n, a_n, \sigma_n) \qquad (5.5)$$

$$= P(\sigma_0) \cdot \prod_{i=1}^{n} P(l_i, a_i, \sigma_i | \sigma_0, l_1, a_1, \sigma_1, .., l_{i-1}, a_{i-1}, \sigma_{i-1}) \qquad (5.6)$$

Here we assume that σ_i contains all the information of its preceding parse derivation that has any effect on the probability of the next transition, namely:

$$P(l_i, a_i, \sigma_i | \sigma_0, l_1, a_1, \sigma_1, \ldots, l_{i-1}, a_{i-1}, \sigma_{i-1}) = P(l_i, a_i, \sigma_i | \sigma_{i-1}) \qquad (5.7)$$

This assumption simplifies equation (5.6) to:

$$P(T) = \prod_{i=1}^{n} P(l_i, a_i, \sigma_i | \sigma_{i-1}) \qquad (5.8)$$

Next we show how we estimate each transition probability $P(l_i, a_i, \sigma_i | \sigma_{i-1})$, which can be decomposed as in (5.9):

$$P(l_i, a_i, \sigma_i | \sigma_{i-1}) = P(l_i | \sigma_{i-1}) \cdot P(a_i | \sigma_{i-1}, l_i) \cdot P(\sigma_i | \sigma_{i-1}, a_i, l_i) \qquad (5.9)$$

To begin with, we estimate the first factor $P(l_i | \sigma_{i-1})$ as follows:

Case 1. $i = 1$:

$$P(l_1 | \sigma_0) = P(l_1 | s_0) \qquad (5.10)$$

Case 2. The previous action a_{i-1} is a shift action, i.e. $a_{i-1} \in A_s$. We assume that only the current stack-top state $s_{i-1} = top(\sigma_{i-1})$ has any effect on the probability of the next input symbol l_i. This means that:

$$P(l_i|\sigma_{i-1}) = P(l_i|s_{i-1}) \qquad (5.11)$$

where

$$\sum_{l \in La(s)} P(l|s) = 1 \qquad (5.12)$$

Case 3. The previous action a_{i-1} is a reduce action, i.e. $a_{i-1} \in A_r$. Unlike Case 2, the input symbol does not get consumed for reduce actions, and thus the next input symbol l_i is always identical to l_{i-1}; l_i can be deterministically predicted. Therefore,

$$P(l_i|\sigma_{i-1}) = 1 \qquad (5.13)$$

Next, we estimate the second factor $P(a_i|\sigma_{i-1}, l_i)$ relying on the analogous assumption that only the current stack-top state s_{i-1} and input symbol l_i have any effect on the probability of the next action a_i:

$$P(a_i|\sigma_{i-1}, l_i) = P(a_i|s_{i-1}, l_i) \qquad (5.14)$$

where

$$\sum_{a \in Act(s,l)} P(a|s,l) = 1 \qquad (5.15)$$

Finally, given the current stack σ_{i-1} and action a_i, the next stack σ_i can be uniquely determined:

$$P(\sigma_i|\sigma_{i-1}, l_i, a_i) = 1 \qquad (5.16)$$

Equation (5.16) can be derived from the LR parsing algorithm; given an input symbol $l_{i+1} \in La(top(\sigma_i))$ and an action $a_{i+1} \in Act(top(\sigma_i), l_{i+1})$, the next (derived) stack $next(\sigma_i, a_{i+1})$ ($= \sigma_{i+1}$) can always be uniquely determined as follows:

- If the current action a_{i+1} is a shift action for an input symbol l_{i+1}, then the parser consumes l_{i+1}, pushing l_{i+1} onto the stack, and then pushes the next state s_{i+1}, which is uniquely specified by the LR table, onto the stack.

- If the current action a_{i+1} is a reduction by a rule $A \rightarrow \beta$, the parser derives the next stack as follows. The parser first pops $|\beta|$ grammatical symbols together with $|\beta|$ state symbols off the stack, where $|\beta|$ is the length of β. In this way, the stack-top state s_j is exposed. The parser then pushes A and s_{i+1} onto the stack, with s_{i+1} being the entry specified in the LR goto table for s_j and A. All these operations are executed deterministically.

As shown in equations (5.11) and (5.13), the probability $P(l_i|\sigma_{i-1})$ should be estimated differently depending on whether the previous action a_{i-1} is a shift action or a reduce action. Fortunately, given the current stack-top state s_{i-1}, it is always possible to determine whether the previous action a_{i-1} was a shift or reduction. Thus, we divide the set of LR parse states S into two subsets: S_s, which is the set containing s_0 and all the states reached immediately after applying a shift action, and S_r, which is the set of states reached immediately after applying a reduce action:

$$S_s \overset{\text{def}}{=} \{s_0\} \cup \{s|\exists a \in A_s, \sigma : s = top(next(\sigma, a))\} \quad (5.17)$$

$$S_r \overset{\text{def}}{=} \{s|\exists a \in A_r, \sigma : s = top(next(\sigma, a))\} \quad (5.18)$$

$$S = S_s \cup S_r \quad \text{and} \quad S_s \cap S_r = \emptyset \quad (5.19)$$

where s_0 is the initial state. See Appendix A for a proof of the mutual exclusiveness between S_s and S_r. Equations (5.9) through (5.18) can be summarized as:

$$P(l_i, a_i, \sigma_i|\sigma_{i-1}) = \begin{cases} P(l_i, a_i|s_{i-1}) & \text{(for } s_{i-1} \in S_s) \\ P(a_i|s_{i-1}, l_i) & \text{(for } s_{i-1} \in S_r) \end{cases} \quad (5.20)$$

Since S_s and S_r are mutually exclusive, we can assign a single probabilistic parameter to each action in an LR table, according to equation (5.20). To be more specific, for each state $s \in S_s$, we associate a probability $p(a)$ with each action $a \in Act(s, l)$ (for $l \in La(s)$), where $p(a) = P(l, a|s)$ such that:

$$\sum_{l \in La(s)} \sum_{a \in Act(s,l)} p(a) = 1 \quad \text{(for } s \in S_s) \quad (5.21)$$

On the other hand, for each state $s \in S_r$, we associate a probability $p(a)$ with each action $a \in Act(s, l)$ (for $l \in La(s)$), where $p(a) = P(a|s, l)$ such that:

$$\sum_{a \in Act(s,l)} p(a) = 1 \quad \text{(for } s \in S_r) \quad (5.22)$$

Through assigning probabilities to actions in an LR table in this way, we can estimate the probability of a stack transition sequence T as given in (5.4) by computing the product of the probabilities associated with all the actions included in T:

$$P(T) = \prod_{i=1}^{n} p(a_i) \quad (5.23)$$

Before closing this section, we describe the advantages of our PGLR model. Our model inherits some of its advantages from the B&C model. First, the model captures context as in equation (5.14): the probabilistic distribution of each parsing action depends on both its left context (i.e. LR parse state) and right context (i.e. input symbol). We elaborate this through an example in Section 4. Second, since the probability of each parse derivation can be estimated simply as the product of the probabilities associated with all the actions in that derivation, we can easily implement a probabilistic LR parser through a simple extension to the original LR parser. We can also easily train the model, as we need only count the frequency of application of each action in generating correct parse derivations for each entry in the training corpus. Third, both the B&C model and our model are expected to be able to allow the parser to prune improbable parse derivations at an equivalently fine-grained level as that for Wright and Wrigley's statistical parser, since these two models assign probabilities to both shift and reduce actions. Furthermore, since our model assigns a single probabilistic parameter to each action in an LR table similarly to the B&C model, the algorithm proposed by Carroll and Briscoe (Carroll and Briscoe 1992) for efficient unpacking of packed parse forests with probability annotations can be equally applicable to our model. Finally, although not explicitly pointed out by Briscoe and Carroll, it should also be noted that PCFGs give global preference over structures but do not sufficiently reflect local bigram statistics of terminal symbols, whereas both the B&C model and our PGLR model reflect these types of preference simultaneously. $P(l_i|s_{i-1})$ in equation (5.11) is a model that predicts the next terminal symbol l_i for the current left context $s_{i-1} \in S_s$. In this case of $s_{i-1} \in S_s$, since s_{i-1} uniquely specifies the previous terminal symbol l_{i-1}, $P(l_i|s_{i-1}) = P(l_i|s_{i-1}, l_{i-1})$, which is a slightly more context-sensitive version of the bigram model of terminal symbols $P(l_i|l_{i-1})$. This feature is expected to be significant particularly when one attempts to integrate syntactic parsing with morphological analysis in the GLR parsing framework (e.g. Li 1995), since the bigram model of terminal symbols has been empirically proven to be effective in morphological analysis.

Besides these advantages, which are all shared with the B&C model, our model overcomes the drawback of the B&C model; namely, our model is based on a probabilistically well-founded formalization, which is expected to improve the parsing performance. We discuss this issue in the remaining sections.

3   COMPARISON WITH BRISCOE AND CARROLL'S MODEL

In this section, we briefly review the B&C model, and make a qualitative comparison between their model and ours.

In our model, we consider the probabilities of transitions between stacks as given in equation (5.8), whereas Briscoe and Carroll consider the probabilities of transitions between *LR parse states* as below:

$$P(T) = \prod_{i=1}^{n} P(l_i, a_i, s_i | s_{i-1}) \tag{5.24}$$

$$= \prod_{i=1}^{n} P(l_i, a_i | s_{i-1}) \cdot P(s_i | s_{i-1}, l_i, a_i) \tag{5.25}$$

Briscoe and Carroll initially associate a probability $p(a)$ with each action $a \in Act(s, l)$ (for $s \in S, l \in La(s)$) in an LR table, where $p(a)$ corresponds to the first factor in (5.25):

$$p(a) = P(l, a | s) \tag{5.26}$$

such that:

$$\forall s \in S. \sum_{l \in La(s)} \sum_{a \in Act(s,l)} p(a) = 1 \tag{5.27}$$

In this model, the probability associated with each action is normalized in the same manner for any state. However, as discussed in the previous section, the probability assigned to an action should be normalized differently depending on whether the state associated with the action is of class S_s or S_r as in equations (5.21) and (5.22). Without this treatment, the probability $P(l_i | s_{i-1})$ in equation (5.11) could be incorrectly duplicated for a single terminal symbol, which would make it difficult to give probabilistically well-founded semantics to the overall score. As a consequence, in the B&C formulation, the probabilities of all the complete parse derivations may not sum up to one, which would be inconsistent with the definition of $P(T)$ (see equation (5.2)).

To illustrate this, let us consider the following grammar $G1$.

Grammar G1:

```
(1)   S  →  X u
(2)   S  →  X v
(3)   X  →  x .
```

This grammar allows only two derivations as shown in Figure 5.1. Suppose that we have tree (a) with frequency m, and (b) with frequency n in the training set. Training the B&C model and our model with these trees, we obtain the models as shown in Table 5.1, where, for each LR parse state, each bracketed value in the top of each row denotes the number of occurrences of the action associated with it, and the numbers in the middle and bottom of each row denote the probabilistic parameters of the B&C model and our model, respectively.

Given this setting, the probability of each tree in Figure 5.1 is computed as follows (see Figure 5.1, where each circled number denotes the LR parse state

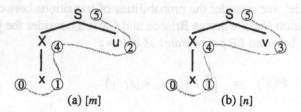

Figure 5.1 Parse trees derived from grammar $G1$. (The square-bracketed value below each tree denotes the number of occurrences of that tree.)

state	action				goto	
	u	v	x	$	X	S
0			**sh1** $(m+n)$		4	5
(S_s)			1			
			1			
1	**re3** (m)	**re3** (n)				
(S_s)	$m/(m+n)$	$n/(m+n)$				
	$m/(m+n)$	$n/(m+n)$				
2				**re1** (m)		
(S_s)				1		
				1		
3				**re2** (n)		
(S_s)				1		
				1		
4	**sh2** (m)	**sh3** (n)				
(S_r)	$m/(m+n)$	$n/(m+n)$				
	1	1				
5				**acc** $(m+n)$		
(S_r)				1		
				1		

Table 5.1 LR table for grammar $G1$, with trained parameters. (The numbers given in the middle and bottom of each row denote the parameters for the B&C model and our model, respectively.)

reached after parsing has proceeded from the left-most corner to the location of that number):

$$P_{\text{B\&C}}(\text{tree(a)}) = 1 \cdot \frac{m}{m+n} \cdot \frac{m}{m+n} \cdot 1 = \left(\frac{m}{m+n}\right)^2 \quad (5.28)$$

$$P_{\text{B\&C}}(\text{tree(b)}) = 1 \cdot \frac{n}{m+n} \cdot \frac{n}{m+n} \cdot 1 = \left(\frac{n}{m+n}\right)^2 \quad (5.29)$$

$$P_{\text{PGLR}}(\text{tree(a)}) = 1 \cdot \frac{m}{m+n} \cdot 1 \cdot 1 = \frac{m}{m+n} \quad (5.30)$$

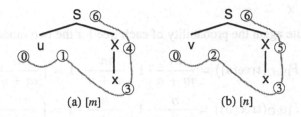

Figure 5.2 Parse trees derived from grammar $G2$

$$P_{\text{PGLR}}(\text{tree(b)}) = 1 \cdot \frac{n}{m+n} \cdot 1 \cdot 1 = \frac{n}{m+n} \tag{5.31}$$

where B&C denotes the B&C model and PGLR denotes our model. This computation shows that our model correctly fits the distribution of the training set, with the sum of the probabilities being one. In the case of the B&C model, on the other hand, the sum of these two probabilities is smaller than one. The reason can be described as follows. After shifting the left-most input symbol x, which leads the process to state 1, the model predicts the next input symbol as either u or v, and chooses the reduce action in each case, reaching state 4. So far, both the B&C model and our model behave in the same manner. In state 4, however, the B&C model again predicts the next input symbol u (or v), despite it already having been determined in state 1. This duplication makes the probability of each tree smaller than what it should be. In our model, on the other hand, the probabilities in state 4, which is of class S_r, are normalized for each input symbol, and thus the prediction of the input symbol is not duplicated.

Briscoe and Carroll are also required to include the factor $P(s_i|s_{i-1}, l_i, a_i)$ in (5.25) since this factor does not always compute to one. In fact, if we have only the information of the current stack-top state s_{i-1} and apply a reduce action in that state, the next state s_i is not always uniquely determined. For this reason, Briscoe and Carroll further subdivide probabilities assigned to reduce actions according to the stack-top states exposed immediately after the pop operations associated with those reduce actions. In our model, by contrast, given the current stack, the next stack after applying any action can be uniquely determined as in (5.16), and thus we do not need to subdivide the probability for any reduce action.

To illustrate this, let us take another simple example in grammar $G2$ as given below, with all the possible derivations shown in Figure 5.2. Further, the LR table is shown in Table 5.2.

Grammar G2:

(1)   S → u   X

(2)   S → v   X

(3)   X → x

Let us compute again the probability of each tree for the two models:

$$P_{\text{B\&C}}(\text{tree(a)}) = \frac{m}{m+n} \cdot 1 \cdot \frac{m}{m+n} \cdot 1 = \left(\frac{m}{m+n}\right)^2 \quad (5.32)$$

$$P_{\text{B\&C}}(\text{tree(b)}) = \frac{n}{m+n} \cdot 1 \cdot \frac{n}{m+n} \cdot 1 = \left(\frac{n}{m+n}\right)^2 \quad (5.33)$$

$$P_{\text{PGLR}}(\text{tree(a)}) = \frac{m}{m+n} \cdot 1 \cdot 1 \cdot 1 = \frac{m}{m+n} \quad (5.34)$$

$$P_{\text{PGLR}}(\text{tree(b)}) = \frac{n}{m+n} \cdot 1 \cdot 1 \cdot 1 = \frac{n}{m+n} \quad (5.35)$$

In the B&C model, the probability assigned to the reduce action in state 3 with the next input symbol being $ is subdivided according to whether the state exposed by the pop operation is state 1 or 2 (see Table 5.2). This makes the probability of each tree smaller than what it should be.

The above examples illustrate that, in the B&C model, the probabilities of all the possible parse trees may not necessarily sum up to one, due to the lack of probabilistically well-founded normalization, which would be inconsistent with the definition of $P(T)$ (see equation (5.2)). In our model, on the other hand, the probabilities of all the parse trees are guaranteed to always sum to one[1]. This flaw in the B&C model can be considered to be related to Briscoe and Carroll's claim that their model tends to favor parse trees involving fewer grammar rules, almost regardless of the training data. In the B&C model, stack transition sequences involving more reduce actions tend to be assigned much lower probabilities for the two reasons mentioned above: (a) the probabilities assigned to actions following reduce actions tend to be lower than what they should be, since the B&C model again predicts the next input symbols immediately after reduce actions, (b) the probabilities assigned to reduce actions tend to be lower than what they should be, since they are further subdivided according to the stack-top states exposed by the stack-pop operations. Therefore, given the fact that stack transition sequences involving fewer reduce actions correspond to parse trees involving fewer grammar rules, it is to be expected that the B&C model tends to strongly prefer parse trees involving fewer grammar rules. To solve this problem, Briscoe and Carroll proposed calculating the geometric mean of the probabilities of the actions involved in each stack transition sequence. However, this solution makes their model even further removed from a probabilistically well-founded model. In our model, on the other hand, any bias toward shorter derivations is expected to be much weaker, and thus we do not require the calculation of the geometric mean.

One may wonder to what extent these differences matter for practical statistical parsing. Although this issue needs to be explored through large-scale

state	action				goto	
	u	v	x	$	X	S
0	**sh1** (m)	**sh2** (n)				6
(S_s)	$m/(m+n)$	$n/(m+n)$				
	$m/(m+n)$	$n/(m+n)$				
1			**sh3** (m)		4	
(S_s)			1			
			1			
2			**sh3** (n)		5	
(S_s)			1			
			1			
3				**re3** $(m+n)$		
(S_s)				$^{(1)}m/(m+n)$; $^{(2)}n/(m+n)$		
				1		
4				**re1** (m)		
(S_r)				$^{(0)}$1		
5				**re2** (n)		
(S_r)				$^{(0)}$1		
				1		
6				**acc** $(m+n)$		
(S_r)				1		
				1		

Table 5.2   LR table for grammar $G2$, with trained parameters. (Each middle bracketed number denotes the state exposed by the stack-pop operation associated with the corresponding reduce action.)

empirical evaluation, it is worthwhile to consider some likely cases where the difference discussed here will influence parsing performance. We discuss such a case through a further example in the next section.

4   EXPECTED IMPACT ON PARSING PERFORMANCE

In this section, we first demonstrate through an example how the B&C model and our model, which we class as GLR-based models here, capture richer context than the PCFG model. We then return to the issue raised at the end of the previous section.

Suppose we have the following grammar $G3$.

Grammar G3:

(1)   S → u S

(2)   S → v S

(3)   S → x

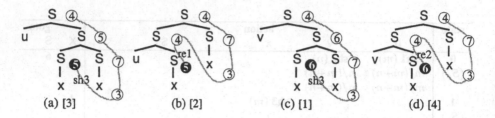

Figure 5.3   Training set for grammar $G3$

(4)   S → S S

Further, let us assume that we train the PCFG model, the B&C model, and our PGLR model, respectively, using a training set as shown in Figure 5.3, where trees (a) and (b) are the parse trees for input sentence $W_1 =$ uxx, and (c) and (d) are those for $W_2 =$ vxx. Table 5.3 shows the LR table for grammar $G3$, with the trained parameters[2].

According to the training data in Figure 5.3, where the square-bracketed value below each tree denotes the number of occurrences of that tree, right branching (i.e. tree (a)) is preferred for input sentence W_1, whereas left branching (i.e. tree (d)) is preferred for input sentence W_2. It is easy to see that the PCFG model does not successfully learn these preferences for either of the sentences, since all the parse trees produced for each sentence involve the same set of grammar rules.

Unlike the PCFG model, both the GLR-based models can learn these preferences in the following way. In the LR parsing process for sentence W_1, the point where the parser must choose between parse trees (a) and (b) is in state 5, which is reached after the reduction of the left-most x into S (see Figure 5.3). In state 5, if the shift action is chosen, parse tree (a) is derived, while, if the reduce action is chosen, (b) is derived. Thus, the preference for (a) to (b) is reflected in the distribution over the shift-reduce conflict in this state. Table 5.3 shows that both the B&C model and our model correctly prefer the shift action in state 5 with the next input symbol being x. For input sentence W_2, on the other hand, the left branching tree (d) is preferred. This preference is also reflected in the distribution over the shift-reduce conflict in the state reached after the reduction of the left-most x into S, but, this time, the relevant state is state 6 instead of state 5. According to Table 5.3, state 6 with the next input symbol being x correctly prefers the reduce action, which derives the left-branching tree (d). In sum, the different preferences for W_1 and W_2 are reflected separately in the distributions assigned to the different states (i.e. states 5 and 6).

As illustrated in this example, for each parsing choice point, the LR parse state associated with it can provide a context for specifying the preference for

state			action		goto
	u	v	x	$	S
0	sh1	sh2	sh3		4
(S_s)	.5	.5	0		
	.5	.5	0		
1	sh1	sh2	sh3		5
(S_s)	0	0	1		
	0	0	1		
2	sh1	sh2	sh3		6
(S_s)	0	0	1		
	0	0	1		
3	re3	re3	re3	re3	
(S_s)	0	0	[1].25 ; [2].25	[4].3 ; [5].15 ; [6].05	
	0	0	.5	.5	
4	sh1	sh2	sh3	acc	7
(S_r)	0	0	.38	.62	
	1	1	1	1	
5	sh1/re1	sh2/re1	sh3/re1	re1	7
(S_r)	0/0	0/0	.38/[1].25	[0].38	
	.5/.5	.5/.5	.6/.4	1	
6	sh1/re2	sh2/re2	sh3/re2	re2	7
(S_r)	0/0	0/0	.17/[2].67	[0].17	
	.5/.5	.5/.5	.2/.8	1	
7	sh1/re4	sh2/re4	sh3/re4	re4	7
(S_r)	0/0	0/0	0/0	[0].6 ; [1].3 ; [2].1	
	.5/.5	.5/.5	.5/.5	1	

Table 5.3 LR table for grammar $G3$

that parse choice. This feature of the GLR-based models enables us to take richer context into account than the PCFG model. Furthermore, although not explicitly demonstrated in the above example, it should also be noted that the GLR-based models are sensitive to the next input symbol as shown in (5.14) in Section 2.

Now, let us see how the probabilities assigned to LR parsing actions are reflected in the probability of each parse tree. Table 5.4 shows the overall distributions provided by the PCFG model, the B&C model, and our model, respectively, to the trees in Figure 5.3[3]. According to the table, our model

	$P(a|W_1)$	$P(b|W_1)$	$P(c|W_2)$	$P(d|W_2)$
PCFG	.50	.50	.50	.50
B&C	.28	.72	.003	.997
PLR	.60	.40	.20	.80
training data	.60	.40	.20	.80

Table 5.4 Distributions over the parse trees from Figure 3. (Trees (a) and (b) are the parse trees for the input sentences $W_1 = \text{uxx}$, and (c) and (d) are those for $W_2 = \text{vxx}$).

accurately learns the distribution of the training data, whereas the B&C model does not fit the training data very well. In particular, for sentence W_1, it goes as far as incorrectly preferring parse tree (b). This occurs due to the lack of well-founded normalization of probabilities as discussed in Section 3. As mentioned above, the B&C model correctly prefers the shift action in state 5, as does our model. However, for the rest of the parsing process, the B&C model associates a considerably higher probability to the process from state 4 through 3 and 7 to 4, which derives tree (b), than the process from 3 through 7 and 5 to 4, which derives tree (a), since in their model the former process is inappropriately supported by the occurrence of tree (d). For example, in both parsing processes for (b) and (d), the pop operation associated with the reduction in state 3 exposes state 4, and the B&C model thus assigns an inappropriately high probability to this reduction, compared to the reduction in state 3 for tree (a).

Of course, as far as various approximations are made in constructing a probabilistic model similar to both the B&C model and our model, it is always the case that the model may not fit the training data precisely due to the insufficiency of the model's complexity. Analogous to the B&C model, our model does not always fit the training data precisely due to the independence assumptions such as equations (5.7), (5.11), etc. However, it should be noted that, as illustrated by the above example, there is reason to believe that the B&C model not fitting the training data is due not only to the insufficient complexity, but also to the lack of well-founded normalization.

5   CONCLUSION

In this chapter we presented a new formalization of probabilistic LR parsing. Our modeling inherits some of its features from the B&C model. It captures derivational context to a greater degree then the PCFG model, and naturally integrates local bigram statistics of terminal symbols and global preference over structures of parse trees. Furthermore, since the model is tightly coupled with GLR parsing, it can be easily implemented and trained. Inheriting these advantages, our formalization additionally overcomes an important drawback of the B&C model: the lack of well-founded normalization of probabilities.

We demonstrated through examples that this refinement is expected to improve parsing performance. Those examples may seem to be relatively artificial and forced. However, our claims have also been empirically supported through large scaled experiments (see (Sornlertlamvanich et al. 1997; Sornlertlamvanich et al. 1999) for our experiments and Carroll and Briscoe 1998 for experiments conducted by other research groups).

It should also be noted that our modeling is equally applicable to both CLR tables and LALR tables. As far as the results of our experimental comparison are concerned, the effectiveness of PGLR using an LALR table is comparable with that of PGLR using an CLR table (Sornlertlamvanich et al. 1999). For a qualitative comparison see our discussion in Appendix B and Inui et al., 1997b.

Other approaches to context-sensitive statistical parsing have also been proposed (such as Magerman and Marcus 1991; Black et al. 1993; Kita, 1994; Sekine and Grishman 1995). Theoretical and empirical comparisons between these models and ours still have to be made. The significance of introducing lexical sensitivity into language models has also been established: (e.g. Schabes 1992; Collins 1996; Collins 1997; Li 1996; Charniak 1997; Haruno et al. 1998; Fujio and Matsumoto 1998; Uchimoto et al. 1999). Our work in this area is reported in Inui et al., 1997a; Shirai et al. 1998.

Acknowledgments

The authors would like to thank the reviewers for their constructive comments. They would also like to thank Masahiro Ueki and Kiyoaki Shirai (Tokyo Institute of Technology) for their fruitful discussion on the formalization of the proposed model, and John Carroll (University of Sussex) for his constructive comments and empirical support for our claim. Finally, they would like to thank Timothy Baldwin (Tokyo Institute of Technology) for his help in writing this chapter.

Appendix A: Proof of the mutual exclusiveness between S_s and S_r

It is obvious from the algorithm for generating an LR(1) goto graph (Aho et al. 1986) that, for each state s ($\neq s_0$), if there exist states s_i and s_j whose goto transitions on symbol X_i and X_j, respectively, both lead to s, then $X_i = X_j$. Namely, for any given state s, the symbol X required to reach s by way of a goto transition is always uniquely specified. On the other hand, if the current state is in S_s, then it should have been reached through a goto transition on a certain terminal symbol $X \in V_t$, whereas, if the current state is in S_r, then it should have been reached through a goto transition on a certain nonterminal symbol $X \in V_n$. Given these facts, it is obvious that S_s and S_r are mutually exclusive.

Appendix B: An LALR-based model

Let us consider equation (5.1) again. In this equation, we implicitly assume the range of T to be all the possible parse tree candidates, i.e. the set of all the complete and *acceptable* stack transition sequences, which we refer to as $\mathcal{T}_{acc}$. Thus, the second factor $P(T)$ in equation (5.1) should be interpreted as a distribution over $\mathcal{T}_{acc}$ such that:

$$\sum_{T \in \mathcal{T}_{acc}} P(T) = 1$$

However, what is estimated by a PGLR model $P_{PGLR}(T)$ is not a distribution over $\mathcal{T}_{acc}$ but over $\mathcal{T}$, which is the set of all the possible complete transition sequences – whether acceptable or rejected –, such that:

$$\sum_{T \in \mathcal{T}} P_{PGLR}(T) = 1$$

Obviously, this difference does not matter in the case of a CLR-based model, since $\mathcal{T}_{acc} = \mathcal{T}$. On the other hand, if one considers an LALR-based model, since there may be rejected transition sequences in $\mathcal{T}$, $\mathcal{T}_{acc} \subseteq \mathcal{T}$. In spite of this, however, one can still rank complete and acceptable stack transition sequences using a PCFG model $P_{PGLR}(T)$, since $P(T)$ can be estimated using $P_{PGLR}(T)$ as follows:

$$P(T) = \left(\sum_{T \in \mathcal{T}_{acc}} P_{PGLR}(T) \right)^{-1} \cdot P_{PGLR}(T)$$

where the first factor is a constant that is independent of T, and thus can be neglected in ranking T. To conclude, one can rank the parse tree candidates for any given input sentence according to $P_{PGLR}(T)$ and $P(W|T)$, whether one bases the model on canonical LR, LALR, or even LR(0) (i.e. SLR).

Notes

1. More precisely, this is the case if the model is based on a canonical LR (CLR) table. In the case of lookahead LR (LALR) tables, the probabilities of all the parse trees may not sum up to one even for the case of our model, since some stack transitions may not be accepted (for details of CLR and LALR, see, for example, Aho 1986; Chapman 1987). However, this fact will never prevent our model from being applicable to LALR. For further discussion, see Appendix B and (Inui et al., 1997b).

2. In practical applications, when computing parameters one would need to use some smoothing technique in order to avoid assigning zero to any parameter associated with an action that had never occurred in training.

3. Although Briscoe and Carroll proposed to take the geometric mean of peripheral distributions as mentioned in Section 3, we did not apply this operation when computing the probabilities in Table 5.4, to give the reader a sense of the difference between the probabilities given by the B&C model and our model. Note that, in our example, since the number of state transitions involved in each parse tree is always the same for any given sentence, taking the geometric mean would not change the preference order.

References

Aho, A., S. Ravi, and J. Ullman (1986) *Compilers, Principle, Techniques, and Tools.* Reading, MA: Addison Wesley.

Black, E., F. Jelinek, J. Lafferty, D. Magerman, R. Mercer, and S. Roukos (1993) Towards history-based grammars: Using richer models for probabilistic parsing. In *Proceedings of the 31st Annual Meeting of the Association for Computational Linguistics*, pp. 31–37.

Briscoe, T. and J. Carroll (1993) Generalized probabilistic LR parsing of natural language (corpora) with unification-based grammars. *Computational Linguistics* 19 (1): 25–60.

Carroll, J. and E. Briscoe (1992) Probabilistic normalization and unpacking of packed parse forests for unification-based grammars. In *Proceedings, AAAI Fall Symposium on Probabilistic Approaches to Natural Language*, pp. 33–38.

Carroll, J. and E. Briscoe (1998) Can subcategorisation probabilities help a statistical parser? In *Proceedings of the 6th ACL/SIGDAT Workshop on Very Large Corpora* pp. 92–100.

Chapman, N. (1987) *LR Parsing – Theory and Practice.* Cambridge University Press.

Charniak, E. (1997) Statistical parsing with a context-free grammar and word statistics In *Proceedings of the National Conference on Artificial Intelligence*, pp. 598–603.

Collins, M. (1996) A new statistical parser based on bigram lexical dependencies. In *Proceedings of the 34th Annual Meeting of the Association for Computational Linguistics* pp. 184–191.

Collins, M. (1997) Three Generative, Lexicalised Models for Statistical Parsing. In *Proceedings of the 35th Annual Meeting of the Association for Computational Linguistics* pp. 16-23.

Fujio, M. and Y. Matsumoto (1998) Japanese dependency structure analysis based on lexicalized statistics. In *Proceedings of the 3rd Conference on Empirical Methods in Natural Language Processing*, pp. 88–96.

Haruno, M., S. Shirai, and Y. Ooyama (1998) Using Decision trees to construct a practical parser. In *Proceedings of COLING-ACL'98*, pp. 505–511.

Inui, K., K. Shirai, H. Tanaka, and T. Tokunaga (1997) Integrated probabilistic language modeling for statistical parsing. Technical Report TR97-0005, Dept. of Computer Science, Tokyo Institute of Technology. Available from *http://www.cs.titech.ac.jp/tr.html*.

Inui, K., V. Sornlertlamvanich, H. Tanaka, and T. Tokunaga (1997) A new probabilistic LR language model for statistical parsing. Technical Report TR97-0004, Department of Computer Science, Tokyo Institute of Technology. Available from *http://www.cs.titech.ac.jp/tr.html*.

Kita, K. (1994) Spoken sentence recognition based on HMM-LR with hybrid language modeling. *IEICE Trans. Inf. & Syst.*, Vol. E77-D, No. 2.

Li, H. (1996) A probabilistic disambiguation method based on psycholinguistic principles. In *Proceedings of the Fourth Workshop on Very Large Corpora (WVLC-4)*. Available from cmp-lg/9606016.

Li, H. and H. Tanaka (1995) A method for integrating the connection constraints into an LR table. In *Proceedings of Natural Language Processing Pacific Rim Symposium '95*, pp. 703–708.

Magerman, D. and M. Marcus (1991) Pearl: A probabilistic chart parser. In *Proceedings of the 5th Conference of European Chapter of the Association for Computational Linguistics*, pp. 15–20.

Schabes, Y. (1992) Stochastic lexicalized tree-adjoining grammars. In *Proceedings of the 14th International Conference on Computational Linguistics*, Vol. 2, pp. 425–432.

Sekine, S. and R. Grishman (1995) A corpus-based probabilistic grammar with only two non-terminals. In *Proceedings of the Fourth International Workshop on Parsing Technologies*. Prague: Charles University, pp. 216–223.

Shirai, K., K. Inui, T. Tokunaga and H. Tanaka (1998) An empirical evaluation of statistical parsing of Japanese sentences using a lexical association statistics. *Proc. 3rd Conference on Empirical Methods in Natural Language processing*, pp. 80–87.

Sornlertlamvanich, V., K. Inui, K. Shirai, H. Tanaka, and T. Tokunaga (1997) Empirical Evaluation of Probabilistic GLR Parsing. In *Proceedings of the Natural Language Processing Pacific Rim Symposium*, pp. 169–174.

Sornlertlamvanich, V., K. Inui, K. Shirai, H. Tanaka, T. Tokunaga, and T. Takezawa (1999) Empirical Support for New Probabilistic Generalized LR Parsing. *Journal of Natural Language Processing*, Vol. 6, No. 2, pp. 3-22.

Su, K., J.-N. Wang, M.-H. Su, and J.-S. Chang (1991) GLR parsing with scoring. In M. Tomita (1991), *Efficient Parsing for Natural Language*, pp. 93–112.

Tomita, M. (1986) *Efficient Parsing for Natural Language*. Boston (Mass): Kluwer.

Tomita, M. (ed.) (1991) *Generalized LR Parsing*. Boston (Mass): Kluwer.

Uchimoto, K., S. Sekine, and H. Isihara (1999) Analysis of Japanese sentences using an integrated statistical language model. In *Proceedings of the 13th Conference of the European Chapter of the ACL* pp. 196-203.

Wright, J. and E. Wrigley (1991) GLR parsing with probability. In M. Tomita (1991), *Efficient Parsing for Natural Language*, pp. 113–128.

Chapter 6

PROBABILISTIC PARSING USING LEFT CORNER LANGUAGE MODELS

Christopher D. Manning
Department of Computer Science, Stanford University, Stanford CA 94305-9020, USA
manning@cs.stanford.edu

Bob Carpenter
Lucent Technologies Bell Labs, 600 Mountain Avenue (2D-453), Murray Hill NJ 07974, USA
carp@research.bell-labs.com

Abstract   We introduce a novel probabilistic grammar model based on a probabilistic version of a left-corner parser. The left-corner strategy is attractive because rule probabilities can be conditioned on both top-down goals and bottom-up derivations. We develop the underlying theory and explain how a grammar can be induced from analyzed data. We show that the left-corner approach provides an advantage over simple top-down probabilistic context-free grammars in parsing the *Wall Street Journal* using a grammar induced from the Penn Treebank. We also conclude that the Penn Treebank provides a fairly weak testbed due to the flatness of its bracketings and to the obvious overgeneration and undergeneration of its induced grammar.

1   INTRODUCTION

For context-free grammars (CFGs), there is a well-known standard probabilistic version, Probabilistic Context-Free Grammars (PCFGs), which have been thoroughly investigated (Booth, 1969; Suppes, 1970; Sankoff, 1971; Baker, 1979; Lari and Young, 1990; Kupiec, 1991, Jelinek et al., 1992; Charniak, 1993).

Under this model, one assigns probabilities to different rewrites of a nonterminal. Or in other words, one is giving the probability of a local subtree given the mother node. So, for example, we might have:

$$P(\text{NP} \rightarrow \text{DT NN}|\text{NP}) = 0.2$$

105

H. Bunt and A. Nijholt (eds.), Advances in Probabilistic and Other Parsing Technologies, 105–124.
© 2000 *Kluwer Academic Publishers.*

$$P(\text{NP} \rightarrow \text{PRP}|\text{NP}) \quad = \quad 0.1$$

where in general, for all nonterminals A, $\sum_\gamma P(A \rightarrow \gamma|A) = 1$.

But standard PCFGs are only one way to make a probabilistic version of CFGs. If we think in parsing terms, a PCFG corresponds to a probabilistic version of top down parsing, since at each stage we are trying to predict the child nodes given knowledge only of the parent node. Other parsing methods lend themselves to different models of probabilistic conditioning. Usually, such conditioning is a mixture of top-down and bottom-up information. This chapter discusses some initial results from another point in this parameter space where the conditioning reflects a left-corner parsing strategy, yielding what we will call probabilistic left-corner grammars (PLCGs).[1] Left-corner parsers simultaneously work top-down from a goal category and bottom-up from the left corner of a particular rule. For instance, a rule such as S $\rightarrow$ NP VP has the left-corner NP and will be fired whenever an NP has been derived and an S is a possible leftmost daughter of the eventual goal category. In this chapter, we present algorithms for PCLG parsing, present some results comparing PCLG parsing with PCFG parsing, and discuss some mechanisms for improving results.

Why might one want to employ PLCGs? While the main perceived weakness of PCFGs is their lack of lexicalization, they are also deficient on purely structural grounds (Briscoe and Carroll, 1993). Inherent to the idea of a PCFG is that probabilities are context-free: for instance, the probability of a noun phrase expanding in a certain way is independent of where the NP is in the tree. Even if we in some way lexicalize PCFGs to remove the other deficiency, this assumption of structural context-freeness remains.[2] But this context-free assumption is actually quite wrong. For example, table 6.1 shows how the probabilities of expanding an NP node (in the Penn Treebank) differ wildly between subject position and object position. Pronouns, proper names and definite NPs appear more commonly in subject position while NPs containing post-head modifiers and bare nouns occur more commonly in object position. (This reflects the fact that the subject normally expresses the sentence-internal topic; see Manning (1996).)

Another advantage of PLCGs is that parse probabilities are straightforwardly calculated from left to right, which is convenient for online processing and integration with other linear probabilistic models.[3]

2   PROBABILISTIC LEFT CORNER GRAMMARS

Left corner parsers (Rosenkrantz and Lewis II, 1970; Demers, 1977) work by a combination of bottom-up and top-down processing. One begins with a goal category (the root of what is currently being constructed), and then looks at the left corner of the string (i.e., one shifts the next terminal). If the left

Expansion	% as Subj	% as Obj
NP → PRP	13.7%	2.1%
NP → NNP	3.5%	0.9%
NP → DT NN	5.6%	4.6%
NP → NN	1.4%	2.8%
NP → NP SBAR	0.5%	2.6%
NP → NP PP	5.6%	14.1%

Table 6.1 Selected common expansions of NP as Subject vs. Object

corner is the same category as the goal category, then one can stop. Otherwise, one projects a possible local tree from the left corner. The remaining children of this projected local tree then become goal categories and one recursively does left corner parsing of each. When this local tree is finished, one again recursively does left-corner parsing with this subtree as the left corner, and the same goal category. To make this description more precise, pseudocode for a simple left corner recognizer is shown in figure 6.1. This particular parser assumes that lexical material is introduced on the right-hand side of a rule, e.g., as N → *house*, and that the top of the stack is to the left when written horizontally.[4] The parser works in terms of a stack of found and sought constituents, the latter being represented on the stack as categories with a bar over them. We use α to represent a single terminal or non-terminal (or the empty string, if we wish to accommodate empty categories in the grammar), and γ to stand for a (possibly empty) sequence of terminals and non-terminals.

The parser has three actions, *shifting*, *projecting*, and *attaching*. To produce a language model that reflects the operation of a left corner parser, we have to provide probabilities for the different actions in figure 6.1. When to shift is deterministic: If the thing on top of the stack is a sought category $\overline{C}$, then one must shift, and one can never successfully shift at other times. But there will be a probability distribution over what is shifted. At other times we must decide whether to attach or project. The only interesting choice here is deciding whether to attach in cases where the left corner category and the goal category are the same. Otherwise we must project. Finally we need probabilities for projecting a certain local tree given the left corner (lc) and the goal category (gc). Under this model, we might have probabilities for this last operation like this:

$$P_{proj}(\text{SBAR} \to \text{IN S}|lc = \text{IN}, gc = \text{S}) = 0.25$$
$$P_{proj}(\text{PP} \to \text{IN NP}|lc = \text{IN}, gc = \text{S}) = 0.55$$

// Initialization
Place the predicted start symbol $\overline{S}$ on top of the stack
// Parser
while (an action is possible) **do** one of the following
    actions
        [Shift] If a barred (goal) category is on top of the stack,
            push the next input symbol on top of the stack
        [Attach] If $\alpha\overline{\alpha}$ is on top of the stack, remove both
        [Project] If α is on top of the stack and $A \rightarrow \alpha\,\gamma$,
            replace α by $\overline{\gamma}A$
    endactions
endwhile
// Termination
if empty(input) **and** empty(stack) **then**
  exit success
else
  exit failure
fi

Figure 6.1 An LC stack parser.

How to make probabilities out of the above choices is made precise in the next section.

2.1 THE LC PROBABILITY OF A PARSE

In this section, we provide probabilities for left-corner derivations. These form the basis for a language model that assigns probabilities to sentences. We start by observing that the probability of a sentence s according to a grammar G is:

$$P(s|G) = \sum_t P(s,t|G), \quad t \text{ a parse tree of } s$$

$$= \sum_{\{t:\ \text{yield}(t)=s\}} P(t|G)$$

The last line follows since the parse tree determines the terminal yield. It is therefore sufficient to be able to calculate the probability of a (parse) tree. Below we suppress the conditioning of the probability according to the grammar.

We can express the probability of a parse tree in terms of the sum of the probabilities of derivations of that parse tree:

$$P(t) = \sum_{d \text{ a LC derivation of } t} P(d)$$

The steps of the derivation reflect the operation of a left corner parser. We can generate trees using left corner probabilities by regarding each step of the derivation as a step in a left corner parsing operation. But under left corner parsing, each parse tree has a unique derivation and so the summation sign can be dropped from the above equation.

Now, without any assumptions, the probability of a derivation can be expressed as a product in terms of the probabilities of each of the individual operations in the derivation. Suppose that $(C_1, \ldots, C_m)$ is the sequence of operations in the LC parse derivation d of t. Then, by the chain rule, we have:

$$P(t) = P(d) = \prod_{i=1}^{m} P(C_i | C_1, \ldots, C_{i-1})$$

In practice, we cannot condition the probability of each parse decision on the entire history, but rather we need to condition on equivalence classes of histories. The simplest model, which we will explore for the rest of this section, is to assume that the probability of each parse decision is largely independent of the parse history, and just depends on the state of the parser. In particular, we will assume that it depends simply on the left corner and top goal categories of the parse stack. This drastic assumption nevertheless gives us a model that uses slightly more conditioning information than a PCFG, because elementary left-corner parsing actions are conditioned by the goal category, rather than simply being the probability of a local tree. For instance, the probability of a certain expansion of NP may be different in subject position and object position, because the goal category is different.

Each elementary operation of a left corner parser is either a shift, an attach or a left corner projection. Under the independence assumptions mentioned above, the probability of a shift will simply be the probability of a certain left corner daughter (lc) being shifted given the current goal category (gc), which we will model by P_{shift}. Recall that when to shift is deterministic. If one is not shifting, one must choose to attach or project, which we model by P_{att}. Attaching only has a non-zero probability if the left corner and the goal category are the same, but we define it for all pairs. If we do not attach, we project a constituent based on the left corner with probability P_{proj}. Thus the probability of each elementary operation C_i can be expressed in terms of probability distributions P_{shift}, P_{att}, and P_{proj} as follows:

$$P(C_i = \text{shift } lc) = \begin{cases} P_{shift}(lc|gc) & \text{if top of the stack is } gc \\ 0 & \text{otherwise} \end{cases}$$

$$P(C_i = \text{attach}) = \begin{cases} P_{att}(lc, gc) & \text{if top of the stack is not } gc \\ 0 & \text{otherwise} \end{cases}$$

$$P(C_i = \text{proj } A \rightarrow \gamma) = \begin{cases} (1 - P_{att}(lc, gc))P_{proj}(A \rightarrow \gamma|lc, gc) \\ \qquad \text{if top is not } gc \\ 0 \qquad \text{otherwise} \end{cases}$$

Rule	Freq.	PCFG Prob.	Rule	Freq.	PCFG Prob.
PP → IN NP	76617	0.81	NP → PRP	17323	0.06
NP → NP PP	34965	0.11	ADVP → RB	14228	0.72
NP → DT NN	29351	0.09	NP → NN	13586	0.04
S → NP VP	28292	0.30	NP → NNS	13318	0.04
S → VP	23559	0.25	VP → TO VP	12900	0.09
S → NP VP	17703	0.19	NP → NNP	12575	0.04

Table 6.2   Highest frequency CFG rules in Penn Treebank

These operations obey the following:

$$\sum_{lc} P_{shift}(lc|gc) = 1$$

$$\text{If } lc \neq gc, \; P_{att}(lc, gc) = 0$$

$$\sum_{\{A \to \gamma : \gamma = lc \ldots\}} P_{proj}(A \to \gamma|lc, gc) = 1$$

From the above we note that the probabilities of the choice of projections sums to one, and hence, since other probabilities are complements of each other, the probabilities of the actions available for each elementary operation sum to one. There are also no dead ends in a derivation, because unless A is a possible left corner constituent of gc, $P(A \to \gamma|lc, gc) = 0$. Thus we have shown that these probabilities define a language model.[5] That is, $\sum_s P(s|G) = 1$. It is possible to extend the PLCG model in various ways to include more probabilistic conditioning, as we discuss briefly later, but our current results reflect this model.

3   PARSING EXPERIMENTS

3.1   PCFG EXPERIMENT

Training and testing were done on Release 2 of the Penn Treebank (Marcus et al., 1993), published in 1995. As in other recent work (Magerman, 1995; Collins, 1996), training was done on sections 02–21 of the Wall Street Journal portion of the treebank (approximately 40,000 sentences, 780,153 local trees) and final testing was done on section 23, which contains 2416 sentences. Counts of how often each local tree occurred in the treebank were made, and these were used directly to give probabilities for rewriting each nonterminal. The highest frequency rules are given in table 6.2. Local trees were considered down to the level of preterminals (i.e., part of speech tags); lexical information was ignored.[6] Every tree was given a new root symbol 'ROOT', attached by

2–12 word sentences	this chapter	Charniak, 1996
Grammar (rules)	14 971	10 605
% sent. length < cutoff	16.6%	
Test set size (sentences)	401	
Average Length (words)	8.3	8.7
Precision	89.8%	88.6%
Recall	90.7%	91.7%
Labelled Precision	83.5%	
Labelled Recall	82.9%	
Labelled Precision +1	87.1%	
Labelled Recall +1	85.2%	
Average CBs	0.27	
Non-crossing accuracy	95.8%	97.9%
Sentences with 0 CBs	84.5%	

Table 6.3   PCFG results

a unary branch to the root in the treebank. Empty nodes (of which there are several kinds in the treebank) were ignored, and nonterminals above them that dominated no pronounced words were also deleted.[7] No attempt was made to do any smoothing. While in a few cases this would clearly be useful (e.g., the training data allows a compound noun to be modified by four adjectives, but not a simple noun), in practice the induced treebank grammar is hugely ambiguous, and greatly overgenerates. Thus, while the lack of smoothing in principle disallows some correct parses from being generated, the treebank grammar can always produce some parse for a sentence (Charniak, 1996) and adding unseen rules with low probabilities is unlikely to improve bottom line performance, because these added rules are unlikely to appear in the maximum probability parse. A better solution would be to use a covering grammar with fewer rules and a more deeply nested structure.[8]

A vanilla PCFG model was tested by chart-parsing the part of speech tags of the sentences (i.e., ambiguities in part of speech assignment were assumed to be successfully resolved). An exhaustive chartparse was done and the highest probability (Viterbi) parse was selected, in the standard way (Charniak, 1993). Results from such parsing are shown in table 6.3 together with results from Charniak (1996). The measures shown have been used in various earlier works, and draw from the Parseval measures (Black et al., 1991). Precision is how many brackets in the parse match those in the correct tree (perhaps also examining labels), recall measures how many of the brackets in the correct tree are in the parse. The unmarked measures ignore unary constituents, the ones marked +1 include unary constituents.[9] Crossing brackets (CBs) measures

2/4–40 word sentences	PCFG	Magerman	Collins
% sent. length < cutoff	92.9%		
Test set size (sentences)		1759	2416
Average Length (words)	21.9	22.3	
Precision	78.8%	86.3%	
Recall	80.4%	85.8%	
Labelled Precision		84.5%	86.3%
Labelled Recall		84.0%	85.8%
Average CBs		1.33	1.14
Non-crossing accuracy	87.7%		
Sentences with 0 CBs		55.4%	57.2%

Table 6.4   PCFG (Charniak, 1996) vs. Magerman (1995) / Collins (1996) comparison

record how many brackets in the parse cross bracketings in the correct tree, with the non-crossing accuracy measuring the percent of brackets that are not CBs. The '% sent. length < cutoff' says what percentage of sentences within the 2416 sentence test section were shorter than the cutoff and thus used in the test set for the current experiment. Our results are not directly comparable to Charniak's since he was using an earlier release of the Penn Treebank. Further, he used two strategies that aimed at increasing performance: recoding auxiliaries from their Penn tag (which is undistinguished from other verbs) to special auxiliary tags, and adding a (crude) correction factor to the PCFG model so that it uniformly favored right-branching trees rather than being context free. Whether the former change was shown to be beneficial is not discussed, but the later correction factor improved results by about two percent. The fact that the results are mixed between the two systems suggests that the quality of the Penn Treebank has improved in the second release, and these gains roughly match the gains from these factors. It is useful that the results are roughly comparable since we can then use Charniak's results as a rough benchmark for PCFG performance on longer sentences, which we have not obtained.[10]

Charniak's central contention is that purely structural parsing like this using treebank grammars works much better than community lore would have one believe. Indeed, as the comparison in table 6.4 suggests, it does not work much worse than Collins (1996) a leading recent parser that includes lexical content. That is, it seems one can score well in the Parseval measures using purely structural factors, and that the use of lexical factors in other models is at present only adding a little to their performance.[11] This is in part because the Penn treebank does not represent certain semantic 'attachment' decisions, and the structure of the trees minimizes the penalty for other 'attachment' errors, as we discuss in the last section of this chapter.

	Parser results			2–12 Error Reduction
Sentence Lengths	2–12	2–16	2–25	
Beam size	50 000	50 000	40 000	
% sent. length < cutoff	16.6%	28.1%	60.2%	
Test set (sentences)	401	680	1454	
Average length (words)	8.3	10.9	16.3	
Precision	92.0%	90.1%	84.6%	21.6%
Recall	92.3%	89.5%	83.2%	17.2%
Labelled Precision	87.1%	86.0%	81.1%	21.8%
Labelled Recall	86.7%	84.9%	79.6%	22.2%
Labelled Precision +1	88.6%	87.7%	83.5%	11.6%
Labelled Recall +1	88.3%	86.3%	81.5%	20.9%
Average CBs	0.21	0.43	1.25	22.2%
Non-crossing accuracy	96.8%	94.7%	89.6%	23.8%
Sentences with 0 CBs	87.5%	76.0%	52.0%	19.4%

Table 6.5 Left Corner Parser results from n-ary grammar.

3.2   LC PARSING RESULTS

The probabilistic left corner parser is implemented as a beam parser in C. As a k-best beam parser, it is not guaranteed to find the best parse (or indeed any parse), unless the beam is effectively infinite. Space requirements depend on the size of the beam, and the length of the sentence, but are considerably more reasonable than those for the chart parser used above. Nevertheless, the branching factor in the search space is very high because there are many rules possible with a certain left corner and goal category (especially for a grammar induced from the Penn Treebank in the manner we have described). Therefore, a huge beam is needed for good results to be obtained. A way of addressing this problem by binarizing the grammar is discussed in the next section.

The parser maintains two beams, one containing partial LC parses of the first i words, and another in which is built a beam of partial LC parses of the first $i + 1$ words. The partial parses are maintained as pointers to positions in trie data structures that represent the list of parser actions to this point and the current parse stack. At the end of parsing, the lists of parser actions can be easily turned into parse trees for the n-best parses in the beam.

Results are shown in table 6.5. They reflect the same training and testing data as described above. The results show a small increase in performance for PLCGs. This is shown more dramatically in the right-hand column of table 6.5, which shows that the extra information provided by the Left Corner goal category reduces parsing errors by about 20% over our PCFG results on 2–12 word sentences.

4   BINARIZATION

For the parser above, use of a beam search is quite inefficient because, for a given left corner and goal category, there are often hundreds of possible local trees that could be projected, and little information is available at the time this decision is made, since the decision mainly depends on words that have not yet been shifted. Therefore the beam must be large for good results to be obtained, and, at any rate, the branching factor of the search space is extremely high, which slows parsing. One could imagine using various heuristics to improve the search, but the way we have investigated combatting this problem is by binarizing the grammar.

The necessary step for binarization is to eliminate productions with three or more daughters. We carried this out by merging the tails, so that a rule such as $NP \rightarrow DT\ JJ\ NN$ is replaced by two rules, $NP \rightarrow DT\ NP_{DT}$ and $NP_{DT} \rightarrow JJ\ NN$. This is carried out recursively until only binary rules remain. As a result of this choice of right binarization, n-ary rules that share the same mother and left corner category all reduce to a single rule. This greatly cuts the branching factor of the search space and allows decisions to be put off during parsing, until more of the input has been seen, at which point alternative continuations can be better evaluated. Furthermore, the weights for such rules all combine into a larger weight for the combined rule.[12]

It is important to note that the resulting model is *not* equivalent to our original model. While the straightforward way of binarizing a PCFG yields the same probability estimates for trees as the n-ary grammar, this is not true for our PLCG model since we are now introducing new estimates for shifting terminals for each of our newly created non-terminals. Slightly different probability estimates result, and further work is needed to investigate what relationship exists between them and the probability estimates of the original grammar.

Prior to the above binarization step, one might also wish to eliminate unary productions, much as we earlier eliminated empty categories. This can be done in two ways. One way is to fold them upwards. This preserves lexical tagging. That is, if there is a category A dominating only a tree rooted at B, then the category A is eliminated and the tree rooted at B moved upwards. This may cause the number of rules to increase, because a local tree that started with a daughter A will now show up with daughter B in the same place. The alternative is to eliminate B and replace it with A. This can also create a new local tree instance because the daughters of B now show up with a new mother A. In this way, lexical tags can be changed. For instance, consider a rule $NP \rightarrow NNP$ for a noun phrase rewriting as a proper noun. In the context

		Parser Results			2–25 Error Reduction
Sentence Lengths	2–12	2–16	2–25	2–40	
Beam size	40 000	40 000	40 000	40 000	
% sent. length < cutoff	16.3%	28.1%	60.2%	91.8%	
Test set (sentences)		680	1454	2216	
Average length (words)	8.3	10.9	16.3	21.6	
Precision	93.5%	91.4%	86.6%	83.0%	13.0%
Recall	92.8%	89.9%	84.3%	80.7%	6.5%
Labelled Precision	89.8%	88.1%	83.4%	79.9%	12.2%
Labelled Recall	88.4%	86.3%	81.0%	77.6%	6.9%
Labelled Precision +1	90.0%	89.0%	85.1%	81.9%	9.7%
Labelled Recall +1	89.5%	87.2%	82.6%	79.5%	5.9%
Average CBs	0.17	0.39	1.09	1.99	12.8%
Non-crossing accuracy	97.2%	95.2%	90.9%	87.6%	12.5%
Sentences with 0 CBs	89.8%	78.2%	55.8%	41.5%	7.9%

Table 6.6   Left Corner Parser results with binarized grammar

of eliminating empty categories upward, we get a new rule S → NNP VP, whereas by eliminating empty categories downward we would have produced a new lexical entry NP → *Jones*. Our current results do not reflect the elimination of unary rules, but we hypothesize that doing this would further improve the measures that do not consider unary nodes, while probably harming the results on measures that do include unary nodes.

Table 6.6 shows that binarization brings a further modest improvement in results. The righthand column shows the percent error reduction on 2–25 word sentences between the n-ary grammar and the binary grammar.

5   EXTENDED LEFT CORNER MODELS

More sophisticated PLCG parsing models will naturally provide greater conditioning of the probability of an elementary operation based on the parse history. There are a number of ways that one could proceed. From the background of work on LC parsing, a natural factor to consider is the size of the parse stack, and we will briefly investigate incorporating this factor.

For left corner parsing, the stack size is particularly interesting. Stabler (1994) notes that in contrast to bottom-up and top-down parsing methods, left-corner parsers can handle arbitrary left-branching and right-branching structures with a finitely bounded stack size. Furthermore, left-corner parses of center embedded constructions have stack lengths proportional to the amount of embedding. This is not actually true for the stack-based LC parser presented earlier which has the stack growing without bound for rightward-branching trees. To gain the desirable property that Stabler notes, one needs to do stack composition by deciding immediately whether to attach whenever one projects a category that matches the current goal category, rather than delaying the attachment until after the left corner constituent is complete. If one decides to attach, the goal barred category and the mother category are immediately removed from the stack. This is implemented by replacing the actions in figure 6.1 by the ones in figure 6.2.

> **actions**
> [Shift] If a barred (goal) category is on top of the stack,
>   push the next input symbol on top of the stack
> [Project] If α is on top of the stack and $A \rightarrow \alpha \gamma$,
>   replace α by $\overline{\gamma}A$
> [ProjectAttach] If $\alpha\overline{A}$ is on top of the stack, and $A \rightarrow \alpha \gamma$,
>   replace $\alpha\overline{A}$ by $\overline{\gamma}$
> **endactions**

Figure 6.2   Altered code for an LC parser that does stack composition

All else being equal, this change makes no difference to the probabilistic model presented earlier. In practice though, this formulation makes a beam search less effective since we are bringing forward the decision of whether to attach or not, and often both alternatives must be tried which fills out the beam unnecessarily.

Given human intolerance for center embeddings and ease of parsing left and right branching structures, we would expect the stack sizes to stay low. The prediction is that the probability of not attaching (composing) decreases slightly with the size of the stack. This prediction is borne out by empirical measurement. The counts for the Penn Treebank, after binarization (including removal of unary rules), are given in table 6.7. Once one looks beyond the odd-even effect in the data, the decreasing probability of not attaching can be clearly seen.

To incorporate stack length into the model, we wish to more accurately predict: $P(C_i|C_1, \ldots, C_{i-1})$. Previously, histories of parse steps were equivalenced according to just the goal category and the left corner (if present). Now, we are going to additionally differentiate parse histories depending on ℓ, the length of the stack after C_{i-1}. As before, if the top of the stack is a predicted category, we will shift; otherwise we cannot shift. In the latter case, we will predict $P_\delta(\delta|\ell, gc, lc)$, the probability of various changes in the stack size, based on the stack size, the goal category, and the left corner.

Let us assume that rules are at most binary, as discussed above. Then the possible change in the stack length from a single elementary operation is between -2 and $+1$. Given that we are not shifting, we have the following:

Stack		Stack size change		
Size	Total	−1	0	+1
8	23	20 (87%)	3 (13%)	0
7	160	86 (54%)	54 (34%)	20 (13%)
6	1291	987 (76%)	218 (17%)	86 (7%)
5	3745	1393 (37%)	1365 (36%)	987 (26%)
4	17000	12116 (71%)	3491 (21%)	1393 (8%)
3	39105	12241 (31%)	14748 (38%)	12116 (31%)
2	108544	63160 (58%)	33143 (31%)	12241 (11%)
1	71681	8521 (12%)	0	63160 (88%)

Table 6.7 Changes in stack size for Penn Treebank

Stack Delta	Rule Type
−2	unary left corner projection and attach
−1	binary left corner projection and attach
0	unary left corner (no attach)
+1	binary left corner (no attach)

The probability of each elementary operation will then be the probability of a certain stack delta (given the stack size, left corner and goal category) times the probability of a certain rule, given the left corner, the goal category, and the stack delta. Whether we attach (compose) or not is deterministic given the stack delta, and so we no longer need to model the P_{att} distribution. Under this model, the probability of different projection actions (given that we are not in a position to shift) becomes:

$$P(C_i = \text{proj } A \to lc, \text{attach}) = P_\delta(-2|\ell, lc, gc)P_{lc'}(A \to lc|lc, gc, \ell, \delta)$$
$$P(C_i = \text{proj } A \to lc, \neg\text{attach}) = P_\delta(0|\ell, lc, gc)P_{lc'}(A \to lc|lc, gc, \ell, \delta)$$
$$P(C_i = \text{proj } A \to lc\, c_2, \text{attach}) = P_\delta(-1|\ell, lc, gc)P_{lc'}(A \to lc\, c_2|lc, gc, \ell, \delta)$$
$$P(C_i = \text{proj } A \to lc\, c_2, \neg\text{attach}) = P_\delta(+1|\ell, lc, gc)P_{lc'}(A \to lc\, c_2|lc, gc, \ell, \delta)$$

A variety of other extended models are possible. Note that the model does not need to be uniform, and that we can estimate different classes of elementary operations using different probabilistic submodels. In particular, at the level of preterminals, we can incorporate a tagging model. Given the structure of the Penn Treebank, a terminal w_j is always dominated by a unary rule giving the terminal's part of speech p_j. In line with our basic model above, the choice of part of speech for a word (where the word now counts as the left corner) will certainly depend on the current goal category. However, we can also condition it on other preceding parse decisions, in particular on the part of speech of the preceding two words, or, perhaps, in certain circumstances, on the particular word that preceded. Taking the former possibility, we can say, for cases where C_i involves predicting a preterminal (through a left corner projection step),

$$P(C_i|C_1,\ldots,C_{i-1}) = P(p_j|w_j, gc, C_1,\ldots, C_{i-1})$$
$$\approx P(p_j|w_j, gc, p_{j-2}, p_{j-1})$$

Assuming – perhaps rashly – independence between the conditioning variables that we have been using before (lc, gc) and the new ones (p_{j-1}, p_{j-2}), then we have a decomposable model Bruce and Wiebe, (1994):[13]

$$P(p_j|w_j, gc, p_{j-2}, p_{j-1}) \approx \frac{P(p_j|w_j, gc)P(p_j|p_{j-2}, p_{j-1})}{P(p_j)}$$

This is nice in part because we can calculate it using just the statistics previously gathered and a simple trigram model over POS tags. (An incidental nice property is that the probability is for the POS given the word, and not the other way round, as in the 'unintuitive' $P(w|p)$ term of standard Markov model POS taggers.)

6   COMPARISON WITH OTHER WORK

Previous work on non-lexicalized parsing of Penn Treebank data includes Schabes et al. (1993) and Charniak (1996), but the work perhaps most relevant to our own is that of Briscoe and Carroll (1993) and Carroll and Briscoe (1996), which also seeks to address the context-freeness assumption of PCFGs. They context-freeness assumption of PCFGs. They approach the problem by using a probabilistic model based on LR parse tables. Unfortunately, many differences of approach make meaningful comparisons difficult, and a comparable study of using PLCGs versus Probabilistic LR parsing remains to be done. Briscoe and Carroll use their Probabilistic LR Grammar to guide the actions of a unification-based parser which uses a hand-built grammar. While we are sympathetic with their desire to use a more knowledge-based approach, this means thattheir language model is deficient, since probability mass is given to derivations which are ruled out because of unification failures; that the coverage of their parser is quite limited because of limitations of the grammar used; and that much time needs to be expended in developing the grammar, whereas our grammar is acquired automatically (and quickly) from the treebank. Moreover, while results are not directly comparable, our parsers seem to do rather better on precision and recall than the parser described in Carroll and Briscoe (1996), while performing somewhat worse on crossing brackets measures. However, Carroll and Briscoe's inferior results probably reflect the fact that the parse trees of their grammar do not match those of their treebank more than anything else.[14]

Since this work was done, Roark and Johnson (1999) have experimented with probabilistic left corner parsing not through building a custom parser, but by transforming the treebank grammar into a grammar that, when used by a top-down parser, follows the same search path as a left corner parser, as in Rosenkrantz and Lewis II (1970). They suggest that most of the advantage of left corner parsing comes from the extra non-local information provided by conditioning on the goal category, and compare this with providing extra non-local information to a top-down parser by also conditioning on the grandmother node. This grandmother conditioning is also helpful, but their experiments suggest some distinction between the information given by grandmother conditioning and the form of left corner conditioning explored here.

7   OBSERVATIONS ON WHY PARSING THE PENN TREEBANK IS EASY

How is it that the purely structural – and context free even in structural terms – PCFG parser manages to perform so well? An important observation is that the measures of precision and recall (labelled or not) and crossing brackets are actually quite easy measures to do well on. It is important to notice that they are measuring success at the level of individual decisions – and normally what makes NLP hard is that you have to make many consecutive decisions correctly to succeed. The overall success rate is then the nth power of the individual decision success rate – a number that easily becomes small.

But beyond this, there are a number of features particular to the structure of the Penn Treebank that make these measures particularly easy. Success on crossing brackets is helped by the fact that Penn Treebank trees are quite flat. To the extent that sentences have very few brackets in them, the number of crossing brackets is likely to be small. Identifying troublesome brackets that would lower precision and recall measures is also avoided. As a concrete instance of this, one difficulty in parsing is deciding the structure of noun compounds (Lauer, 1995). Noun compounds of three or more words in length can display any combination of left- or right-branching structure, as in [[cable modem] manufacturer] vs. [computer [power supply]]. But such fine points are finessed by the Penn Treebank, which gives a completely flat structure to a noun compound (and any other pre-head modifiers) as shown below (note that the first example also illustrates the rather questionable Penn Treebank practice of tagging hyphenated non final portions of noun compounds as adjectives!).

(NP a/DT stock-index/JJ arbitrage/NN sell/NN program/NN)
(NP a/DT joint/JJ venture/NN advertising/NN agency/NN)

Another case where peculiarities of the Penn Treebank help is the (somewhat nonstandard) adjunction structures given to post noun-head modifiers, of the general form (NP (NP the man) (PP in (NP the moon))). A well-known parsing

Penn VP attach	(VP saw (NP the man) (PP with (NP a telescope)))
Penn NP attach	(VP saw (NP (NP the man) (PP with (NP a telescope))))
Another VP attach	(VP saw (NP the (N' man)) (PP with (NP a telescope)))
Another NP attach	(VP saw (NP the (N' man (PP with (NP a telescope)))))

Table 6.8   Penn trees versus other trees

ambiguity is whether PPs attach to a preceding NP or VP – or even to a higher preceding node – and this is one for which lexical or contextual information is clearly much more important than structural factors (Hindle and Rooth, 1993). Note now that the use of the above adjunction structure reduces the penalty for making this decision wrongly. Compare Penn Treebank style structures, and another common structure in the examples in table 6.8. Note the difference in the results:

| | Error | Errors assessed | | |
		Prec.	Rec.	CBs
Penn	VP instead of NP	0	1	0
	NP instead of VP	1	0	0
Another	VP instead of NP	0	1	0
	NP instead of VP	1	0	0
Another	VP instead of NP	1	2	1
	NP instead of VP	2	1	1

The forgivingness of the Penn Treebank scheme is manifest. One can get the attachment wrong and not have any crossing brackets.[15]

8   CONCLUSIONS

This chapter introduces probabilistic left-corner grammars (PLCGs), a probabilistic grammar model based on the left-corner parsing of context-free grammars. The ability of left corner parsers to support lefcorner parsing of context-free grammars. The ability of left corner parsers to support left-to-right online parsing makes themmars. The ability of left corner parsers to support left-to-right online parsing makes them promising for many tasks. The different conditioning model is slightly richer than that of standard PCFGs, and this was shown to bring worthwhile performance improvements over a standard PCFG when used to parse Penn Treebank sentences. Beyond this, the model can be extended in variouentences. Beyond this, the model can be extended in various ways, an avenue that we have onlyan be extended in various ways, an avenue that we have only just begun exploring. Because the left-corner component of the grammar is purely structural, it can be combined with other models that include lexical attachment preferences and preferences for basic phrasal chunking (both incorporated into Collins' parser).

Acknowledgments

We thank Edward Stabler and Mark Johnson for getting us interested in left corner parsing, and Mark more particularly for valuable discussion of some of the work in this chapter.

Notes

1. This name may appear strange since the symbolic part of the grammar is unchanged and still context-free. But if we regard the probabilistic conditioning as part of the grammar, then we do have a different kind of grammar. We should then perhaps call the result a LCPG, but we place the P in initial position for reasons of tradition.

2. Note, though, that context-freeness is as much a matter of the grammar as of the PCFG formalism. An alternative way to capture the conditioning shown in table 6.1 would be to subcategorize NPs into NP[Subj] and NP[Obj]. Such equivalences between enriching the contextual conditioning and enriching the grammar are further discussed in Roark and Johnson (1999) and Manning and Schütze (1999), 437–439.

3. Note however, that while the obvious way of calculating PCFG probabilities does not allow incremental processing, incremental calculation is possible, as discussed by Jelinek et al. (1992).

4. In general, empty categories can be accommodated by allowing a category to be introduced for completion without shifting a word off the input stack.

5. Formally, this is subject to showing that the probability mass accumulates in finite trees, but this holds when the probabilities are estimated from treebanks (Manning and Schütze, 1999, 388).

6. Of course, we could easily integrate our model with a tagging model.

7. Simply eliminating empties in the treebank is dangerous because they are the only trace of unbounded dependency constructions. This leads to ridiculous rules like S → VP (with 23559 appearances in the treebank) stemming from S → NP VP where there is a trace subject NP. A purely context-free solution would be to introduce slash percolation, as in Collins (1997).

8. See Krotov et al. (1998) for one attempt at compacting the Penn Treebank covering grammar.

9. The original PARSEVAL measures (because they were designed for comparing different parsers that used different theories of grammar) ignored node labels entirely, discarded unary brackets, and performed other forms of tree normalization to give special treatment to certain cases such as verbal auxiliaries. While such peculiarities made some sense in terms of the purpose for which the measures were originally developed, it is not clear that they are appropriate for the use of these measures within the statistical NLP community. Thus people often report labelled measures, but it is often unclear whether the other rules and transformations of the standard have been employed, even though this affects the results reported. In this chapter, unary nodes are deleted in measures except those marked +1, but none of the special case tree transformations in the PARSEVAL standard are applied. All punctuation and all constituent labels (but not functional tags) are also retained. Note in particular that the unary measures include the unary rule expanding the ROOT node, which has been omitted in other reported results.

10. Our PCFG parser builds a complete chart, which leads to unviable space requirements for long sentences.

11. Again, results are not strictly comparable. The comparison is unfair to Magerman and Collins' systems since they are also doing part of speech tagging, whereas the PCFG is not. But on the other hand, Magerman and Collins' parsers conflate the ADVP and PRT labels and ignore punctuation, which improves their reported results.

12. The form of binarization we use is refered to by Roark and Johnson (1999) as RB2. If we apply this continuation-style transformation even to binary rules to produce a unary residue, so that NP → DT NN is transformed into the rules NP → DT NP_{DT} and NP_{DT} → NN, and then optionally eliminate unary rules downward rather than upward, then for every left corner C and mother G there will be a unique rule $G → C\ G_C$. As Roark and Johnson (1999) point out, this transformation (which they refer to as RB1) would have been superior as it delays the decision as to the identity of the right child of the original rule. Note also that an effect of right binarization transformations is to move a lot of the probabilistic information out of the P_{proj} probabilities, and into the P_{shift} probabilities.

13. Below is a derivation of this equation, written in a simplified form with three variables. We assume b and c are independent, and the result then follows by using Bayes' rule followed by the definition of conditional probability:

$$P(a|b,c) = \frac{P(a)P(b,c|a)}{P(b,c)} = \frac{P(a)P(b|a)P(c|a)}{P(b)P(c)} = \frac{P(a)P(b,a)P(c,a)}{P(a)^2 P(b)P(c)} = \frac{P(a|b)P(a|c)}{P(a)}$$

14. See also the discussion of Caroll and Briscoe's model by Inui et al. in this volume.

15. If one includes unary brackets (recall footnote 8), then the contrast becomes If one includes unary brackets (recall footnote 8), then the contrast becomes even more marked, since there would be 2 precision and recall errors each under the alternative parse trees.

References

Baker, J. K. (1979). Trainable grammars for speech recognition. In Klatt, D. H. and Wolf, J. J., editors, *Speech Communication Papers for the 97th Meeting of the Acoustical Society of America*, pp. 547–550.

Black, E., Abney, S., Flickinger, D., Gdaniec, C., Grishman, R., Harrison, P., Hindle, D., Ingria, R., Jelinek, F., Klavans, J., Liberman, M., Marcus, M., Roukos, S., Santorini, B., and Strzalkowski, T. (1991). A procedure for quantitatively comparing the syntactic coverage of English grammars. In *Proceedings, Speech and Natural Language Workshop, Pacific Grove, CA*, pp. 306–311. DARPA.

Booth, T. L. (1969). Probabilistic representation of formal languages. In *Tenth Annual IEEE Symposium on Switching and Automata Theory*, pp. 74–81.

Briscoe, T. and Carroll, J. (1993). Generalized probabilistic LR parsing of natural language (corpora) with unification-based methods. *Computational Linguistics*, 19:25–59.

Bruce, R. and Wiebe, J. (1994). Word-sense disambiguation using decomposable models. In *Proceedings of the 32nd Annual Meeting of the Association for Computational Linguistics*, pp. 139–146.

Carroll, J. and Briscoe, T. (1996). Apportioning development effort in a probabilistic LR parsing system through evaluation. In *Proceedings of the Conference on Empirical Methods in Natural Language Processing (EMNLP-96)*, pp. 92–100, University of Pennsylvania.

Charniak, E. (1993). *Statistical Language Learning*. MIT Press, Cambridge, MA.

Charniak, E. (1996). Tree-bank grammars. In *Proceedings of the Thirteenth National Conference on Artificial Intelligence*, pp. 1031–1036.

Collins, M. J. (1996). A new statistical parser based on bigram lexical dependencies. In *Proceedings of the 34th Annual Meeting of the Association for Computational Linguistics*, pp. 184–191.

Collins, M. J. (1997). Three generative, lexicalised models for statistical parsing. In *Proceedings of the 35th Annual Meeting of the Association for Computational Linguistics*, pp. 16–23.

Demers, A. (1977). Generalized left corner parsing. In *Proceedings of the Fourth Annual ACM Symposium on Principles of Programming Languages*, pp. 170–181.

Hindle, D. and Rooth, M. (1993). Structural ambiguity and lexical relations. *Computational Linguistics*, 19:103–120.

Inui, K., Sornhertlamvanich, V., Tanaka, H. and Tokunaga, T. (2000). Probabilistic GLR parsing. *This volume*, pp. 87–106.

Jelinek, F., Lafferty, J. D., and Mercer, R. L. (1992). Basic methods of probabilistic context free grammars. In Laface, P. and De Mori, R., editors, *Speech Recognition and Understanding: Recent Advances, Trends, and Applications*, volume 75 of *Series F: Computer and Systems Sciences*. Springer Verlag.

Krotov, A., Hepple, M., Gaizauskas, R., and Wilks, Y. (1998). Compacting the penn treebank grammar. In *COLING/ACL '98*, volume I, pp. 699–703.

Kupiec, J. (1991). A trellis-based algorithm for estimating the parameters of a hidden stochastic context-free grammar. In *Proceedings of the Speech and Natural Language Workshop*, pp. 241–246. DARPA.

Lari, K. and Young, S. J. (1990). The estimation of stochastic context-free grammars using the inside-outside algorithm. *Computer Speech and Language*, 4:35–56.

Lauer, M. (1995). *Designing Statistical Language Learners: Experiments on Noun Compounds*. PhD thesis, Macquarie University, Sydney, Australia.

Magerman, D. M. (1995). Statistical decision-tree models for parsing. In *Proceedings of the 33st Annual Meeting of the Association for Computational Linguistics*, pp. 276–283.

Manning, C. D. (1996). *Ergativity: Argument Structure and Grammatical Relations*. CSLI Publications, Stanford, CA.

Manning, C. D. and Schütze, H. (1999). *Foundations of Statistical Natural Language Processing*. MIT Press, Cambridge MA.

Marcus, M. P., Santorini, B., and Marcinkiewicz, M. A. (1993). Building a large annotated corpus of English: The Penn treebank. *Computational Linguistics*, 19:313–330.

Roark, B. and Johnson, M. (1999). Efficient probabilistic top-down and left-corner parsing. In *Proceedings of the 37th Meeting of the Association for Computational Linguistics*, pp. 421–428.

Rosenkrantz, S. J. and Lewis II, P. M. (1970). Deterministic left corner parser. In *IEEE Conference Record of the 11th Annual Syposium on Switching and Automata*, pp. 139–152.

Sankoff, D. (1971). Branching processes with terminal types: applications to context-free grammars. *Journal of Applied Probability*, 8:233–240.

Schabes, Y., Roth, M., and Osborne, R. (1993). Parsing the Wall Street Journal with the Inside-Outside algorithm. In *Proceedings of the Sixth Conference of the European Chapter of the Association for Computational Linguistics*, pp. 341–347, University of Utrecht.

Stabler, E. P. (1994). The finite connectivity of linguistic structure. In Clifton, C., Frazier, L., and Rayner, K., editors, *Perspectives on Sentence Processing*, pp. 303–336. Lawrence Erlbaum, Hillsdale, NJ.

Suppes, P. (1970). Probabilistic grammars for natural languages. *Synthese*, 22:95–116.

Chapter 7

A NEW PARSING METHOD USING A GLOBAL ASSOCIATION TABLE

Juntae Yoon, Seonho Kim and Mansuk Song
Department of Computer Science
Yonsei University
Seoul 120-749, Korea
{ jtyoon, pobi, mssong } @december.yonsei.ac.kr

Abstract   This chapter presents a new parsing method using statistical information extracted from a corpus, especially for Korean. In Korean, structural ambiguities occur in the dependency relations between words. While figuring out the correct dependency, lexical associations play an important role. Our parser uses statistical co-occurrence data to compute lexical associations. We show that sentences can be parsed deterministically by means of global management of the associations. The global association table (GAT) is defined, and we describe how the associations between words are recorded in the GAT. We present a hybrid semi-deterministic parser that is controlled by the association values between phrases. Whenever the expectation of the parser fails, it chooses an alternative using a chart to avoid backtracking.

1   INTRODUCTION

Word associations can play an important role in finding out the dependency relation between them. The associations among words or phrases are indicators of lexical preference. Several studies have shown that the association value computed with statistical information gives good results in resolving structural ambiguities (Hindle and Rooth, 1993; Magerman, 1995; Collins, 1996) Statistical information has been used in recent research in automatic syntactic analysis not only for the recognition of sentences by a given grammar, but also for finding the correct analysis among multiple parse trees.

A chart parser that is used to produce all possible analyses of a sentence generates many structures, which makes it difficult to find the correct one. While reading a sentence, a reader can in many cases make decisions without

125

H. Bunt and A. Nijholt (eds.), Advances in Probabilistic and Other Parsing Technologies, 125–139.
© 2000 *Kluwer Academic Publishers.*

examining the entire sentence. Deterministic parsers have been designed to work similarly, following the *determinism hypothesis* for natural language parsing (Marcus, 1980; Faisal and Kwasny, 1994); however, the deterministic parser may give erroneous results because of its limited fixed lookahead.

This chapter presents a new parsing method that uses lexical associations for parsing sentences semi-deterministically. First, a global association table (GAT) is defined to record and manage the associations. As all the associations can be globally observed through the GAT, the parser can obviate errors caused by limited lookahead. The associations among words are estimated on the basis of lexical associations calculated using data acquired from a corpus. Next, a parsing algorithm is described using the GAT. The parser selects the next action according to the association among the nodes presented by the GAT. That is, the parser is controlled not by condition-action rules, but by the associations between phrases. It merges one phrase with another phrase that has the highest association value, or will wait until it meets the most probable candidate indicated by the GAT. In sum, our system is a parser with sentence length lookahead buffer. Experiments show that this does not cause any loss of accuracy, and that it is equally efficient as the deterministic parser.

2   CHARACTERISTICS OF KOREAN

2.1   SENTENCE STRUCTURES

Korean is an agglutinative language and has different features than an inflectional language such as English. A sentence consists of a sequence of *eojeol*s composed of a content word and functional words. A content word determines the characteristics of a phrase. For instance, an eojeol whose content word is a verb, an adjective, or a copula, functions as a predicate. A functional word directs the grammatical function of an eojeol. For example, '*eul/reul*' is the postposition (functional word) that makes a nominal eojeol an object; '*seup-nika*' is the sentential ending for a question, and '*t/eot*' converts a predicate to the past tense.

> (7.1) <u>*Na-neun*</u>   <u>*sae*</u>   <u>*chaek-eul*</u>   <u>*sa-t-da*</u>.
>   I   new   book   bought.
>   → I bought a new book.

'*Na-neun*' is the subject of the above sentence, and '*chaek-eul*', the object.

Second, Korean is an SOV (*Subject Object Verb* order) language, where the head always follows its complements: a head eojeol follows its complement eojeols. A new phrase is generated when one or more eojeols are merged, and the head of the phrase is always the last eojeol of the phrase.

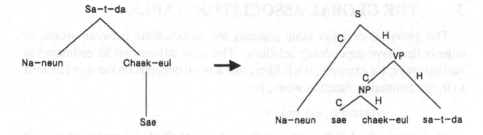

Figure 7.1 Dependency tree and binary tree for example sentence (7.1)

(7.2) *Keu-ga* <u>*norae-reul*</u> *booreu-myu* <u>*hakkyo-e*</u> *ga-t-da*.
He   a song   singing   to school went
→ He went to school singing a song.

Both '*booreu-myu*' and '*ga-t-da*' have verbs as their content words. Predicative eojeols are the heads for nominal eojeols and follow the eojeols, '*keu-ga*', '*norae-reul*', and '*hakkyo-e*', respectively.

Third, the grammatical dependency relation is determined decisively by functional words. For example, '*in the box*' in English can modify both a noun and a verb. By contrast, in order that '*sangja*', which means *box*, modifies a noun, it has to have the postposition '*ui*' in Korean. Whenever it has another postposition, it is the complement of a verb. There are syntactic levels in Korean, and the dependency relation of an eojeol is fixed according to the level.

2.2 SYNTACTIC ANALYSIS

The dependency tree of a sentence is built up through parsing. For deterministic parsing, the dependency tree is represented by a binary phrase structure tree that has one child node for a complement and one for a head. The complement node is the dependent node of the dependency tree and the head node is the head of the dependent node. Consequently, the parser uses binary grammar rules with feature structures describing the morphemes that constitute an eojeol. The parent node inherits the features of its head node. Since the head follows its complement in Korean, the root node of the parse tree inherits the features of the last eojeol in the sentence.

Figure 7.1 shows the dependency tree and our parse tree of example sentence (7.1). '*Na-neun*(I)' is a nominal eojeol and dependent on the predicative eojeol, '*sa-t-da*(bought)'. The feature structure of '*sa-t-da*' is placed in the root node of the parse tree because it is the head of the sentence.

3 THE GLOBAL ASSOCIATION TABLE

The global association table contains the associations between words or eojeols that have dependency relations. The associations can be estimated in various ways; for example, if it is likely that a word depends on the word nearest to it, the estimation function would be:

$$Assoc(e_i, e_j) = 1/d$$

(with distance d). Let the row and the column of the GAT represent eojeols occurring to the left-hand side and to the right-hand side, respectively, in the parsing process. The left-hand side eojeol is a complement, and the right-hand side the candidate for its head. $GAT(i, j)$ indicates the degree of association in case the ith eojeol is dependent on the jth eojeol. Because the head follows its complement in Korean, the table is a triangular matrix.

3.1 ESTIMATION FUNCTION FOR ASSOCIATIONS

Two kinds of co-occurrence data were extracted from a corpus containing 30 million eojeols. One is for compound noun analysis, the other is for noun-verb dependency analysis. The associations of modifier-head relations such as adverb-verb, or prenoun-noun, are estimated by their distance. A distance measure is also used in case there are no co-occurrence data, due to data sparseness. Distance has been shown to be the most plausible estimation method in the absence of any linguistic knowledge (Collins, 1996; Kurohashi and Nagao, 1994).

First of all, co-occurrence pairs of two nouns were collected using the method presented in Pustejovksy et al. (1993). Let N be the set of eojeols consisting of only a noun and NP the set of eojeols composed of a noun with a postposition. From e_1, e_2, e_3 ($e_1 \notin N$, $e_2 \in N$, $e_3 \in NP$), we can obtain noun compounds (n_2, n_3) such that n_2 and n_3 are the nouns that belong to the eojeols e_2 and e_3, respectively. The parser analyzes compound nouns, based on the complete noun compounds. Table 7.1 shows an example of compound noun pairs.

Modifying Noun	Head Noun
saengsan/NN(production)	*soodan*/NN(method)
dambae/NN(tobacco)	*nongsa*/NN(farming)
sooyo/NN(demand)	*byunhwa*/NN(variation)
france/NN(France)	*moonhak*/NN(literature)

Table 7.1 Examples of co-occurrence pairs of two nouns

The association between nouns is computed using the co-occurrence data extracted by the above method. Let $N = \{n_1, \ldots, n_m\}$ be the set of nouns.

Given $n_1, n_2 \in N$, the association score $Assoc_{NN}$ for n_1 and n_2 is defined to be

$$Assoc_{NN}(n_1, n_2) = P(n_1, n_2)$$
$$= \frac{freq(n_1, n_2)}{\sum_i \sum_j freq(n_i, n_j)}$$

As mentioned above, the distance measure is suggested in the absence of any cooccurrence data. Therefore, these estimators are sequentially applied for two eojeols in the following way. Here, e_i and e_j are the ith and the jth nominal eojeols, and n_i and n_j the nouns that belong to these eojeols.

> If $Assoc_{NN}(n_i, n_j) \neq 0$
> then $Assoc(e_i, e_j) = Assoc_{NN}(n_i, n_j)$
> else $Assoc(e_i, e_j) = 1/d$

Because the associations are calculated and compared for all e_j on which e_i have the possiblity to be dependent, the compound noun analysis is based on the dependency model rather than on the adjacency model (Kobayasi *et al.*, 1994; Lauer, 1995). Because the two estimation functions are used, an extra comparison routine is required. It will be explained in the next section.

Predicate	Noun	Postposition
gada/VB(go)	*gajok*/NN(family)	*ga*(SUBJ)
gada/VB(go)	*keu*/PN(he)	*ga*(SUBJ)
gada/VB(go)	*kang*/NN(river)	*e*(TO)
masida/VB(drink)	*maekjoo*/NN(beer)	*reul*(OBJ)
masida/VB(drink)	*mool*/NN(water)	*reul*(OBJ)
masida/VB(drink)	*neo*/PN(he)	*ga*(SUBJ)

Table 7.2 Examples of triples extracted from the text

Second, the co-occurrence pairs of nominal eojeols and predicative eojeols were extracted by partial parsing from a corpus. Table 7.2 shows an example of the triples generated from the text. The triple ⟨*masida*/VB, *mool*/NN, *reul*/OBJ⟩ indicates that the verb, '*masida*', and the noun, '*mool*,' which mean 'drink' and 'water' respectively, co-occur under the grammatical circumstance '*reul*' which is the postposition that makes a noun an object.

The association between a verb and a noun is evaluated based on the triples obtained by the above method. Let V, N, S be the sets of predicates, nouns and syntactic relations respectively:

$$V = \{v_1, \ldots, v_l\},$$
$$N = \{n_1, \ldots, n_m\}$$

$$S = \{ga, reul, e, \ldots\}$$

Given $v \in V, s \in S, n \in N$, the association score $Assoc_{VN}$ for v and n with syntactic relation s is defined to be

$$Assoc_{VN}(n, s, v) = (\lambda_1 P(n, s|v) + \lambda_2 P(s|v)) \times D(v, n)$$
$$(\lambda_1 \gg \lambda_2)$$

The conditional probability $P(n, s|v)$ measures the strength of the statistical association between the verb v and the noun n, with the given syntactic relation s. That is, it favors those associations that have more co-occurrences of nouns and syntactic relations for verbs. However, the above formula, including the maximum likelihood estimator, suffers from the problem of data sparseness. For smoothing, the probability $P(s|v)$ is introduced that indicates how strongly the verb requires the given syntactic relation. Lastly, $D(v, n)$ is the distance between two eojeols, which was experimentally determined according to the number of eojeols between the two.

These estimators (plus the distance measure) are applied sequentially in the following way. Let e_i be the ith eojeol and e_j the jth eojeol; n_i and s_i the noun and the postposition in the nominal eojeol e_i, and v_j the verb in the predicative eojeol e_j. Then

> If $Assoc_{VN}(n_i, s_i, v_j) \neq 0$
> then $Assoc(e_i, e_j) = Assoc_{VN}(n_i, s_i, v_j)$
> else $Assoc(e_i, e_j) = 1/d$

3.2   CONSTRUCTING THE GLOBAL ASSOCIATION TABLE

The association value of two eojeols is recorded in the GAT only when the eojeols have a dependency relation. First of all, the dependency relation of two eojeols is therefore checked. For two eojeols to have a dependency relation indicates that they have a possibility to be combined in parsing. For example, a nominal eojeol with postpositional case marking depends on a predicative eojeol that follows it. Second, if a dependency relation can be assigned to two eojeols, the association value is calculated using the estimators described in the previous section.

The association is represented by a pair ⟨*method, association-value*⟩. If a sentence consists of n eojeols, the GAT used is an $n \times n$ triangular matrix. As mentioned in the previous section, each eojeol has its own syntactic level in Korean, and an eojeol can be combined with either a predicate or a noun. Therefore an eojeol doesn't have a dependency relation to the nominal eojeol whenever it is dependent on the predicative eojeol, and *vice versa*. Be-

	0	1	2	3	4	5	6
0	-	(2,0.1)	(1,1/2)	-	(1,1/3)	-	-
1	-	-	(1,1)	-	(1,1/2)	-	-
2	-	-	-	(2,0.11)	-	(1,1/2)	(2,0.02)
3	-	-	-	-	(2,0.15)	-	-
4	-	-	-	-	-	(1,1)	(2,0.52)
5	-	-	-	-	-	-	(1,1)
6	-	-	-	-	-	-	-

Table 7.3   Global association table for example sentence (7.3)

cause different estimators are applied for the analysis of compound nouns and predicate-argument combinations, no collision occurs in the comparison of the associations $Assoc_{NN}$ and $Assoc_{VN}$. The GAT is sorted by the association values in order to find the most probable phrase in the parsing process and is implemented by means of a global association list. The algorithm for generating the GAT is represented in Figure 7.2. Table 7.3 shows the GAT for example sentence (7.3).

> **Construction of GAT**
> for each eojeol e_i $0 <= i <= n - 2$
>   1. for each eojeol e_j $i + 1 <= j <= n - 1$
>   if (depend_on (e_i, e_j))
>   then compute $g_i(j) = < method, Assoc(e_i, e_j) >$
>   2. sort $g_i(i + 1), \ldots, g_i(n - 1)$ and refer it to $G(i)$

Figure 7.2   Algorithm for constructing global association table

(7.3) (0)*computer*   (1)*hwamyon-ui*   (2)*gusuk-e*   (3)*natana-n*
    (0)computer   (1)of screen   (2)in the corner   (3)appeared
    (4)*sutja-ga*   (5)*paru-ge*   (6)*olaga-t-da.*
    (4)the number   (5)fast   (6)scrolled up
$\rightarrow$ The number to appear in the corner of the computer screen
    scrolled up fast.

In Table 7.3, '-' means that two eojeols have no dependency relation. The first element of a pair is the method of measurement and the second is the association value. The pair (1, 1/2) in GAT(0,2), indicates that the distance measure is 1/2. The pair (2, 0.11) in GAT(2,3) means that the association value is 0.11 and that it is estimated with co-occurrence relations. The *method* has priority for the comparison of associations. Therefore, (2,0.02) is greater than (1,0.5) because the method of the first is greater than that of the second. Since

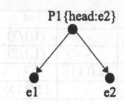

P1{head:e2}

e1   e2

Figure 7.3   Index to which the parent node refers

the rows of the table are sorted for parsing, GAT[2] can be represented in the form of a list of eojeols as follows.

$$GAT[2] \rightarrow \langle 3,(2,0.11) \rangle \rightarrow \langle 5,(2,0.02) \rangle \rightarrow \langle 6,(1,1/2) \rangle$$

This association list informs the parser that the eojeol e_2 has the possibility to merge with the eojeols e_3, e_5 or e_6, and that the most probable one is e_3. The function $max(G(i))$ is defined to return the most probable candidate for the head of the ith eojeol, e_i, in the GAT.

4   PARSING ALGORITHM

4.1   GAT-DRIVEN STRATEGY

The parser presented here consists of a stack and a buffer. For Korean, a two-item lookahead buffer is sufficient to make good decisions. The grammatical structures lie in the parsing stack and a set of actions operate on the buffer. Unlike the deterministic parser where the set of rules directs the operation, this system parses by applying the association values of the GAT.

Since a head follows its complement in Korean, the head of a phrase is the last eojeol of the phrase. A phrase is generated when two eojeols or two phrases are merged. In this case, Head Feature Inheritance takes care of the assignment of the same value as the head feature. Suppose an eojeol e_1 and an eojeol e_2 merge, and a new phrase P_1 be generated, as shown in Figure 7.3. As the head of P_1 is e_2, the parser uses the subscript of e_2 as the index to the GAT, that is, 2.

The parser uses the basic operations CREATE, ATTACH, and DROP, and its operation is conditioned not by rule matching but by the values of the GAT, as shown in the following description. The function $position(max(G(i)))$ returns the sentential position of the most probable candidate for the head of the ith eojeol, e_i.

CREATE If the most probable candidate for the head of the eojeol e_i is e_j, that is, $j = position(max(G(i)))$, then merge e_i (or the phrase where the last eojeol is e_i) with e_j (or the phrase where the last eojeol is e_j), and generate a new phrase.

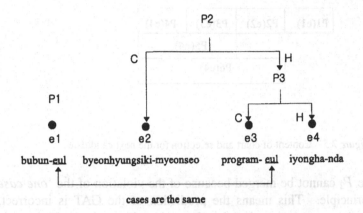

Figure 7.4   Example of prediction failure

ATTACH If the phrase where the e_j is the last eojeol is not the most probable candidate for the head of the eojeol e_i, that is, $e_j \neq max(G(i))$, then wait until e_i meets the most probable candidate indicated by the GAT.

DROP The DROP operation is accompanied by a CREATE operation in our system, because the complement precedes the head and thus the top node of the stack must be dropped and checked for dependency immediately after a new node is generated.

The GAT provides the parser with the prediction of the best candidate for the head of the *i*th eojeol, e_i. This is easy because the GAT is already sorted; however, the expectation is not always correct because the value of the GAT is calculated whenever there is a possible dependency relation between one eojeol and another. That is, the parser constructs the GAT as preparsing and it may happen that the two eojeols or phrases which have the possiblity to have dependency relations cannot be merged in parsing. The *'one case per clause'* principle is violated.

(7.4) *bubun-eul*(part/OBJ) *byeonhyeongsiki-myeonseo*(change)
     program-eul(program/OBJ) *iyongha-nda*(use).
→ The part being changed, the program is used.

In Figure 7.4, e_1 and e_3 are nominal eojeols; e_2 and e_4 are both predicative eojeols. The phrase P_1 consists of e_1, and the phrase P_2 consists of three eojeols, e_2, e_3, e_4. Let the most probable candidate, suggested by the GAT, for both e_1 and e_3 be e_4, where e_1 and e_3 have the same grammatical case because they contain postpositions marking the same case. The phrase P_1

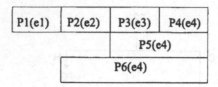

P1(e1)	P2(e2)	P3(e3)	P4(e4)
		P5(e4)	
	P6(e4)		

Figure 7.5 Content of chart and selection for the next candidate

and the phrase P_2 cannot be merged because of the violation of the '*one case per clause*' principle. This means the prediction of the GAT is incorrect, and consequently an analysis using the alternatives is required. If the next candidate is e_2, the grammatical structure in the buffer must be erroneous. The chart presents the phrase suitable for the alternative execution in the buffer. The chart allows the parser to store the partial structure to remove the backtracking. In this case an ALTER operation occurs.

ALTER is required if an eojeol e_i cannot be merged with the eojeol e_j which is the prediction of the candidate for the head of e_i.

When the operation is executed, the structure in the lookahead buffer is backed up into the chart. When the ALTER operation is needed, another candidate taken from the chart has to be put in the buffer. The next candidate, $C(e_i)$ is chosen in the following way. Let i be the left-hand position and k the right-hand position of the erroneous prediction in the GAT. Then $C(e_i)$ is the phrase where the left-hand position is i and the right-hand position is $max(i+1 \leq j \leq k)$, in terms of nodes in the chart. The phrase P_2, including e_2, is then the next candidate in Figure 7.5. The GAT-based parsing algorithm is described in Figure 7.6.

4.2   OPERATION OF THE PARSER

The complexity of making the GAT is $O(N^2)$, where N is the number of eojeols, since the construction of the table tends to $O(N^2)$ and its sorting to $O(NlogN)$. In addition, the observed average complexity of the parser is linear, according to the experiments. Thus, the overall complexity is almost $O(N^2)$, which shows that the parser is quite efficient.

Table 7.4 represents the analysis steps of the sentence in example (7.3). The head on the stack top is the complement, and the candidate for its head lies in the head part of the buffer. In row 7 of the table, the ATTACH operation is executed according to the GAT in Table 7.3, because the lookahead does

For phrases P_i and P_j, let their heads be e_i and e_j, respectively:

if lookahead = nil and there is one parse tree in the stack
then return SUCCESS
else if (GAT(0) = NULL)
    then return FAIL
    else if $(position(G(i)) = j)$
        then begin if (isunifiable(P_i, P_j) = TRUE)
            then CREATE;
            else ALTER;
        end
    else ATTACH.

Figure 7.6   Parsing algorithm using the GAT

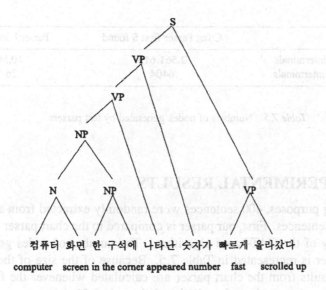

컴퓨터 화면 한 구석에 나타난 숫자가 빠르게 올라갔다
computer screen in the corner appeared number fast scrolled up

Figure 7.7   Binary parse tree for example sentence (7.3) (in Korean)

not provide the best candidate for the head of the complement on the stack top. The eojeol 'sutja-ga' has to wait until it meets its best candidate. A new phrase is created in row 9. The eojeol 'olaga-t-da' is the best candidate for the eojeol 'sutja-ga', as estimated by the GAT. Figure 7.7 represents the parse tree of sentence (7.3), written in Korean.

	OP	Stack Top		First Lookahead	
		Constituents	Head	Constituents	Head
1	A	(computer)	computer	(hwamyon-ui)	hwamyon-ui
2	B	(computer hwamyon-ui)	hwamyon-ui	(han)	han
3	A	(han)	han	(gusuk-e)	gusuk-e
4	A	(computer hwamyon-ui)	hwamyon-ui	(han gusuk-e)	gusuk-e
5	A	((computer hwamyon-ui) (han gusuk-e))	gusuk-e	(natana-n)	natana-n
6	A	(((computer hwamyon-ui) (han gusuk-e)) natana-n)	natana-n	(sutja-ga)	sutja-ga
7	B	((((computer hwamyon-ui) (han gusuk-e)) natana-n) sutja-ga)	sutja-ga	(paru-ge)	paru-ge
8	A	(paru-ge)	paru-ge	(olaga-t-da)	olaga-t-da
9	A	((((computer hwamyon-ui) (han gusuk-e)) natana-n) sutja-ga)	sutja-ga	(paru-ge olaga-t-da)	olaga-t-da

Table 7.4   Analysis of sentence (7.3). (A) CREATE & DROP operation; (B) ATTACH operation

	Chart Parser first S found	Parser Using GAT
Total of gen. nonterminals	2,561,613	10,582
Aver. of gen. nonterminals	6404	26.5

Table 7.5   Numbers of nodes generated by test parsers

5   EXPERIMENTAL RESULTS

For testing purposes, 400 sentences were randomly extracted from a corpus of 3 million sentences. First, our parser is compared to the chart parser to show the efficiency of the GAT-based algorithm. The number of nodes generated by each parser is represented in Table 7.5. Because of the size of the search space, the results from the chart parser are calculated whenever the first S is found. The average number of prediction failures is 0.26 per sentence, that is, the parser has to search for an alternative in the chart once in four sentences. This makes the complexity of the parser a constant.

Figure 7.8 shows the occurrence of ALTER operations per number of words. The average number of ALTER operations is about 0.36 for the sentences with more than 20 words, which confirms the efficiency of our parser.

Second, the precision of the parser is given in Table 7.6.. Precision is defined as the ratio of the correct dependency relations between eojeols in parse trees. No label is attached because the final output is the tree that represents the dependency relations among words. Thus, the number of erroneous and correct

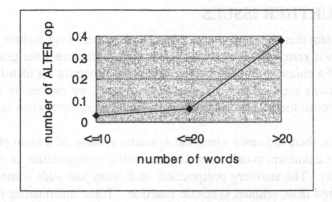

Figure 7.8   Number of ALTER operation per number of words

relations is considered, which can be estimated by the number of crossing brackets.

	CBs		0 CBs		$\leq$ 2 CBs	
(a)	(b)	(c)	(d)	(c)	(d)
378	0.95	176	44.0	323	80.8

Table 7.6   Precision of the parser: (a) number of crossing brackets; (b) average number of crossing brackets per sentence; (c) number of sentences; (d) percentages.
(Crossing Brackets (CBs): number of constituents that violate constituent boundaries with a constituent in the correct parse.)

The cause of incorrect analyses can be traced back to two main reasons. One is the statistical information. We collected the data from a 30 million eojeol corpus. The total number of the data is 2 million and the average frequency of the co-occurrence data is 2.5. The triples with frequencies greater than 2 are about 400,000. The frequency of most data is only 1, which is the primary cause of erroneous results. In addition, the association value of adjuncts and subordinate clauses is estimated by distance. The distance estimator was good but not the best. Semantic information, for instance from a thesaurus, would help to reduce the space of parameters.

Finally, linguistic information is needed, e.g. for light verbs and for the lexical characteristics of individual words. Our parser is a hybrid system which uses both rules and statistical information, and requires linguistic research even though the statistical methods are powerful. In spite of some errors, the parser is satisfactory in that the association values can be computed in various ways and the parser can be extended so as to use them.

6   FURTHER ISSUES

The system that we have proposed has another interesting feature, concerning unknown grammatical case. As functional words direct the grammatical function of a phrase in Korean, postpositions are important for identfying syntactic relations such as case. Due to this property, we can easily recognize syntactic consitituents like subject, object and so on, also when scrambling occurs.

However, there are cases where the syntactic relation of a noun phrase to a predicate is unknown, mainly caused by an auxiliary postposition or an omitted postposition. The auxiliary postposition in Korean just adds some meaning like *only* and *also*, without syntactic function. Trace information in relative clauses is another instance of unknown syntactic relations. Trace information is crucial in machine translation since relative pronouns or relative adverbs would be selected differently according to the syntactic relation. Since there is no indicator such as relative pronoun or relative adverb in Korean, the choice of a translation word is not trivial. Therefore, we should consider methods for identifying syntactic relations in a relative clause, which could be done in Korean by recognizing the semantic relation between the predicate and the noun modified by the clause.

Our system presents an elegant solution to this problem. Because the association between eojeols consists of an association degree and the related case, the unknown case could be guessed while parsing. This is intuitively reasonable, the more since the parsing is based on lexical co-occurrence data, which provides a kind of semantic information. Additional experiments have shown that the accuracy of unknown case guesses is about 87.5%.

7   CONCLUSION

We have shown that it is possible to make parsing decisions semideterministically using a global association table. The GAT is a very effective structure in that it is triangular matrix, because Korean is an SOV language and the dependency relations between words are important. It would have to be transformed for parsing English, because phrase structure grammar is needed for parsing English.

There are many possibilities for improvement. The method described for calculating the lexical associations in the GAT can be modified in various ways. The GAT and the parser can be extended by reconsidering the distance measure and taking coordinate conjunctive structures into account.

References

Allen, J. (1995) *Natural Language Understanding. 2nd Ed.* Benjamin Cummings.

Brill, E. (1993) *A Corpus-Based Approach to Language Learning*. Ph.D. Dissertation, Dept. of Computer and Information Science, Univ. of Pennsylvania.

Briscoe, T. and Waegner, N. (1992) Robust Stochastic Parsing Using the Inside-Outside Algorithm. In *Workshop notes from the AAAI statistically-based NLP Techniques Workshop*.

Charniak, E. (1993) *Statistical Language Learning*. MIT Press.

Collins, M. J. (1996) A New Statistical Parser Based on Bigram Lexical Dependencies. In *Proceedings of 34th Annual Meeting of Association for Computational Linguistics*.

Faisal, K. A. and Kwasny, S. C. (1990) Design of a Hybrid Deterministic Parser. In *Proceedings of COLING-90*.

Framis, F. R. (1994) An Experiment on Learning Appropriate Selectional Restrictions from a Parsed Corpus. In *Proceedings of COLING-94*.

Gazdar G., and Mellish C. (1993) *Natural Language Processing in LISP*. Addison Wesley.

Hindle, D. and Rooth, M. (1993) Structural Ambiguity and Lexical Relations. Computational Linguistics.

Kobayasi Y., Tokunaga T., and Tanaka H. (1994) Analysis of Japanese Compound Nouns using Collocational Information. In *Proceedings of COLING-94*.

Kurohashi S. and Nagao M. (1994) A Syntactic Analysis Method of Long Japanese Sentences Based on the Detection of Conjunctive Structures. Computational Linguistics.

Lauer, M. (1995) Corpus Statistics Meet the Noun Compound: Some Empirical Results. In *Proceedings of 33rd Annual Meeting of Association for Computational Linguistics*.

Marcus, M. (1980) *A Theory of Syntactic Recognition for Natural Language*. Cambridge, MA: MIT Press.

Magerman, D. M. (1995) Statistical Decision-Tree Models for Parsing. In *Proceedings of 33rd Annual Meeting of Association for Computational Linguistics*.

Pustejovsky, J., Bergler, S., and Anick, P. (1993) Lexical Semantic Techniques for Corpus Analysis. Computational Linguistics.

Resnik, P. (1992) Wordnet and Distributional Analysis: A Class-Based approach to Lexical Discovery. In *Proceedings of AAAI Workshop on Statistical Methods in NLP*.

Tomita, M. (1986) Efficient Parsing for Natural Language. Boston: Kluwer Academic Publishers.

Chapter 8

TOWARDS A REDUCED COMMITMENT, D-THEORY STYLE TAG PARSER

John Chen
K. Vijay-Shanker
Department of Computer and Information Sciences, University of Delaware, Newark, DE 19716
{ jchen,vijay } @cis.udel.edu

Abstract   Many traditional TAG parsers handle ambiguity by considering all of the possible choices as they unfold during parsing. In contrast, D-theory parsers cope with ambiguity by using underspecified descriptions of trees. This chapter introduces a novel approach to parsing TAG, namely one that explores how D-theoretic notions may be applied to TAG parsing.

Combining the D-theoretic approach to TAG parsing as we do here raises new issues and problems. D-theoretic underspecification is used as a novel approach in the context of TAG parsing for delaying attachment decisions. Conversely, the use of TAG reveals the need for additional types of underspecification that have not been considered so far in the D-theoretic framework. These include combining sets of trees into their underspecified equivalents as well as underspecifying combinations of trees.

Herein we examine various issues that arise in this new approach to TAG parsing and present solutions to some of the problems. We also describe other issues which need to be resolved for this method of parsing to be implemented.

1   INTRODUCTION

Ambiguity is a central problem in the parsing of natural languages. Within the framework of TAG, a number of approaches have been adopted in trying to deal with this issue. Traditional approaches share the characteristic of exploring all of the choices in the face of ambiguity. To make such a scheme effective, techniques such as structure sharing and dynamic programming are commonly used. In contrast, we explore a different style of parsing that copes with ambiguity through the underspecification of tree structures.

This style of parsing deals with descriptions of trees instead of trees themselves. Notable examples of such parsers include Marcus et al. (1983), Gorrell

141

H. Bunt and A. Nijholt (eds.), Advances in Probabilistic and Other Parsing Technologies, 141–159.
© 2000 *Kluwer Academic Publishers.*

(1995), and Sturt and Crocker (1996). We refer to these as D-theory parsers. Following them, we construct an underspecified representation that captures a set of parses for the input seen so far.

The primitive of dominance is used in the descriptions that our parser manipulates. Its use in parsing has been pioneered by Marcus et al. (1983), and further investigated by the others such as those listed above. It has also been used within the confines of TAG elementary trees, as stated by Vijay-Shanker (1992). Nevertheless, in our context of using domination to handle ambiguity in TAG parsing, we differ from both of these bodies of work. We differ from the latter because our use of domination is not limited to use within TAG elementary trees; it is crucially used here to underspecify ambiguity in the attachment of elementary trees. Thus the domination statements that our parser makes are domination statements between nodes in different elementary trees. We differ from prior work in D-theory parsing because our parser incorporates a specific grammatical formalism and grammar in order to specify syntactically well-formed structures. Moreover, it uses new kinds of representations that have not been considered in D-theory parsing in order to specify ambiguity.

We discuss several novel issues and present our solutions to many of the issues that arise in adopting the use of dominance to parsing TAGs. For example, there is considerable bookkeeping that is necessary to ensure whether a particular underspecified representation conforms to a possible legal TAG derivation. Furthermore, TAG's extended domain of locality presents a problem because it hinders the degree of underspecification that is necessary in order to delay disambiguation decisions. We therefore argue that sets of elementary trees need to be underspecified into single representations. Another problem is that the notion of standard referent, used in D-theory parsing as the default model of a given underspecified representation, needs to be reconceptualized in order to accommodate the novel use of domination that is proposed here.

This chapter is organized as follows. We first consider some broad distinguishing characteristics of our parser in Section 2. Subsequently, we define some terminology in Section 3 as a preparatory for the following sections, which delve into various aspects of our parser. Section 4 gives a high level outline of our parser. Section 5 explicates the mechanism whereby descriptions of trees are combined. Section 6 deals with computing the standard referent. Section 7 discusses the issue of combining a set of elementary trees into a single representation. Finally, concluding remarks are given in Section 8.

2   PARSING FRAMEWORK

Our parser draws on typical characteristics of D-theoretic parsers, such as Marcus et al. (1983) and Gorrell (1995). Such characteristics, as well as their relation to our parser, are discussed in this section. A basic feature of

D-theoretic parsers is that the input sentence is parsed strictly from left to right and a description is constructed that captures a set of parse trees for the input seen.

One of our goals, which is shared by many other D-theoretic parsers, is that of incremental interpretation. This means at each point in the parse, a partial semantic representation is constructed from the sentence prefix that has been input so far, as delineated by the underspecified representation.

The notion of standard referent, as discussed in Marcus et al. (1983) and Rogers and Vijay-Shanker (1996), is included in our parser. Recall that an underspecified representation specifies a set of parse trees, namely those trees which are consistent with every assertion that is embodied by the underspecified representation. The standard referent is that parse tree which is taken to be the default choice from the set of trees that are consistent with a particular underspecified representation. The need for a standard referent would arise from a requirement of incremental interpretation. However, here it is mainly used in determining how structures may be combined.

Our parser subscribes to the notion of informational monotonicity. This means that, during parsing, the assertions that the parser makes are considered to be indelible. This is important because, at any point during parsing, we find that not all of the attachment possibilities that may be expressed by a dominance based description language can be incorporated into the underspecified representation that our parser constructs. Certain ambiguities, for example, may not be expressible in our underspecified representation. Therefore, there is the possibility that one of the assertions that the parser makes will turn out to be incompatible with evidence provided by later input. In that situation, the parser is forced to retract that assertion, leading to backtracking. In the literature on D-theory parsers, it has been commonly conjectured that such backtracking correlates with garden path effects.

3   TERMINOLOGY

Our terminology borrows from TAG and D-Tree Grammar literature. From TAG, the grammar consists of a set of lexicalized trees. The frontier of each elementary tree is composed of a *lexical anchor*; the other nodes on the frontier will either be *substitution* or *foot* nodes. An interior node is commonly considered to be constituted of a top and bottom feature structure. In contrast, we use the terminology introduced by Vijay-Shanker (1992) in that an interior node is considered as a pair of *quasi-nodes*. A domination link connects the *top* and *bottom* quasi-nodes. The path from the root to the lexical anchor of an elementary tree will be called the *trunk*.

We now define the terms component and lowering node. The notion of component is borrowed from D-Tree Grammars, as defined in Rambow et al.

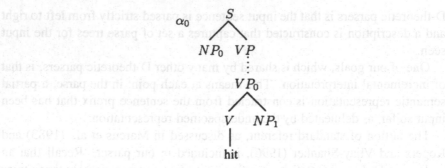

Figure 8.1   A lexicalized TAG tree with two components and two lowering nodes.

(1995). A *component* is a maximal subpart of an underspecified representation that has the property that all of its nodes are connected by immediate domination links. Consider α_0 in Figure 8.1 for example. It consists of two components: the first contains the nodes S, NP_0, and the top VP quasi-node, while the second contains the bottom VP quasi-node (VP_0), the V node, and the NP_1 node. A *lowering node* is the root of a component. It can either be the root of an elementary tree or a bottom quasi-node. We call such nodes lowering nodes because in D-theory, adjunction or substitution at these nodes would mean that these nodes would be lowered, i.e., later input causes some structure to be placed above them. The elementary tree α_0 contains two lowering nodes, S and VP_0.

4   PARSING ALGORITHM

With the terminology so defined, the disquisition of our parsing algorithm can now proceed. At any given time during parsing, we assume that there is a single *underspecified representation* R corresponding to the sentence prefix which has been seen so far. It describes a set of trees that are obtained by combinations of structures anchored by the input encountered. For now, we assume that R is treelike except that some of the nodes may be connected by domination links instead of immediate domination links. The immediate domination links arise only from the immediate domination links that appear in the composed TAG trees. The domination links arise from either those that appear in elementary TAG trees or between nodes in different trees. At the start of parsing, R consists of a single substitution node S.

A provisional description of the parsing process is outlined as follows.

- The next word is input. There will usually be more than one elementary tree corresponding to this word.

■ Those elementary trees that are *structurally* incompatible with the current representation R are removed from consideration. This is addressed in Sections 5.1 and 5.2.

■ The remaining elementary trees must be incorporated into the current representation R to produce the new underspecified representation. If only one elementary tree corresponding to the current input word remained after the second step's filter, then this would be straightforward. On the other hand, there may be cases where more than one tree remains. We propose to address the latter situation by grouping such a set of elementary trees into one underspecified representation, as will be discussed further in Section 7. This would allow us to delay the choice of elementary tree until later while still being consistent with informational monotonicity. Nevertheless, it may still be the case that the remaining set of elementary trees corresponding to the current word cannot be grouped together. In this case, we would have to choose a particular subset of elementary trees as well as how that subset should be attached to the current representation R. We propose that such choices be made according to semantics or lexical frequencies as determined from a corpus.

In what follows, we begin a more detailed discussion of certain essential aspects of our parsing algorithm. We start by considering what structural possibilities the parser needs to consider when it tries to combine the current underspecified representation R with an elementary tree η that is anchored by the next input word.

5   CONTROL STRATEGY

This section describes how representations may be combined. Associated with each representation are expectation lists that encode how it expects to fit into a complete sentence structure. We first describe the nature of expectation lists. Next, we develop the control strategy that is used to check if two representations may be combined, through the use of expectation lists. We also consider what actions may take place if two expectation lists are incompatible.

5.1   EXPECTATIONS

At any given point in the parsing of the input sentence, subsequent input may clearly not be inserted into the part of R that is to the left of that path running from the root of R to the leaf l. Extending the notion of trunk, which has hitherto only been defined for elementary trees, we state that the *trunk* of an underspecified representation R is the path from the root to the last input node. Thus, when inserting new structure into R, only the nodes and domination links on and to the right of the trunk need to be considered. These nodes are contained in what we call the *right expectation list* of R.

Analogous observations hold about the elementary TAG trees. Namely, at each point in parsing, an elementary tree η, representing the next input word, is combined with R. When considering how η may be combined with R, it suffices to consider only those nodes and domination links that appear on or to the left of that path from the root to the anchor. These nodes are contained in the *left expectation list* of η.

Now we will consider how to compute the left expectation list of R and the right expectation list of η. In the relevant subparts of R and η, we need to examine nodes that can be involved in combinations: lowering nodes, substitution nodes, and foot nodes. In our expectation lists, we consider expectations of two types: substitution expectations or lowering expectations. A substitution expectation corresponds to a substitution node or a foot node. Conversely, a lowering expectation corresponds to a lowering node.

Each expectation is characterized as optional or obligatory. Substitution expectations are always obligatory. Lowering expectations may either be optional or obligatory. Suppose there exists a domination link that states that node a dominates node b. The lowering expectation corresponding to node b is obligatory if the labels of a and b do not match.

Expectation lists are *ordered* lists of expectations. The order of expectations for one representation corresponds to the sequence in which the parser will try to assemble it with the other representation. The algorithm that is presented in Figure 8.2 returns an ordered list of expectations when given an underspecified representation or elementary tree and a direction d that specifies whether a left or right expectation list should be found. It first examines the anchor and then makes its way up the trunk of the representation, one node at a time. At each such node n, the algorithm sees if n corresponds to an expectation. If so, this is recorded. It also checks if n has any siblings in the dth direction. If so, each such sibling is scanned in a depth first fashion for any expectations.

Consider the expectations in the right expectation list for α_0 in Figure 8.1. The algorithm starts at the anchor 'hit' and then makes its way up to the V node. The V node has a sibling, NP_1, which is examined in a depth first fashion for any expectations. This yields the first expectation, $NP_{1(oblig,subst)}$. The algorithm continues up the trunk to the bottom VP quasi-node (VP_0), which is associated with another expectation $VP_{(opt,low)}$, which is duly recorded. Continuing further up the trunk, the algorithm finds one more expectation corresponding to the root S, which is $S_{(opt,low)}$. Similarly, the left expectation list of α_0 would be $< VP_{(opt,low)}, NP_{0(oblig,subst)}, S_{(opt,low)} >$.

order_expect(n:node, $d \in$ {left,right})
  case n lies on trunk
    if n is a lowering node
      record n as a lowering expectation
      loop through each *sibling* i of n that appears to the d of n
        from $not : d^1$ to d
        order_expect(i, d)
      if n has a parent p^2
        order_expect(p, d)
  case n does *not* lie on trunk
    if n is a substitution node
      record n as a substitution expectation
    else (n is an interior node)
      if n is a lowering node
        record n as a lowering expectation
        loop through each $child^3$ i of n that appears to the d of n
          from $not : d$ to d
          order_expect(i, d)
      if n is an adjoining node
        record n as a lowering expectation

Figure 8.2   Algorithm that returns an ordered list of left or right expectations.

5.2   COMBINING REPRESENTATIONS

As the parser proceeds through the input sentence from left to right, the parser tries to combine the underspecified representation R with an elementary tree η corresponding to the current input word. Expectation lists encode how a representation to the left may be combined with an elementary tree to the right. We say that the underspecified representation R can be combined with the elementary tree η when the right expectation list of R is *compatible* with the left expectation list of η.

An outline of a proposed procedure to determine the compatibility of two expectation lists is delineated in this section. This procedure has two steps. First, one expectation is taken from the left expectation list of η and the right expectation list of R is searched for a matching expectation. Second, given that the two representations partially combine according to how these first two expectations match, it is seen whether the two representations can be fully combined.

Finding the First Pair of Matching Expectations.   We take the first expectation e_1 from the left expectation list of η. e_1 may either be a substitution expectation or a lowering expectation. If it is the former, we look for a matching lowering expectation in R. Conversely, if it is the latter, we look for a matching substitution expectation.

It may occur that, although e_1 is an obligatory expectation, there is no expectation in R that matches. We need not consider this particular situation further, because the two representations are obviously incompatible. Alternatively, although there may be no matching expectation for e_1, e_1 is an optional expectation. In this case, we can skip to the next expectation on the left expectation list of the elementary tree.

Matching the Rest of the Two Expectation Lists.   Suppose that a matching expectation e_m (in R) for e_1 (in η) is found. Now there are two tasks that must be accomplished. First it must be ensured that this matching expectation can indeed lead to a valid combination of the two representations that are under consideration. This is accomplished as follows. Suppose that n_m and n_1 are the nodes corresponding to the expectations e_m and e_1, respectively. Now let p_m be the path from the root of the underspecified representation R to n_m. Conversely, let p_1 be the path from the root of the elementary tree η to n_1. The task is to find out if the components along the path p_m can be interspersed with the components along the path p_1. This is done by iteratively matching the expectations corresponding to the nodes that lie on path p_m with those that lie on the path p_1, starting from those expectations corresponding to nodes that lie closest to e_m and e_1. Second, any remaining unmatched obligatory expectations in η should be matched, in order of their appearance on the expectation list, by recursively calling the aforementioned procedure.

Representing Ambiguity of Attachment.   Suppose e_1 is a substitution expectation and we find a matching lowering expectation e_m in R. That e_m must be the corresponding attachment site for e_1 does not immediately hold. In Figure 8.3(b), for example, the auxiliary tree could be adjoined at either of the VP's in R. To capture such attachment ambiguity, rather than equating n_1 and n_m (the node corresponding to the first expectation in the expectation list for R that matches e_1), we will say n_1 dominates n_m. On the other hand, in Figure 8.3(a), there is no ambiguity in attachment of the new elementary tree. In this case we can make a stronger statement by equating n_1 and n_m.

In general, the type of attachment ambiguity that we underspecify is where e_1 is a substitution expectation that matches more than one lowering expectation and no obligatory expectations occur between the first and the last matching lowering expectations on the left expectation list of η, inclusively.

Whether such an ambiguity exists is determined as follows. Suppose e_1 is a substitution expectation. Furthermore suppose its combination with e_m, the first matching lowering expectation, does in fact lead to a valid combination of representations. We may find another valid combination by scanning further in the right expectation list of the underspecified representation R, starting from e_m, to find another matching expectation $e_{m'}$ (before encountering an obligatory expectation that does not match e_1) and verifying that it leads to another valid combination of structures, using the same method that we performed for the first matching expectation e_m.

Our underspecified representation captures this ambiguity as follows. Notice that no matter where the elementary tree η is adjoined, it is the case that the node n_1 will always dominate the lowest attachment site n_m. Therefore, in cases of such ambiguity, we stipulate such a domination as shown in Figure 8.3(b). Notice that while the example in Figure 8.3(b) corresponds to adjoining, a similar situation arises even if n_1 is a substitution node.

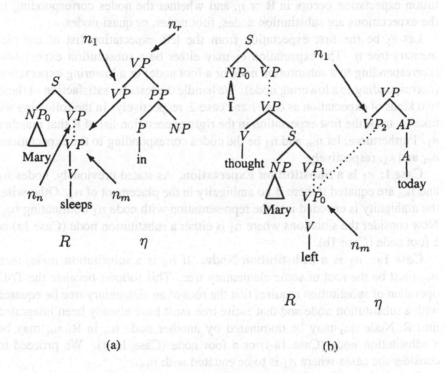

Figure 8.3 Example of case 1 of the algorithm to match expectation lists. (a) is the subcase of unambiguous attachment. (b) is the subcase of ambiguous attachment.

Representing the ambiguity in this way has various repercussions. For example, if the elementary tree that is being ambiguously added is an auxiliary tree, then we should make sure that if disambiguation should subsequently occur, an additional assertion should be made in order to guarantee a proper TAG adjunction. In detail, suppose that γ is the auxiliary tree, and n_1 is the foot node of γ. When disambiguation occurs, n_1 is equated with some bottom quasi-node n_b. In that case, an additional stipulation should be made that the top quasi-node n_t that corresponds to n_b dominates the root of γ. Another consequence is that an underspecified representation R that encodes such ambiguities is no longer the treelike structure that was assumed earlier. This necessitates alterations in our algorithm for computing expectation lists, as will be discussed in Section 6.

Details Behind Matching the First Two Expectations. As noted previously, matching one expectation list against another entails finding a sequence of pairs of corresponding substitution and lowering expectations. Whether two expectations match depends upon various factors, such as whether the substitution expectation occurs in R or η, and whether the nodes corresponding to the expectations are substitution nodes, foot nodes, or quasi-nodes.

Let e_1 be the first expectation from the left expectation list of the elementary tree η. The expectation e_1 may either be a substitution expectation (corresponding to a substitution node or a foot node) or a lowering expectation (corresponding to a lowering node). We handle the tests for satisfaction of these two kinds of expectation as case 1 and case 2, respectively. In the following we take e_m to be the first expectation in the right expectation list of R that matches e_1. Furthermore, let n_m and n_1 be the nodes corresponding to the expectations e_m and e_1, respectively.

Case 1: e_1 is a Substitution Expectation. As stated previously, nodes n_1 and n_m are equated if there is no ambiguity in the placement of n_1. Otherwise, the ambiguity is encoded into the representation with node n_1 dominating n_m. Now consider the situations where n_1 is either a substitution node (Case 1a) or a foot node (Case 1b).

Case 1a: n_1 is a Substitution Node. If n_1 is a substitution node, then n_m must be the root of some elementary tree. This follows because the TAG operation of substitution requires that the root of an elementary tree be equated with a substitution node and that entire tree must have already been integrated into R. Node n_m may be dominated by another node n_n in R. n_n may be a substitution node (Case 1a-i) or a foot node (Case 1a-ii). We proceed to consider the cases where n_1 is to be equated with n_m.

Case 1a-i: n_n is a Substitution Node. Let n_r be the root of η. We can say that it is dominated by n_n if $n_r \in LC(n_n)$[4]. See α_{13} of Figure 8.4 for an example. Otherwise, our original assertion of equality between n_1 and n_n was in error. The use of domination of n_r by n_n is to allow for further material to the right to be inserted between these two.

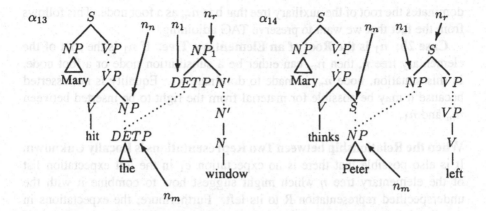

Figure 8.4 Case where stating that NP_0 dominates NP_1 is justified.

Case 1a-ii: n_n **is a Foot Node.** Suppose n_n is a foot node. If $n_r \notin LC(n_n)$ then n_n does not dominate n_r. Otherwise, n_n may or may not dominate n_r; the rest of the expectation lists would have to be checked in order to find out if there is the possibility of ambiguity in the placement of n_r. See α_{14} of Figure 8.4.

Case 1b: n_1 **is a Foot Node.** If n_1 is a foot node, then n_m must be a bottom quasi-node. Analogous to Case 1a, this follows because the TAG operation of adjoining requires that the foot node be equated with a bottom quasi-node. Again, where there is no ambiguity in the placement of n_1, we consider whether n_n is a foot node (Case 1b-i) or a top quasi-node (Case 1b-ii). Note that node n_n cannot be a substitution node because a substitution node cannot occur along the path between a top and bottom quasi-node.

Case 1b-i: n_n **is a Foot Node.** This case is similar to Case 1a-ii.

Case 1b-ii: n_n **is a Top Quasi-node.** If n_n is a top quasi-node, then it dominates n_r. This is to ensure that a valid TAG adjunction is performed. See Figure 8.3(a) for an example.

Case 2: e_1 **is a Lowering Expectation.** Again suppose that n_m and n_1 are the nodes corresponding to the expectations e_m and e_1, respectively. This time e_m must be a substitution expectation. Note that the possible attachment of n_m to more than one node in η does not occur. Because n_1 is a lowering node, it can only be a bottom quasi-node (Case 2a) or a root of an elementary tree (Case 2b).

Case 2a: n_1 **is a Bottom Quasi-node.** If n_1 is a bottom quasi-node, then n_m must be a foot node. It cannot be a substitution node because that would mean that a substitution node exists along the path between a top and bottom quasi-node. Node n_1 is dominated by another node n_k in elementary tree η, which can only be a top quasi-node. Because n_k is a top quasi-node, it dominates the root of the auxiliary tree that has n_m as a foot node. This follows from the fact that we want to preserve TAG adjoining.

Case 2b: n_1 is the Root of an Elementary Tree. If n_1 is the root of the elementary tree η, then n_m can either be a substitution node or a foot node. In this situation, node n_m is made to dominate n_1. Equality is not asserted because it may be possible for material from the right to be inserted between n_m and n_1.

When the Relationship between Two Representations is Locally Unknown. It is also possible that there is no expectation e_1 in the left expectation list of the elementary tree η which might suggest how to combine it with the underspecified representation R to its left. Furthermore, the expectations in that list may have all been optional. In this situation, although no assertion of domination can combine R and η, it is possible that subsequent input may be able to combine them. Call this Case 3. It occurs for example in the context of the sentence *Who does John annoy?* After the prefix *Who does...* has been seen, the parser considers combining the two representations that are shown in Figure 8.5(a), only to find that it is impossible.

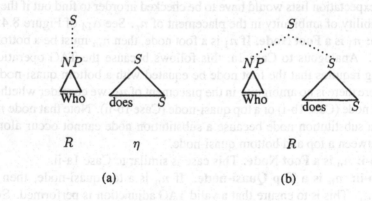

(a)   (b)

Figure 8.5 (a) Representations that are selected when the input *Who does...* is encountered. (b) The same representations combined with domination.

As a general strategy for case 3, we will assume that the disparate representations are combined using dominance where both of the representations are dominated by the lowest node which we know for certain will dominate both. An example is shown in Figure 8.5(b). This strategy would entail complications to the procedure of building expectation lists and checking for the compatibility of expectations. Notice that this strategy is akin to buffering the uncombinable items. There is therefore the problem of determining what, if anything, is the proper buffer size.

6   COMPUTING THE STANDARD REFERENT

In D-theory, the notion of standard referent plays an important role. The standard referent is a minimal model (tree) of a description. It is usually obtained by minimizing the path lengths of all of the domination links. Such a tree would be useful in incremental interpretation. For us the method for obtaining the standard referent is also useful in determining the order in which the components of the current underspecified representation are to be combined with new additional input. Recall that the underspecified representation that our parser produces allows for non-treelike forms in order to describe some forms of attachment ambiguity. On the other hand, the algorithm that was given to compute expectation lists requires a treelike description as input.

Consider the description α_8 in Figure 8.6. The problem here is that obtaining the expectation list for α_8 is not possible because an expectation list requires a unique ordering of domination. In particular, whether XP_3 dominates XP_4 depends on whether or not XP_3 is placed above XP_4. If the standard referent is implicitly assumed to be the default structure, the question arises as to what the standard referent of α_8 is. Such cases have never arisen in previous work on D-theory.[5] In defining the notion of standard referent here, we have to consider disambiguating the attachment ambiguity that is expressed in structures such as α_8. Because the standard referent is usually taken to be the default structure, its definition could also be used to give an ordering for the expectation list.

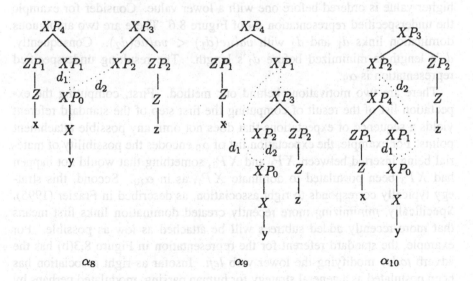

Figure 8.6   An example of our parser's underspecified representation (α_8), its standard referent (α_9), and another representation compatible with α_8 (α_{10}).

The basic strategy that we would like to use in order to determine the standard referent is to minimize the lengths of the domination links. This strategy, however, does not always yield a single standard referent, as seen in α_8 of Figure 8.6. In this case, there is no unique standard referent because the sum of the lengths of the domination links d_1 and d_2 does not vary with the placement of the auxiliary tree that is rooted by node XP_3.[6] The difficulty arises when two domination links reach the same node. We call such pairs of domination links *ambiguous*. In α_8 the pair of domination links d_1 and d_2 are ambiguous because they both dominate the same node XP_3.

In order to guarantee that a single standard referent is obtained, the process of determining a standard referent is divided into two stages. First, all of the ambiguous domination links are disambiguated by minimizing their lengths sequentially according to a predetermined order, yielding an unambiguous representation R'. Second, a single standard referent is determined from R' by minimizing the sums of the lengths of the domination links.

Suppose d_1 and d_2 are any ambiguous pair of domination links in R. d_1 and d_2 state that certain nodes U and V dominate a node X. Clearly, U and V must come from different elementary trees, say β_U and β_V. There must have been an order in which β_U and β_V were introduced into R. This is the order in which the ambiguous domination links d_1 and d_2 are ordered.

Each domination link is assigned a value that specifies the time at which the elementary tree in which the link's parent node resides was introduced into R. In defining the order for an expectation list, the domination link with the higher value is ordered before one with a lower value. Consider for example the underspecified representation α_8 of Figure 8.6. There are two ambiguous domination links d_1 and d_2 with $value(d_1) < value(d_2)$. Consequently, d_2's length is minimized before d_1's length. The resulting underspecified representation is α_9.

There are two motivations behind our method. First, computing the expectation list of the result of computing the first step of the standard referent yields a sequence of expectations that does not omit any possible attachment points. For example, the expectation list of α_9 encodes the possibility of material being inserted between XP_1 and XP_3, something that would not happen had XP_3 been postulated to dominate XP_4, as in α_{10}. Second, this strategy typically corresponds to right association, as described in Frazier (1995). Specifically, minimizing more recently created domination links first means that more recently added subtrees will be attached as low as possible. For example, the standard referent for the representation in Figure 8.3(b) has the adverb *today* modifying the lower verb *left*. Insofar as right association has been postulated as a general strategy for human parsing, modulated perhaps by semantic and discourse factors, it corresponds with this strategy of computing the standard referent, which may be used as the baseline structure for semantic interpretation.

7   ELEMENTARY REPRESENTATIONS

Underspecification plays an important role in reduced commitment parsing. Too great an underspecification means that few constraints are placed on what the final structure of the sentence will look like. It diminishes the predictive ability of the parser and enlarges the range of potential structures that are considered at any given time. Conversely, too little an underspecification leads the parser into making incorrect predictions and reduces the number of sentences that can be parsed without backtracking.

The enlarged domain of locality that TAG provides causes the latter sort of problem in this context. Let us select the strategy of choosing only one elementary tree at each step in the parse. Consider the problems it raises when trying to parse the following pair of sentences: *I know the answer* and *I know the answer is wrong*. Crucially, after having seen the word 'know' the parser cannot predict which elementary tree to select because the extended domain of locality of TAG requires two different elementary trees for 'know', each corresponding to a different subcategorization.

In order to alleviate this problem, it is useful to coalesce different elementary trees into a single representation because at this point, there is no way to tell which is the correct tree to choose. We merge the two elementary trees for the verb 'know' by having the substitution node corresponding to its object ambiguously specified as NP or S. See Figure 8.7(a). We call a single set of assertions with the added proviso of node label underspecification (which represent a set of elementary TAG trees) an *elementary representation*.

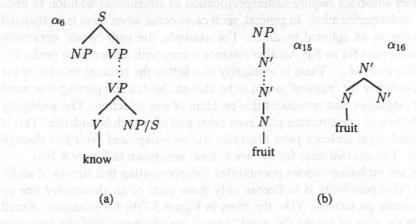

(a)   (b)

Figure 8.7 (a) Elementary representation corresponding to two elementary TAG trees. (b) Elementary trees that require underspecification in order for parser to avoid backtracking.

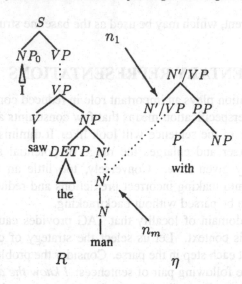

Figure 8.8   Node label underspecification allows us to represent PP attachment ambiguity.

The expedient of node label underspecification is also useful in avoiding backtracking in several other situations. Another example is the ambiguity that is associated with PP attachment. Suppose that a PP may either attach at the N' level or the VP level. The problem is that there is a separate elementary tree for each case. With node label underspecification, these separate elementary trees may be coalesced into one elementary representation. Using such elementary representations, we can delay the PP attachment decision until all of the necessary disambiguating information is encountered, as in Figure 8.8.

Other situations require underspecification of structure in addition to node label underspecification. In general, such cases occur when there is an optional argument or an optional modifier. For example, the verb 'wash' optionally subcategorizes for an NP. Another instance occurs with the sentence prefix *The wedding marked...* There is ambiguity in whether the reduced relative or the main verb tree for 'marked' ought to be chosen. Notice that parsing free word order languages also introduces this problem of tree selection. The ambiguity in selection of tree structure may even cross part of speech boundaries. This is exhibited in the sentence pairs *Fruit flies like an orange* and *Fruit flies through the air.* The relevant trees for the word 'fruit' are shown in Figure 8.7(b).

We are exploring various possibilities for representing this structural ambiguity. One possibility is to license only those parts of an elementary tree up to a certain projection. Take the trees in Figure 8.7(b) for example. Recall that in the case of seeing the word 'know', we underspecified the argument label because it was unavailable. Similarly, upon encountering the word 'fruit' we underspecify the set of two elementary trees because only projection up to the N level is licensed. The method suggested by Evans and Weir (1997) can perhaps be used to coalesce these structures.

8   CONCLUSIONS AND FUTURE WORK

In this work, we consider parsing TAG using underspecified descriptions of trees featuring dominance and underspecified node labels. The prediction component of an Earley parser corresponds to our assertion of domination. The completion component of an Earley parser does not have an analogue in our parser; it is a manifestation of how an Earley parser considers all possible parses while our parser leaves the situation underspecified. Specifically, in order to underspecify the attachment, we find that in most of the cases in Section 5.2, our parser does not immediately perform TAG operations of substitution and adjoining. That would require equating nodes from two different trees. Instead, our parser asserts domination that leaves us uncommitted to a particular attachment site. Nevertheless, when our parser recovers a parse tree from the underspecified representation, it is necessary for our parser to ensure that the resulting tree corresponds to one derived using substitution and adjoining.

In contrast with traditional work in TAG parsing, we envision our parser to be one that delays attachment decisions. However, we would not like our parser to leave the situation completely underspecified, but to reduce the search space through the judicious use of extra information. This is our notion of reduced commitment, the idea that the underspecified representation that the parser constructs encodes only those relations that the parser strongly believes must hold for the entire sentence. This extra information may include semantics, information about thematic roles, selectional restrictions, or frequency data that are collected from a parsed corpus. It is a subject for future work.

While our parser draws elements from D-theory, this work also extends beyond current work on D-theory. Current work on D-theory parsers do not use any explicit grammar formalism or grammar. Our choice of TAG was motivated by several factors. First, TAGs in general have the desirable properties of factoring recursion and localizing dependencies, which provide argument and structural requirements that are needed by D-theory style parsers for making its assertions regarding structures. Second, TAGs encode linguistic knowledge in a declarative format, making it easier to develop and modify than a more procedural design. Third, extensive TAG grammars have already been developed which could be quickly adapted to the deterministic parser that is proposed here.

Our use of TAG notwithstanding, we use dominance in a different manner than is customary with D-theory parsers. D-theory parsers usually construct a treelike description. On the other hand, some of the descriptions that our parser constructs are not necessarily treelike. This was necessary to capture attachment site ambiguity. In these cases, a statement is made that the tree which may be ambiguously placed dominates the lowest possible attachment site. Consequently, this site would be dominated by two structures, each of which is ambiguously ordered with respect to domination.

This ambiguous representation had a direct impact on our computation of the standard referent, another area where we deviate from normal D-theory parsers. We have provided a means of determining a standard referent under these exceptional circumstances. Our solution appears to produce a structure that conforms to right association, which is not the case for all other D-theory parsers. Not only may our standard referent aid in incremental interpretation but in our case it also aids in deciding how representations may be combined.

We have also discussed how representations may be combined through the use of expectation lists. We have provided a taxonomy of expectations. These help define a number of cases that illustrate when domination may be postulated between components of different elementary trees. We have enumerated many of these cases and given examples of their application.

Finally, we have argued that in incorporating TAG into D-theory style parsing, the assumptions that are standardly made about TAG trees can interfere with the goal of delaying attachment decisions. To alleviate this situation, we have suggested how several TAG trees should be coalesced into one elementary representation. An elementary representation represents elementary TAG trees that differ only in their node labels. This underspecification essentially allows the parser to delay the choice of the specific elementary TAG tree until further information can be obtained. We have also enumerated other cases where node label underspecification is insufficient. We have postulated a solution based on limiting how much of a projection of an elementary tree that we would license in a given situation. This is another subject for further investigation.

Acknowledgments

The first author was supported by NSF grants #GER-9354869 and #SBR-9710411.

Notes

1. If d is left (right), then $not : d$ is right (left).

2. Node p is a *parent* of a node c if p is connected to c by a domination or immediate domination link. For example, a top quasi-node is the parent of the corresponding bottom quasi-node.

3. The *child* relation is defined analogously to the parent relation in the previous footnote. For example, a bottom quasi-node is the child of its corresponding top quasi-node.

4. $LC(\nu)$ stands for left corner, by which we include anything that can appear in the left periphery of a tree whose root is ν.

5. See Rogers and Vijay-Shanker (1996) for discussion on the determinism hypothesis in D-theory parsing and the uniqueness of the standard referent.

6. Another possible standard referent of α_8 would be found by equating the two pairs of nodes XP_1 and XP_2, and XP_3 and XP_4, which would result in a parse tree where, for example, ZP_1 and ZP_2 are siblings. Nevertheless, it does not result in a tree obtained by any sequence of TAG operations, assuming that the component that is rooted at XP_4 and the component that is rooted at XP_3 come from different elementary trees. We avoid this undesirable result by never attempting, in computing the standard referent, to equate two nodes simply because they both happen to be asserted as parents of a single node.

References

Evans, R. and Weir, D. (1997). Automaton-based parsing for lexicalized tree adjoining grammars. In *Proceedings of the Fifth International Workshop on Parsing Technologies*, pp. 66–76, Cambridge, MA.

Frazier, L. (1995). Issues of representation in psycholinguistics. In Miller, J. L. and Eimas, P. D., editors, *Speech, Language, and Communication*, pp. 1–27. Academic Press, New York, NY.

Gorrell, P. (1995). *Syntax and Parsing*. Cambridge University Press, Cambridge, United Kingdom.

Marcus, M. P., Hindle, D., and Fleck, M. M. (1983). D-theory: Talking about talking about trees. In *Proceedings of the 21st Annual Meeting of the Association for Computational Linguistics*, pp. 129–136.

Rambow, O., Vijay-Shanker, K., and Weir, D. (1995). D-tree grammars. In *Proceedings of the 33rd Annual Meeting of the Assocation for Computational Linguistics*, pp. 151–158. Cambridge, MA.

Rogers, J. and Vijay-Shanker, K. (1996). Towards a formal understanding of the determinism hypothesis in d-theory. In Bunt, H. and Tomita, M., editors, *Recent Advances in Parsing Technology*, pp. 59–78. Kluwer Academic Publishers, Boston, MA.

Sturt, P. and Crocker, M. W. (1996). Monotonic syntactic processing: A cross-linguistic study of attachment and reanalysis. *Languages and Cognitive Processes*, 11(4):449–494.

Vijay-Shanker, K. (1992). Using descriptions of trees in a tree adjoining grammar. *Computational Linguistics*, 18(4):481–504.

Chapter 9

PROBABILISTIC PARSE SELECTION BASED ON SEMANTIC CO-OCCURRENCES

Eirik Hektoen

Logica UK Limited, Stephenson House, 75 Hampstead Road, London NW1 2PL, UK

HektoenE@logica.com

Abstract   This chapter presents a new technique for selecting the correct parse of ambiguous sentences based on a probabilistic analysis of lexical co-occurrences in semantic forms. The method is called 'Semco' (for semantic co-occurrence analysis) and is specifically targeted at the differential distribution of such co-occurrences in correct and incorrect parses. It uses Bayesian Estimation for the co-occurrence probabilities to achieve higher accuracy for sparse data than the more common Maximum Likelihood Estimation would. It has been tested on the *Wall Street Journal* corpus (in the Penn Treebank) and shown to find the correct parse of 60.9% of parseable sentences of 6–20 words.

1   INTRODUCTION

In recent years there have been many proposals for probabilistic natural language parsing techniques, that is, techniques which not only find the possible syntactic derivations for a sentence, but also attempt to determine the most likely parse according to some probabilistic model. A basic example is a probabilistic context-free grammar (PCFG), in which each production rule is associated with the conditional probability of it being applied when the left-hand non-terminal occurs in the generation of a sentence (e.g., Baker, 1982; Kupiec, 1991; Pereira and Schabes, 1992). This effectively regards the derivation of a sentence as a top–down recursive stochastic process, starting with the sentence non-terminal and ending with a random sentence in the language being modelled. While a PCFG is a pleasingly simple model, the fact that it assumes the choice of production at each step is only conditional on the left-hand non-terminal is a limitation to its accuracy. Some variations have therefore been proposed, by which the probability of a rule (or more generally, a parse derivation step) is made conditional on an extended view of the preceding derivation. For example,

161

H. Bunt and A. Nijholt (eds.), Advances in Probabilistic and Other Parsing Technologies, 161–175.
© 2000 *Kluwer Academic Publishers.*

Briscoe and Carroll (1993) associate probabilities with transitions in an LR(1) parse table (partly reflecting the left context and a one-word lookahead), while Black *et al.* (1993) present a model in which virtually any aspect of the partial parse at any point in a derivation may be taken into account.

Both Briscoe and Carroll and Black *et al.* tie the probabilistic analysis to the precise parsing algorithm being used, effectively shifting the emphasis from modelling sentence generation to parse selection as a goal in its own right. Others take this further by separating the parsing and the parse selection completely. Hindle and Rooth (1993), for example, propose a system for resolving PP attachment ambiguities by comparing the degree of statistical association between the possible verb/preposition/noun triples after an arbitrary parser has produced a set of syntactically possible parses. This approach is attractive because it is based on lexical co-occurrences, which may reflect the acceptability of the meaning of a parse, but is less comprehensive than the other methods mentioned, since only a particular kind of ambiguity is covered.

Yet others have made the opposite move, and presented parsing methods where the probabilistic analysis is used as the main driving force for the parser independently of any linguistically motivated grammar. Both Magerman (1995) and Collins (1996) propose such systems, where complex statistical patterns extracted from a treebank constitute both the (shallow) syntactic grammar and selectional criteria. The results are systems which are comprehensive in the types of ambiguities they can handle and designed to extract a highly detailed and wide ranging statistical data from the training corpus, but which do not take any advantage of the analytical syntactic rules encoded in a formal grammar, and which do not support the derivation of semantic forms.

The system presented in this chapter is essentially a specialised parse selector based on semantic forms derived from the parses found by a separate parser, and can therefore be used with any grammar and parser supporting formal semantics. It is based on lexical co-occurrences in terms of the predicates in the semantic forms, but handles all predicates uniformly and is therefore generally comprehensive in the types of ambiguities covered. It uses a complex statistical analysis to extract a large set of probabilistic parameters from the training corpus, but does not abandon the use of a formal grammar. Significantly, the system uses *Bayesian Estimation*[1] rather than simple Maximum Likelihood Estimation (MLE) for determining co-occurrence probabilities. This appears to be a sufficient response to the high degree of sparseness in the lexical co-occurrence data without the blurring associated with smoothing and clustering techniques (generally required for MLE). It seems reasonable to expect that a parse selection system should benefit from being trained on the same form of data that it is to be applied to – that is, specifically on the selection of the correct parse in sets of possible parses for different sentences rather than the unconditional probability of correct parses in isolation. The focus of the training in this system is therefore the differential distribution of co-occurrences in correct versus incorrect parses. The system is called 'Semco' (for semantic co-occurrence analysis), and has been trained and tested on (separate parts of) the *Wall Street Journal* corpus in the Penn Treebank.

2 DEFINITIONS

The aim of the Semco analysis is to model co-occurrences of lexical predicates in semantic forms for the purpose of parse selection. A semantic form is here assumed to be a logical expression or description (including unscoped or quasi logical forms) derived in a compositional manner from a syntactic parse tree, and thus in general representing one of several possible interpretations of a sentence. A *co-occurrence* should represent the variable semantic linking of the predicates (generally representing lexical items from the sentence) in such expressions, and is therefore defined as the coincidence of two predicates being applied to the same element (a quantified variable or a constant). More precisely, if the ith argument of the predicate Q and the jth argument of the predicate R are the same, the semantic form is said to include the co-occurrence $(Q.i, R.j)$ understood as an unordered pair.

To see how such co-occurrences can be used for sentence disambiguation, consider the following exchange (from Andy Warhol, 1975):

(9.1)   *B: Is that a female impersonator?*
         A: Of what?

The expression *female impersonator* is so commonly used as a noun–noun compound ('an impersonator of a female'), that it comes as a surprise here when A's reply requires an alternative reading in which *female* is used as an adjective (giving 'an impersonator who is female'). The difference between the two readings is represented by the semantic predicates and co-occurrences shown in Table 9.1. Note that the co-occurrences are concise representations of the facts that *female* and *impersonator* form a noun compound in Reading 1, while *female* is used as an adjectival modifier of *impersonator* in Reading 2.

The probabilistic analysis treats co-occurrences as elementary, atomic units, so that for a given grammar and lexicon there is a finite set C of possible co-occurrences. As far as this analysis is concerned, a parse, or *derivation*, is regarded as a set of co-occurrences, with the set of all parses being $\mathcal{D} = \{d \mid d \subseteq C\}$. Similarly, a sentence is regarded as a set of possible parses, such that the set of all possible sentences is $\mathcal{S} = \{s \mid s \subseteq \mathcal{D}\}$.

For each co-occurrence, parse and sentence there is a corresponding *event* – conventionally represented by the corresponding capital letter – referring to the status of a random sentence. More precisely:

- C is the event that the correct parse of the sentence includes the co-occurrence c.

	Reading 1	Reading 2
Categories	*female*$_N$ *impersonator*$_N$	*female*$_{Adj}$ *impersonator*$_N$
Predicates	(female x)	(female x)
	(impersonator y)	(impersonator x)
	(NCOMP y x)	
Co-occurrences	(female.0 NCOMP.1)	(female.0 impersonator.0)
	(impersonator.0 NCOMP.0)	

Table 9.1   Example predicates and co-occurrences

- D is the event that the correct parse is d. It can be expressed as the conjunction of the co-occurrence events for all the co-occurrences in d and the negated co-occurrence events for all other co-occurrences:

$$D = \bigwedge_{c \in d} C \wedge \bigwedge_{c \notin d} \neg C \qquad (9.2)$$

- S is the event that the correct parse is an element of s, and is simply the disjunction of the corresponding parse events:

$$S = \bigvee_{d \in s} D \qquad (9.3)$$

3   THE EVENT SPACE

Given the above definitions of co-occurrence, parse and sentence events, one's first reaction may be to regard the associated probabilities as the relative frequencies of the respective entities in the language – that is, in the correct analyses of the sentences in the training corpus. This is not the only possible definition, however, and would have serious disadvantages for the following analysis. For example, it would mean that the model should reflect the typical number of co-occurrences in an average sentence, making any assumption of independence between co-occurrences inappropriate (since the probabilities of any additional co-occurrence would diminish once the number has passed this average). It would also make it impossible for the training to be based on the differential distribution of co-occurrences in correct and other syntactically possible, but incorrect, parses of the training sentences, since such alternative parses would have no particular status in the model.

Alternative definitions of the basic probabilities are possible because all actual references to probabilities will be conditional on some given sentence.

The only requirement of the probabilistic model is that it predicts the relative, conditional probabilities for different parses for any given sentence, while the unconditional probabilities of different sentences in the corpus are never directly relevant.

To derive a suitable definition of the basic event space here, we will take the presumed independence of all co-occurrence events as the starting point, based on the view that the model ought to satisfy the following basic assumption:

(9.4)   **Basic Assumption:** The relative probabilities of any two parses depends only on the co-occurrences that distinguish between them, and not on any co-occurrence present in both of them, any co-occurrence absent in both of them, or any further possible parses of the same sentence.

The independence of the co-occurrence events follows by considering two parses, d_1 and d_2, that are only distinguished by a single co-occurrence c, say $c \in d_1$ and $d_2 = d_1 \setminus c$. By the basic assumption, the ratio $P(D_1|S) : P(D_2|S)$ is invariant for any such d_1 and d_2 and $s \supseteq \{d_1, d_2\}$, and this ratio must be $P(C) : P(\neg C)$. From the independence of the co-occurrence events and (9.2) it follows that the unconditional probability of a parse event D is given by

$$P(D) = \prod_{c \in d} P(C) \prod_{c \notin d} P(\neg C). \tag{9.5}$$

4   CO-OCCURRENCE PROBABILITY ESTIMATION

The co-occurrence probabilities $P(C)$ represent the basic parameters in the analysis and need to be estimated from the training corpus. In many other probabilistic analyses of corpus data the basic parameters are estimated as the observed relative frequencies of sentences displaying the relevant characteristics, but such a simple approach is not possible here. Instead, Bayesian estimation (see e.g. Freund, 1992) is used, by which the estimate is defined in terms of the distribution of the probability to be estimated regarded as a continuous probabilistic variable.

More precisely, the unknown probability $P(C)$ for a given c is regarded as the continuous probabilistic variable Θ with a value θ in the interval $(0, 1)$. Let s_i for i in $0, \ldots, t$ be all the sentences in the training corpus, and let d_i be the correct parse of each s_i. Let also S_i be the event corresponding to s_i, and let C_i be the event associated with the co-occurrence c with respect to the sentence s_i. The overall status of the corpus with respect to c can then be expressed as the conjunction of the events $\hat{S} = \bigwedge S_i$ and

$$\hat{C} = \bigwedge_{c \in d_i} C_i \wedge \bigwedge_{c \notin d_i} \neg C_i. \tag{9.6}$$

The distribution of Θ given the observed status of the corpus can then be expressed as the probability density function $\phi(\theta|\hat{C}, \hat{S})$, which according to Bayes's law is given by

$$\phi(\theta|\hat{C}, \hat{S}) = P(\hat{C}|\theta, \hat{S})\frac{h(\theta|\hat{S})}{P(\hat{C}|\hat{S})}. \tag{9.7}$$

Here $h(\theta|\hat{S})$ is the probability density function for the distribution of Θ given only the sentences in the corpus (i.e., not knowing the correct parses), and $P(\hat{C}|\hat{S})$ is the (discrete) probability of $\hat{C}$ not knowing θ. In other words, $h(\theta|\hat{S})$ is effectively (for our purposes) the *prior* distribution of Θ (regarding $\hat{S}$ as fixed), while $\phi(\theta|\hat{C}, \hat{S})$ is the *posterior* distribution of the same given the correct disambiguation of the sentences implied by $\hat{C}$.

The probability $P(\hat{C}|\theta, \hat{S})$, that is, the probability of the correct (observed) parse selections in the corpus in terms of the co-occurrence c and given $\theta = P(C)$, is given according to (9.6) and the fact that each sentence represents an independent draw in the event space by the product

$$P(\hat{C}|\theta, \hat{S}) = \prod_{c \in d_i} P(C_i|\theta, \hat{S}) \prod_{c \notin d_i} (1 - P(C_i|\theta, \hat{S})). \tag{9.8}$$

To determine $P(C_i|\theta, \hat{S})$, let n_i and m_i be the number of parses of s_i which do and do not, respectively, include c. Since the ratio of the probabilities of each of the former to each of the latter is $\theta : (1 - \theta)$, we get

$$P(C_i|\theta, \hat{S}) = \frac{n_i\theta}{n_i\theta + m_i(1 - \theta)}. \tag{9.9}$$

Returning to equation (9.7), the probability $P(\hat{C}|\hat{S})$ can now be determined from $P(\hat{C}|\theta, \hat{S})$ by the integral

$$P(\hat{C}|\hat{S}) = \int_0^1 P(\hat{C}|\theta, \hat{S})h(\theta|\hat{S})\, d\theta. \tag{9.10}$$

This leaves only the prior distribution, $h(\theta|\hat{S})$, which cannot be determined analytically, but which may be estimated empirically from a preliminary estimation of all the co-occurrences in the corpus (e.g., using $h(\theta|\hat{S}) = 1$ as a temporary simplification without seriously affecting the overall distribution).

Having found the posterior distribution $\phi(\theta|\hat{C}, \hat{S})$, a straightforward application of the Bayesian estimation method would be to estimate the unknown probability $P(C)$ as the *expected* value of Θ, that is

$$E(\Theta|\hat{C}, \hat{S}) = \int_0^1 \phi(\theta|\hat{C}, \hat{S})\, \theta\, d\theta. \tag{9.11}$$

A slight variation of this will be used here, however, based on the observation that the expected value operator in (9.11) essentially represents a continuous, arithmetic mean of the co-occurrence probability θ weighted by the distribution function $\phi(\theta|\hat{C}, \hat{S})$. As such, it would represent a reasonable estimation of $P(C)$ if the result were to be used as a term in a sum of such results, but according to (9.5) the main use of a co-occurrence probability will be represented by a factor of either $P(C)$ or $1 - P(C)$ in a parse probability. As the net effect of the presence or absence of the co-occurrence in a parse thus is to either multiply or divide the parse probability by $\frac{\theta}{1-\theta}$, a more suitable estimate of $P(C)$ is found by applying the expected value operator to $\ln \frac{\theta}{1-\theta}$, that is, defining the estimate as $\tilde{p}_c$ given by the equation[2]

$$\ln \frac{\tilde{p}_c}{1 - \tilde{p}_c} = E(\ln \frac{\theta}{1 - \theta}|\hat{C}, \hat{S}) = \int_0^1 \phi(\theta|\hat{C}, \hat{S}) \ln \frac{\theta}{1 - \theta} d\theta. \qquad (9.12)$$

From (9.7), (9.8), (9.10) and (9.12), noting that the integral in (9.10) does not depend on θ and can therefore be moved outside that in (9.12), we then get the following overall expression for the co-occurrence probability estimate:

$$\ln \frac{\tilde{p}_c}{1 - \tilde{p}_c} = \frac{\int_0^1 P(\hat{C}|\theta, \hat{S})h(\theta|\hat{S}) \ln \frac{\theta}{1-\theta} d\theta}{\int_0^1 P(\hat{C}|\theta, \hat{S})h(\theta|\hat{S}) d\theta}. \qquad (9.13)$$

To summarise, the effect of all this is that the posterior probabilistic distribution of the co-occurrence probability is determined from the prior distribution of such probabilities and the observations relating to this co-occurrence in the corpus. The posterior distribution represents the full knowledge we have of the likelihood of different possible values of the co-occurrence probability, and the final estimate is defined as that which represents the best approximation (for our purposes) of this as a fixed value.

5   IMPLEMENTATION NOTES

The previous section derived (9.13) in conjunction with (9.8) and an empirical estimation of $h(\theta|\hat{S})$ as the main expression for the estimate $\tilde{p}_c$ of a co-occurrence probability $P(C)$. In practice, only sentences with at least one parse that includes c and one that doesn't, that is, for which $n_i, m_i > 0$, have any effect on the result. For any such sentence, moreover, it is enough to record the ratio

$$r_i = \frac{n_i}{m_i} \qquad (9.14)$$

in the training data. Then, by defining

$$f(\theta) = \left[\prod_{n_i, m_i > 0} f_i(\theta) \right] h(\theta|\hat{S}) \qquad (9.15)$$

and

$$f_i(\theta) = \begin{cases} P(C_i|\theta, \hat{S}) = r_i\theta/(r_i\theta + 1 - \theta) & \text{if } c \in d_i \\ P(\neg C_i|\theta, \hat{S}) = (1 - \theta)/(r_i\theta + 1 - \theta) & \text{otherwise,} \end{cases} \qquad (9.16)$$

equation (9.13) is reduced to

$$\ln \frac{\tilde{p}_c}{1 - \tilde{p}_c} = \frac{\int_0^1 f(\theta) \ln \frac{\theta}{1-\theta}\, d\theta}{\int_0^1 f(\theta)\, d\theta}. \qquad (9.17)$$

The functions $f_i(\theta)$ and $f(\theta)$ represent scaled probability density functions of Θ: $f_i(\theta)$ is (proportional to) the apparent distribution based only on sentence i; $f(\theta)$ is (proportional to) the posterior distribution based on all the relevant sentences as well as the prior distribution $h(\theta|\hat{S})$. Fig. 9.1 shows some typical examples of the $f_i(\theta)$ functions, the $h(\theta|\hat{S})$ found to represent the distribution of co-occurrence probabilities in the *Wall Street Journal* corpus, and two possible forms of $f(\theta)$ derived from them.

The actual computation of $\tilde{p}_c$ will have to be by numerical integration of (9.17) based on the r_i values extracted from the training corpus for each co-occurrence.[3] This may seem rather costly in computational terms, but is feasible in practice with a careful implementation. In particular, it is generally not necessary to compute $\tilde{p}_c$ for all the co-occurrences in the training corpus, since in most cases only a small fraction of them will ever be required. Instead, a practical implementation may compile indexed files with the r_i values extracted from the corpus for each co-occurrences and compute the small number of co-occurrence probabilities required for any sentence when the need arises.

6   TEST RESULTS

An implementation of the Semco analysis has been tested with a feature unification-based, medium-wide coverage, syntactic/semantic grammar and sentences from the bracketted form of the *Wall Street Journal* part of the Penn Treebank. Due to limitations in the grammar and parser, the corpus had to be restricted in different ways: It was first limited to sentences of 6–20 words (after the deletion of parenthetical material) which parsed successfully with at most 100 parses (as more ambiguous ones would add disproportionately to the overall cost of the computation). It was further reduced by rejecting sentences for which no parse achieved a minimum threshold similarity with the corpus bracketting, or for which more than 30% of the parses achieved the same, maximal such similarity.

The parse/bracketting similarity measure used was a weighted sum of different counts based on shared constituents (with or without matching labels), crossing brackets, and the overall length of the sentence (for normalising the

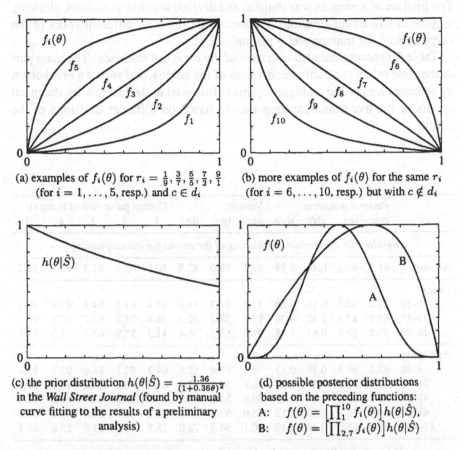

(a) examples of $f_i(\theta)$ for $r_i = \frac{1}{9}, \frac{3}{7}, \frac{5}{5}, \frac{7}{3}, \frac{9}{1}$ (for $i = 1, \ldots, 5$, resp.) and $c \in d_i$

(b) more examples of $f_i(\theta)$ for the same r_i (for $i = 6, \ldots, 10$, resp.) but with $c \notin d_i$

(c) the prior distribution $h(\theta|\hat{S}) = \frac{1.36}{(1+0.36\theta)^2}$ in the *Wall Street Journal* (found by manual curve fitting to the results of a preliminary analysis)

(d) possible posterior distributions based on the preceding functions:
A: $f(\theta) = \left[\prod_1^{10} f_i(\theta)\right] h(\theta|\hat{S})$,
B: $f(\theta) = \left[\prod_{2,7} f_i(\theta)\right] h(\theta|\hat{S})$

Figure 9.1   Co-occurrence probability density functions. All functions are scaled to give a maximum value of 1 with no significance for the co-occurrence probability estimation.

result). The threshold was set to correspond, typically, to a parse including about three-quarters of the corpus constituents with no crossing brackets. Multiple parses achieving the same, maximal score above this threshold (within the limit mentioned above) were presumed 'equally correct' for training and testing purposes. The number of sentences left in the corpus after each step in the selection process were:

Number of sentences of length 6–20 words	20155
... which parsed successfully	12162
... which had up to 100 parses	10852
... which met the similarity measure requirements	7887

The final set of sentences was shuffled and divided into five partitions, allowing a cycle of five training/testing iterations to be run with different splits of the corpus into $\frac{4}{5}$ for training and $\frac{1}{5}$ testing.

Table 9.2 shows a detailed overview of the main test statistics. The main part of the table refers to a particular division of the corpus, and shows a breakdown by sentence length and ambiguity. This is followed in the last row by the mean results of the five training/testing rounds based on different divisions of the corpus.

	Parseval measures				Variants			Correct parse ranked in top n				
	prec	rec	xb/c	xb/p	nxpr	lpre	lrec	1	2	3	4	5
Results with the original partitioning of the corpus for training/testing:												
All sents	61.3	87.2	0.40	0.79	93.1	58.0	82.5	60.8	75.1	81.3	85.6	89.2
Length												
6–10	70.0	94.3	0.12	0.20	97.2	67.7	91.2	82.4	91.2	94.2	97.0	98.7
11–15	61.5	87.1	0.41	0.76	93.5	58.2	82.5	58.9	75.3	82.7	87.2	90.6
16–20	57.2	83.7	0.67	1.45	91.0	53.5	78.4	41.2	57.9	65.7	71.3	77.1
Ambiguity												
1–20	62.8	89.9	0.31	0.53	95.1	59.8	85.6	69.3	83.1	88.6	92.9	95.6
21–40	59.0	83.1	0.63	1.20	90.9	55.3	77.9	42.5	60.2	69.2	74.7	80.1
41–60	58.1	81.4	0.69	1.47	89.6	54.2	75.8	37.9	56.0	64.7	67.2	71.6
61–80	56.8	78.7	0.59	2.12	85.0	53.4	73.9	35.1	45.9	51.4	55.4	63.5
81–100	58.2	83.2	0.44	1.40	90.1	54.5	78.0	38.5	46.2	51.9	55.8	61.5
The mean results over a cycle of five different partitionings of the corpus:												
All sents	61.3	87.4	0.41	0.77	93.4	58.0	82.7	60.9	74.7	82.2	85.9	89.3

All entries are in %, except xb/c and xb/p which are per sentence. Definitions:

prec	*precision*, the proportion of the constituents in the parses also found in the corpus
rec	*recall*, the proportion of the constituents in the corpus also found in the parses
xb/c, xb/p	*crossing brackets rate*, counted in the corpus form or selected parse, resp.
nxpr	*non-crossing precision*, constituents in the parse that don't cross any brackets in the corpus
lpre, lrec	*labelled precision/recall*, where the syntactic labels in the parse and the corpus must match
1–5	*n best correct selection rate*, sentences for which the correct parse (i.e., the best match with the corpus bracketting) is ranked in the top n parses by the selection algorithm

Table 9.2   Parse selection accuracy test results

The Parseval measures in the table have become a frequently used, common standard for comparison of different systems, but are only partly relevant for a system such as this. The fact that they are taken at constituent level means that they primarily measure the ability of the system to reproduce the precise bracketting in the corpus rather than the correct selection of parses as such. As a result, fully correct parses receive reduced scores where the grammar used by the parser differs significantly from that assumed in the corpus, while incorrect parses are credited to the extent that some of their constituents coincide with those in the corpus. In this system the grammar generally produces much more detailed parses than the corpus (i.e., with many more constituents, e.g. at bar-1 level), meaning that the *precision* rate is severely reduced and effectively rendered meaningless, while the *recall* rate is not similarly badly affected. This systematic imbalance between the corpus bracketing and the parses also prompted the inclusion of two *crossing brackets* rates: where four words are bracketed as '$(w_1\ w_2)\ w_3\ w_4$' in the corpus but parsed as '$w_1\ ((w_2\ w_3)\ w_4)$', for example, it counts as one crossed bracket in the corpus ('xb/c') but two in the parse ('xb/p'). Again, the generally greater number of constituents in the parses than in the corpus means that the latter is artificially high and a poor basis for comparison with other systems.

The table includes three variant Parseval measures. The 'non-crossing precision', which is like the standard precision rate except that any constituent in the parse that does not actually cross brackets with the corpus form is assumed to be correct, is intended as an illustration of a possible way to deal with the problem discussed above. The labelled precision and recall rates are the common variations of the Parseval measures where constituents are required to have matching syntactic labels.

The measures that most directly reflect the practical accuracy of the Semco system in my opinion are those headed 'Correct parse ranked in top n', as these show the relative frequencies of fully correct, sentence-level disambiguations ($n = 1$) and near-misses (n in 2–5). In the compilation of these figures, the 'correct' parse of each sentence was identified by comparison with the corpus bracketting using the same similarity formula that was used for the training of the system.

The table shows, as one would expect, that the selection accuracy tends to diminish as sentences increase in length or ambiguity, but the differences in the three higher bands of ambiguities are relatively minor (indeed, for many measures the sentences with 81–100 parses do better than those of 41–60 parses). This indicates that the decision to omit sentences of more than 100 parses from the testing is not likely to have affected the overall performance of the system greatly.

	Sentence lengths	Precision	Recall	Labelled precision	Labelled recall	Crossing brackets
Semco	6–20	61.3	87.4	58.0	82.7	0.41
	11–20	59.8	85.8	56.3	80.9	0.51
Magerman (1995)	10–20	90.8	90.3	89.0	88.5	0.49
(SPATTER)	4–40	86.3	85.8	84.5	84.0	1.33
Collins (1996)	1–40			86.3	85.8	1.14

Entries are in %, except the crossing brackets rate, which is per sentence. Note that the *precision* and *labelled precision* rates are poor measures of the Semco system's accuracy because of the more detailed parses produced by the grammar compared to the corpus annotations. The crossing brackets rate included for Semco is that counted against the corpus bracketting ('xb/c').

Table 9.3   Parseval measures of parse accuracy of different systems

7   CONCLUSIONS

The results in Table 9.2 show that the Semco technique achieves relatively high levels of parse selection accuracy, and that it therefore may represent a good practical method of sentence disambiguation. This is reflected in the Parseval recall rate of 87.4%, the average of only 0.41 crossing brackets per sentence (with respect to the corpus bracketting), and in the correct disambiguation of 60.9% of the sentences (with this figure increasing to 74.7% and 82.2% if near-misses ranked 2nd or 3rd are included).

Comparison with other published work is made difficult by the problems with the Parseval measures discussed above and by other incompatibilities between the different systems and the precise corpora used. Table 9.3 shows, however, the main figures from the Semco system and results published by Magerman (1995) (for his 'SPATTER' system) and Collins (1996). Considering the strong relationship between sentence length and accuracy shown in Table 9.2, the most comparable figures in Table 9.3 are those for Semco with 11-20 words and Magerman's SPATTER system with 10–20 words. Disregarding the precision rates, which are severely biased against Semco, the table shows that while SPATTER performs somewhat better in terms of recall, the difference in the crossing brackets rates is insignificant. (Collins only includes results for sentence of 1-40 words, making any direct comparison with Semco dubious, but the results are broadly similar to Magerman's for 4–40 words.)

To be fair, the Semco results are based only on a subset of suitable, parseable sentences in the corpus (about 39% of the original sentences within the length range), but this is an inevitable consequence of the major differences between the systems. Magerman's and Collins's systems are both based on extracting local syntactic structures along with their statistical distribution directly from the corpus annotation, and are therefore independent of any linguistic analysis of the corresponding syntax. This robustness can be an important advantage – it is very hard to write a formal grammar with something approaching full coverage of naturally occurring languages – but has several disadvantages too. In particular, the lack of a linguistic analysis means that there is no guarantee that a parse generated by these systems represents a meaningful sentence-wide syntax, and the models cannot support interpretation through compositional semantics.

The Semco system is compatible with any parsing technique capable of supporting formal semantics, making it potentially much more useful in a wider, practical NLP system where any form of interpretation is required. The lack of robustness in the experimental set-up discussed in this chapter is not a consequence of the Semco technique, but a reflection of the limited coverage of the grammar used. In future developments of this work, it is intended that the Semco system will be used with a fully wide-coverage natural language grammar and an n-best parser that includes mechanisms for handling undergeneration.

To conclude, the main novel aspect of the Semco analysis is the way the probabilistic model is based on the differential distribution of co-occurrences in correct and incorrect parses. This requires an analysis in which probabilities don't represent direct frequencies in the data, but rather correspond to a hypothetical event universe of which real sentences are only a small fragment. Simply put, the event universe includes sentences with any number of co-occurrences – whether they require a million words or ten – but this is no problem for the practical application of the system which is always conditional on a concrete, given sentence. There is no need for normalisation of the probabilities of parses with different numbers of co-occurrences in this analysis, sine the presence and absence of any co-occurrence are regarded as complementary events.

The use of Bayesian estimation for the basic co-occurrence probabilities is partly a requirement from the probabilistic model, but is also a means of dealing with the highly sparse data in a theoretically motivated manner. Where MLE tends to be highly inaccurate for very sparse data – requiring clustering or smoothing – and directly inappropriate for unseen data, Bayesian estimation finds the result *theoretically expected* to represent the best approximation of the true probability based on a full analysis of the latter's continuous probability distribution. The result is unable to distinguish between different co-occurrences with the same observations (e.g., unseen), as smoothing or clustering might, but are statistically unbiased such that the random errors in the probability estimates for a set of co-occurrences will tend to cancel out and lead to improved accuracy in the parse probabilities. More detailed experiments by Hektoen

(1997) show, moreover, that clustering the co-occurrence data in combination with Bayesian estimation reduces the accuracy of the parse selection.

Acknowledgments

This research was performed at the Computer Laboratory, University of Cambridge, Pembroke Street, Cambridge CB2 3QG, UK. I am very grateful to Ted Briscoe, John Carroll, Miles Osborne, John Daugman, Gerald Gazdar, Steve Young and the anonymous IWPT-97 reviewers for their valuable advice. The work was made possible by a generous grant from the Norwegian Research Council (*Norsk Forskningsråd*, ST.30.33.221752) and an Overseas Research Students Award from the Committee of Vice-Chancellors and Principals of the Universities of the United Kingdom (ORS/9109219).

Notes

1. Note that *Bayesian Estimation* (following e.g. Freund, 1992) refers not merely to the use of Bayes's law, but to the particular technique of estimating unknown probabilities by integration over a continuous probability distribution applied in Section 4.

2. The convergence of the integral in (9.12), although $\ln \frac{\theta}{1-\theta} \to \pm\infty$ for $\theta \to 0$ and $\theta \to 1$, follows from the well-known convergence of $\int_0^1 \ln \theta \, d\theta = -1$ and the fact that the relevant probability distribution functions are finite.

3. To avoid arithmetic overflow at or near $\theta = 0$ and $\theta = 1$, however, it is convenient to rewrite the nominator in (9.17) as $\int_0^1 \big([f(\theta) - f(0)] \ln \theta - [f(\theta) - f(1)] \ln(1 - \theta) \big) d\theta - f(0) + f(1)$, and omit the logarithms when the preceding factors are 0.

References

Baker, J. (1982). Trainable Grammars for Speech Recognition. *Speech Communication Papers for the 97th Meeting of the Acoustical Society of America*, pp. 547–550.

Black, E., Jelinek F., Lafferty J., Magerman D., Mercer R. and Roukos S., (1993). Towards History-based Grammars: Using Richer Models for Probabilistic Parsing. In *Proceedings, 31st Annual Meeting of the Association for Computational Linguistics*, pp. 31–37.

Briscoe, T and Carroll J., (1993). Generalized Probabilistic LR Parsing of Natural Language (Corpora) with Unification-Based Grammars. *Computational Linguistics*, 19(1):25–59.

Collins, M. J., (1996). A New Statistical Parser Based on Bigram Lexical Dependencies. In *Proceedings, 34th Annual Meeting of the Association for Computational Linguistics*, pp. 184–191.

Freund, J. E. (1992). *Mathematical Statistics*, 5th edition. Englewood Cliffs: Prentice–Hall International, Inc.

Hektoen, E. (1997). *Statistical Parse Selection using Semantic Co-occurrences*. PhD thesis, Churchill College.

Hindle, D. and Rooth M., (1993). Structural Ambiguity and Lexical Relations. *Computational Linguistics*, 19(1):103–120.

Kupiec, J., (1991). A Trellis-Based Algorithm for Estimating the Parameters of a Hidden Stochastic Context-Free Grammar. *DARPA Speech and Natural Language Workshop*, Asilomar, California, USA.

Magerman, D. M., (1995). Statistical Decision-Tree Models for Parsing. In *Proceedings, 33rd Annual Meeting of the Association for Computational Linguistics*, pp. 276–283.

Pereira, F. and Schabes Y., (1992). Inside–Outside Re-estimation for Partially Bracketed Corpora. In *Proceedings, 30th Annual Meeting of the Association for Computational Linguistics*, pp. 128–135.

Schabes, Y. (1992). Stochastic Lexicalised Tree-Adjoining Grammars. In *Proceedings of the fifteenth International Conference on Computational Linguistics: COLING-92*, volume 2, pp. 426–432.

Warhol, A. 1975. *The Philosophy of Andy Warhol*. Harcourt Brace Jovanovich, San Diego.

Chapter 10

LET'S PARSETALK –
MESSAGE-PASSING PROTOCOLS
FOR OBJECT-ORIENTED PARSING

Udo Hahn
Freiburg University, Freiburg, Germany
hahn@coling.uni-freiburg.de

Norbert Bröker
SAP AG, Walldorf, Germany
norbert.broeker@sap.com

Peter Neuhaus
Isys GmbH, Freiburg, Germany
neuhaus@isys.de

Abstract   As a response to the requirements imposed by real-world natural language processing, we argue for a design of natural language grammars and their associated
parsers in which declarative knowledge about language structure and procedural
knowledge about language use are equally balanced within a strictly object-
oriented specification and implementation framework. In particular, we introduce fundamental message-passing protocols for object-oriented parsing, which
include, besides the one for basic dependency parsing, protocols for ambiguity
handling, robustness, backtracking, preferential and predictive parsing, as well as
textual reference resolution. Based on an empirical evaluation, we also provide
reasons for sacrificing completeness of the parse in favor of efficiency gains.

1   INTRODUCTION

Over the past decades the design of natural language grammars and their
parsers was almost entirely based on *competence* considerations (Chomsky,
1965). These hailed pure declarativism (Shieber, 1986) and banned procedural

H. Bunt and A. Nijholt (eds.), Advances in Probabilistic and Other Parsing Technologies, 177–201.
© 2000 *Kluwer Academic Publishers.*

aspects of natural language use out of the domain of language theory. The major premises of that approach were to consider sentences as the object proper of linguistic investigation, to focus on syntactic descriptions, and to rely upon perfectly well-formed utterances for which complete grammar specifications of arbitrary depth and sophistication were available. In fact, promising efficiency results can be achieved for parsers operating under such optimal laboratory conditions. Considering, however, the requirements of natural language understanding, i.e., the integration of syntax, semantics, and discourse pragmatics, together with an often explosive growth of the number of ambiguities emerging at each of these levels, the processing costs of such 'ideal' competence-based devices either tend to increase at excessive rates, or linguistic processing fails completely. This is particularly true of real-world NLP scenarios where ill-formed input and incomplete knowledge have to be taken into consideration.

As a consequence, the challenge to meet the specific requirements imposed by real-world text analysis has led many researchers in the NLP community to re-engineer competence grammars and their parsers and to include various add-ons in terms of constraints, procedural heuristics or statistical criteria, in order to express processing priorities, preferences, or simple rules of thumb. In contradistinction to these approaches, our principal goal has been to incorporate performance conditions already in the design of natural language grammars, yielding so-called *performance grammars*.

One of the earliest suggestions under this label, using criteria for lexical and rule selection or parse preferences, was made by Robinson (1975) and has, in the meantime, developed into sophisticated models of probabilistic grammars for NL parsing (e.g., Collins, 1997 or Charniak, 1997). Some of these ideas have also been incorporated into hitherto entirely declarative grammar frameworks (Uszkoreit, 1991). Another approach considers formal restrictions on the expressive power of the underlying grammars as the crucial factor for meeting performance criteria, e.g., LR(k) grammars (Marcus, 1980) or even more constrained finite automata (Church, 1980).

However, performance phenomena can also be considered at the algorithmic level only. One approach favors parsing preferences such as minimal attachment or right association (Hobbs & Bear, 1990; Huyck & Lytinen, 1993), work that is strongly motivated by psycholinguistic evidences. Another major stream of research considers various models for differential resource allocations. These can be divided into ones with a compile-time flavor, e.g., skimming parsers (DeJong, 1979; Jacobs, 1990), and those employing run-time decision mechanisms such as anytime algorithms (Menzel, 1994). Note that any of these parsing-oriented strategies yields a more or less significant amount of reduction of complexity which pays off in terms of efficiency gains, but must also be traded off against the lack of completeness and the quality, i.e., the precision of the analytic results.

From these considerations, we derive the requirements that not only declarative knowledge (as is common for competence grammars), but also procedural knowledge (about control and parsing strategies, resource limitations, etc.) has to be taken into consideration at the grammar specification level proper. This can be achieved by providing self-contained description primitives for the expression of procedural knowledge. However, one has to take care to transparently separate declarative (structure-oriented) from procedural (process-oriented) knowledge pieces. Hence, we have chosen a formally homogeneous, highly modularized object-oriented grammar specification framework, *viz.* the actor model of computation which is based on concurrently active objects that communicate by asynchronous message passing (Agha, 1990).

We thus stay on theoretically solid ground and circumvent the major seductions outlined by Kaplan (1987), for any attempt at incorporating performance-related notions into the area of NL parsing. The theoretically unreflected integration of procedural knowledge at the level of parser implementation (Kaplan's *procedural seduction*) is escaped by lifting these specifications to the grammar level, while the demodularization of grammatical knowledge as a consequence of the high degree of interaction between the knowledge sources during natural language understanding (Kaplan's *interaction seduction*) is escaped by embedding that knowledge into an object-oriented specification framework. This approach combines the modularization into objects and disciplined forms of interaction among objects by message passing mechanisms.

The PARSETALK system, whose design is based on these considerations, forms the language processing core of SYNDIKATE, a text knowledge acquisition system, which is operational in two domains, *viz.* as a prototype for the analysis of test reports from the information technology field (Hahn & Romacker, 2000) and medical finding reports (Hahn et al., 1999). The analysis of texts rather than isolated sentences requires, first of all, the consideration of textual phenomena at the micro (text cohesion) and the macro level (text coherence) of textuality. Second, text understanding is based on drawing inferences by which text propositions are integrated on the fly into the text knowledge base with reference to a canonical representation of the underlying domain knowledge. This way, grammatical (language-specific) and conceptual (domain-specific) knowledge are simultaneously accessed in the course of the parsing process. Third, text understanding in humans occurs immediately and at least within specific processing cycles in parallel (Thibadeau et al., 1982). These processing strategies we find in human language processing are taken as hints as to how the complexity of natural language understanding can reasonably be overcome by machines. Thus, (text) parsing devices should operate incrementally and concurrently (Hahn & Adriaens, 1994). In addition, the consideration of real-world texts forces us to supply mechanisms which allow for the robust processing of extra- and ungrammatical input. We take a cautious approach here where – in the light of abundant specification gaps at the grammar and domain representation level – the degree of underspecification of the knowledge sources or the impact of grammar violations directly corresponds to a lessening of the precision and depth of text knowledge representations, thus aiming at a sophisticated fail-soft model of partial text parsing.[1]

2   THE GRAMMAR

The PARSETALK performance grammar we consider contains fully *lexicalized grammar* specifications (Hahn et al., 1994). Each lexical item is subject to configurational constraints on word classes and morphological features as well as conditions on word order and conceptual compatibility which a head places on possible modifiers (cf. Bröker, 1999 for a complete description). Grammatical conditions of these types are combined in terms of *valency* constraints (at the phrasal and clausal level) as well as *textuality* constraints (at the text level), which concrete dependency structures and local as well as global coherence relations must satisfy. The compatibility of grammatical features including order constraints (encapsulated by methods we refer to as SYNTAXCHECK) is computed by a unification mechanism, while the evaluation of semantic and conceptual constraints (which we refer to as CONCEPTCHECK) relies upon the construction of a consistent conceptual representation in terms of description logic expressions, mainly based on terminological classification (Romacker et al., 1999). Thus, while the dependency relations represent the linguistic structure of the input, the conceptual relations yield the targeted representation of the text content (for an illustration, cf. Fig. 10.9).

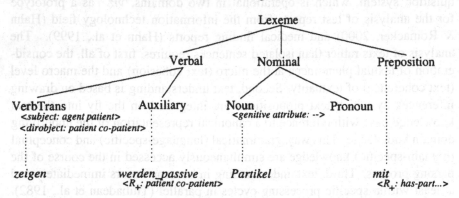

Figure 10.1   Fragment of the word class hierarchy

In order to structure the underlying lexicon, we make heavy use of *inheritance* mechanisms. Lexical specifications are organized along the grammar hierarchy at various abstraction levels, e.g., with respect to generalizations on word classes. In Fig. 10.1, *Verbal* and *Preposition*, e.g., denote word classes, whereas *'zeigen' (show)* and *'mit' (with)* refer to concrete lexemes. For instance, the word class of transitive verbs, *VerbTrans*, contains several generally valid restrictions on the range of semantic interpretations. As far as, e.g., the syntactic dependency relation *subject* is concerned, only agent or patient roles are permitted for semantic mappings (Romacker et al., 1999). This constraint is propagated to all lexical instances of this verb class, e.g., *'zeigen' (show)*, by way of property inheritance. Lexicalization of this form already yields a fine-grained decomposition of declarative grammar knowledge. It lacks, however, an equivalent description at the procedural level. We therefore complement declarative grammar descriptions by procedural ones in terms of lexicalized communication primitives to allow for heterogeneous and local forms of interaction among lexical items.

Following the arguments brought forward, e.g., ow for heterogeneous and local forms of interaction among lexical items.

Following the arguments brought forward, e.g., by Jackendoff (1990) and Allen (1993) at the representational level we do not distinguish between a semantic and a conceptual interpretation of texts. Hence, semantic and domain knowledge specifications are based on a hybrid terminological knowledge representation language (for a survey, cf. Woods & Schmolze, 1992). Ambiguities which result in interpretation variants are managed by a context mechanism of the underlying knowledge base system.

Robustness at the grammar level is achieved by several means. Dependency grammars describe binary, functional relations between words rather than contiguous constituent structures. Thus, ill-formed input often has an (incomplete) analysis in our grammar. Furthermore, it is possible to specify lexical items at different levels of syntactic or semantic granularity such that the specificity of constraints may vary. The main burden of robustness, however, is exicon). The main burden of robustness, however, is assigned to a dedicated message-passing protocol which we will discuss in the next section.

3 THE PARSER

In the PARSETALK parsing system (cf. Neuhaus (1999) for a detailed description), we represent lexical items as *word actors* which are acquainted with other actors representing the heads or modifiers in the current utterance. A specialized actor type, the *phrase actor*, groups word actors which are connected by dependency relations and encapsulates administrative information about each phrase. A message does not have to be sent directly to a specific word actor, but will be sent to the mediating phrase actor which forwards it to an appropriate word actor. Furthermore, the phrase actor holds the communication channel to the corresponding interpretation context in the domain knowledge base system.

A *container actor* encapsulates several phrase actors that constitute alternative analyses for the *same* part of the input text (i.e., structural ambiguities). Container actors play a central role in controlling the parsing process, because they keep information about the *textually* related (*preceding*) container actors holding the left context and the *chronologically* related (*previous*) container actors holding a part of the head-oriented parse history.

Basic Parsing Protocol (incl. Ambiguity Handling).   ambiguity We use a graphical description language to sketch the message-passing protocol for establishing dependency relations as depicted in Fig. 10.2 (the phrase actor's active head is visualized by ⊕). A searchHeadFor message (and *vice versa* a searchModifierFor message if searchHeadFor fails) is sent to the textually preceding container actor (precedence relations are depicted by bold dashed lines), which simultaneously directs this message to its encapsulated phrase actors. At the level of a single phrase actor, the distribution of the searchHeadFor message occurs for all word actors (depicted by ⊙) [2] only at the 'right rim' of the dependency tree. A word actor which receives a searchHeadFor message from another word actor concurrently forwards this message to its head (if any) and tests at its local site independently whether a dependency relation can be established by checking its corresponding valency constraints (running SYNTAXCHECK and CONCEPTCHECK). In the case of a success, a headFound message is returned, the sender and the receiver are copied (to enable alternative attachments in the concurrent system, i.e., no destructive operations are carried out), and a dependency relation, indicated by a dotted line, is established between those copies which join into a phrasal relationship (for a more detailed description of the underlying protocols, cf. Neuhaus & Hahn, 1996).

For illustration purposes, consider in Fig. 10.2 the analysis of a phrase like *'Zenon sells this printer'* covering the content of the phrase actor which textually precedes the phrase actor holding the dependency structure for *'for $2,000'*. The latter actor requests its attachment as a modifier of some head. The resultant new container actor (encapsulating the dependency analysis for *'Zenon sells this printer for $2,000'* in two phrase actors) is, at the same time, the historical successor of the phrase actor covering the analysis for *'Zenon sells this printer'*.

The structural ambiguity inherent in the example is easily accounted for by this scheme. The criterion for a structural ambiguity to emerge is the reception of at least two positive replies to a single searchHeadFor (or searchModifierFor) message by the initiator. The basic protocol already provides for the concurrent copying and feature updates. In the example from Fig. 10.2, two alternative readings are parsed, one phrase actor holding the attachment to the verb (*'sells'*), the other holding that to the noun (*'printer'*). The crucial point about these ambiguous syntactic structures is that they have conceptually

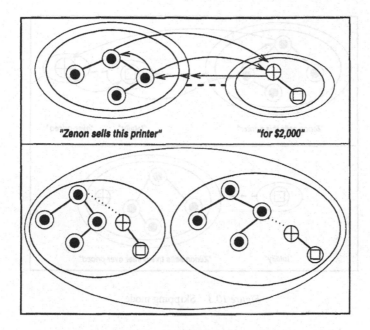

Figure 10.2   Basic mode (incl. structural ambiguities)

different representations in the domain knowledge base. In the case of Fig. 10.2 verb attachment leads to the instantiation of the price slot of the corresponding Sell action, while the noun attachment leads to the corresponding instantiation of the price slot of Printer.

Robustness: Skipping Protocol.   skipping for robustness purposes is a well-known mechanism though limited in its reach (Lavie & Tomita, 1996). However, in free-word-order languages such as German, skipping is, in fact, vital for the analysis of entirely well-formed structures, e.g., those involving scrambling or discontinuous constructions.[3]

The incompleteness of linguistic and conceptual specifications is ubiquitous in real-world applications and, therefore, requires mechanisms for a fail-soft parsing behavior. Fig. 10.3 illustrates a typical 'skipping' scenario. The currently active container addresses a searchHeadFor (or searchModifierFor) message to its textually immediately preceding container actor. If *both* types of messages fail, the immediately preceding container of the active container forwards these messages – in the canonical order – to its immediately preceding container actor. If any of these two message types succeeds after that mediation, a corresponding (discontinuous) dependency structure is built up. Furthermore, the skipped container is moved to the left of the newly built container actor.

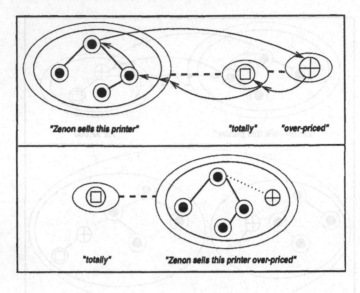

Figure 10.3   Skipping mode

Note that this behavior results in the reordering of the lexical items analyzed so far such that skipped containers are continuously moved to the left.

As an example, consider the phrase *'Zenon sells this printer'* and let us further assume *'totally'* to be a lexically unknown item which is followed by the occurrence of *'over-priced'* as the active container. skipping yields a structural analysis for *'Zenon sells this printer over-priced'*, while *'totally'* is simply discarded from further consideration. This mode requires an extension of the basic protocol in that searchHeadFor and searchModifierFor messages are forwarded across non-contiguous parts of the analysis when these messages do not yield a positive result for the requesting actor relative to the *immediately* adjacent container actor.

Backtracking Protocol.   backtracking, to which we still adhere in our model of constrained concurrency, accounts for a state of the analysis where none of the aforementioned protocols have terminated successfully in *any textually* preceding container.[4] In such a case, several repeated skippings have occurred, until a linguistically plausible clausal or sentential barrier is encountered such as the beginning of a relative clause or particular punctuation marks. Then, backtracking takes place and messages are now directed to historically previous containers, i.e., to containers holding fragments of the parse history.

This is realized in terms of a protocol extension by which searchHeadFor (or searchModifierFor) messages are first reissued to the *textually* immediately preceding container actor which then forwards these messages to its *historically*

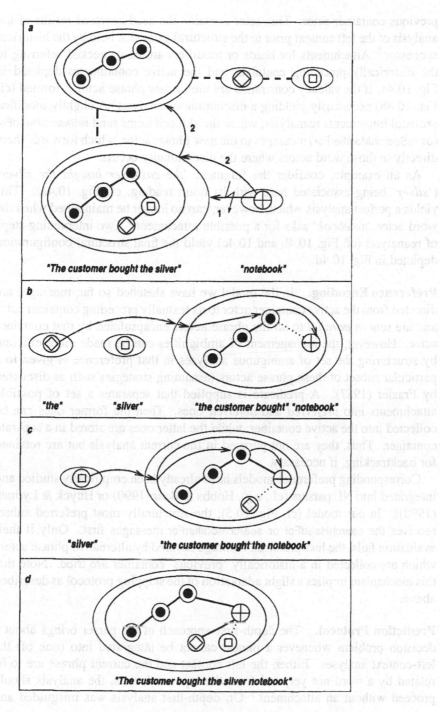

Figure 10.4   Backtracking mode

previous container actor. This actor contains the head-centered results of the analysis of the left context prior to the structural extension held by the historical successor.[5] Attachments for heads or modifiers are now checked referring to the historically preceding container and the active container as depicted in Fig. 10.4a. If the valency constraints are met, a new phrase actor is formed (cf. Fig. 10.4b) necessarily yielding a discontinuous analysis. A slightly modified protocol implements reanalysis, where the skipped items send reSearchHeadFor (or reSearchModifierFor) messages to the new phrase actor, which forwards them directly to those word actors where the discontinuity occurs.

As an example, consider the fragment *'the customer bought the silver'* (*'silver'* being associated here with its noun reading, cf. Fig. 10.4a). This yields a perfect analysis which, however, can no longer be maintained when the word actor *'notebook'* asks for a possible attachment.[6] Two intervening steps of reanalysis (cf. Fig. 10.4b and 10.4c) yield the final structural configuration depicted in Fig. 10.4d.

Preference Encoding.   In the model we have sketched so far, messages are directed from the active container actor to its textually preceding container actor and are sent *in parallel* to *all* the phrase actors encapsulated by that container actor. However, the management of ambiguities can be made more efficient by structuring the set of ambiguous analyses in that preference is given to a particular subset of these phrase actors (assuming strategies such as discussed by Frazier (1987). A predicate is supplied that separates a set of possible attachments into *preferred* and *deferred* ones. Then the former ones can be collected into the active container, while the latter ones are stored in a separate container. Thus, they are not pursued in the current analysis but are retained for backtracking, if necessary.

Corresponding preference models have already been empirically studied and integrated into NL parsers (cf., e.g., Hobbs & Bear (1990) or Huyck & Lytinen (1993)). In our model (cf. Fig. 10.5), the structurally most preferred subset receives the searchHeadFor or searchModifierFor messages first. Only if their evaluation fails, the less preferred readings covered by alternative phrase actors which are collected in a historically 'previous' container are tried. Note that this mechanism implies a slight adaptation of the skipping protocol as described above.

Prediction Protocol.   The depth-first approach of the parser brings about a decision problem whenever a phrase cannot be integrated into (one of) the left-context analyses. Either, the left context and the current phrase are to be related by a word not yet read from the input and, thus, the analysis should proceed without an attachment.[7] Or, depth-first analysis was misguided and

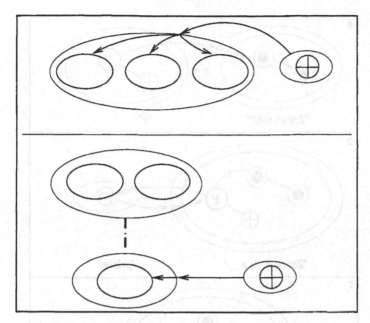

Figure 10.5   Non-preferential message distribution (upper part); preference encoding (lower part)

a backtrack should be invoked to revise a former decision with respect to attachment information in the light of new data read from input.

Prediction can be considered as a reasonable strategy to achieve a more informed selection between these alternatives. Words not yet read, but required for a complete analysis, can be derived from the input analyzed so far, either in a top-down (predicting a modifier) or a bottom-up fashion (predicting a head). Both types of prediction are common in phrase-structure-based parsers, e.g., Earley-style top-down prediction (Earley, 1970) or left-corner strategies with bottom-up prediction (Kay, 1982). Since dependency grammars, in general, do not employ nonlexical categories which can be predicted, so-called *virtual words* are constructed by the parser, which are later to be instantiated with lexical content as it becomes available when the analysis proceeds.

Whenever an active phrase cannot attach itself to the left context, the head of this phrase may predict a virtual word as the tentative head of a new phrase under which it is subordinated. The virtual word is specified with respect to its word class, morphosyntactic features, and order restrictions, but is left vacuous with respect to its lexeme and semantic specification. This way, a determiner immediately constructs an NP (cf. Fig. 10.6a), which can be attached to the left context and may incrementally incorporate additional attributive adjectives until the head noun is found (cf. Fig. 10.6b).[8] The virtual word processes a searchPredictionFor protocol initiated by the next lexical item. The virtual word

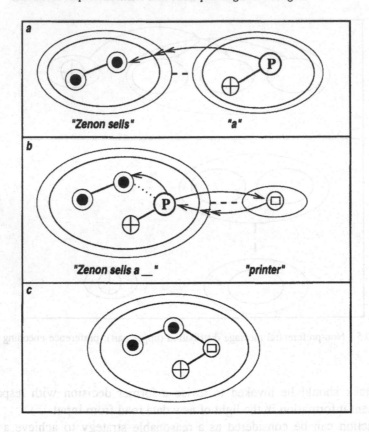

Figure 10.6 Predicting and merging a noun

and this lexical item are *merged* iff the lexical item is at least as specific as the virtual word (concerning word class and features) and it is able to govern all modifiers of the virtual word (cf. Fig. 10.6c).

This last criterion may not always be met, although the prediction, in general, is correct. Consider the case of German verb-final subclauses. A top-down prediction of the complementizer constructs a virtual finite verb (designated by ⓟ), which may govern any number of NPs in the subclause (cf. Fig. 10.7a). If the verbal complex, however, consists of a nonfinite main verb preceding a finite auxiliary, the modifiers of the virtual verb must be distributed over two lexical items.[9] An extension of the prediction protocol accounts for this case: A virtual word can be split, if it can govern the lexical item and some modifiers can be transferred to the lexical item. In this case, the lexical item is subordinated to a newly created virtual word (indicated by ⓟ in Fig. 10.7b) governing the remaining modifiers. Since order restrictions are available for

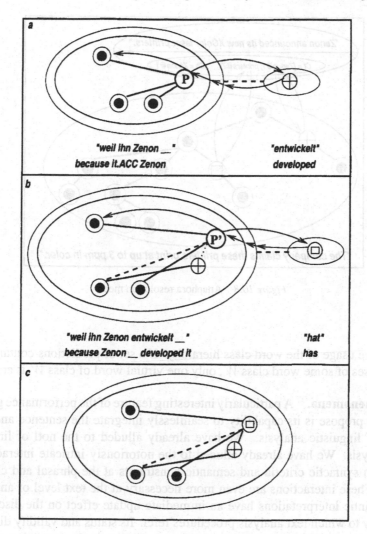

"weil ihn Zenon __"
because it.ACC Zenon

"entwickelt"
developed

"weil ihn Zenon entwickelt __"
because Zenon __ developed it

"hat"
has

Figure 10.7 Predicting and splitting a Verb

virtual words, even nonprojectivities can be accounted for by this scheme (cf. Fig. 10.7b).[10]

Although prediction allows parsing to proceed incrementally and more informed (to the potential benefit of increased efficiency), it engenders possible drawbacks: In underspecified contexts, many false predictions may arise and may dramatically increase the number of ambiguous analyses. Furthermore, the introduction of additional operations (prediction, split, and merge) increases the search space of the parser. Part of the first problem is addressed by our

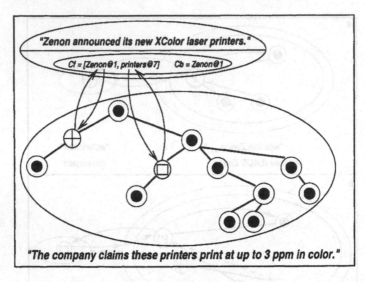

Figure 10.8　Anaphora resolution mode

extensive usage of the word class hierarchy. If a set of predictions contains all subclasses of some word class W, only one virtual word of class W is created.

Text Phenomena.　A particularly interesting feature of the performance grammar we propose is its capability to seamlessly integrate the sentence and text level of linguistic analysis. We have already alluded to the notl of linguistic analysis. We have already alluded to the notoriously intricate interactions between syntactic criteria and semantic constraints at the phrasal and clausal level. These interactions are even more necessary at the text level of analysis as semantic interpretations have an immediate update effect on the discourse memory to which text analysis procedures refer. Its status and validity directly influences subsequent analyses at the sentence level, e.g., by supplying proper referents for semantic checks when establishing new dependency relations. Even more, lacking facilities for the referential resolution of textual forms of pronominal or nominal anaphora (Strube & Hahn, 1995), functional anaphora (Hahn et al., 1996) and metonymies (Markert & Hahn, 1997) result in invalid or incohesive text knowledge representation structures (for a deeper discussion of these notions, cf. Hahn et al., 1999). As an unwarranted consequence, not only invalid parsing results emerge (at the methodological level) but this also precludes proper text knowledge acquisition and subsequent retrieval (at the level of system functionality) (Hahn & Romacker, 2000). Hence, we stress the neat integration of syntactic and semantic checks during the parsing process at the sentence and the text level.

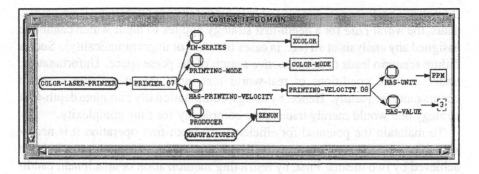

Figure 10.9 Sample output of text parsing

We now turn to text grammar specifications concerned with reference resolution and their realization by a special text parsing protocol. This protocol makes use of a special actor, the *centering actor*, which keeps a backward-looking center (C_b) and a preferentially ordered list of forward-looking centers (C_f) of the previous utterance (we here assume a functional approach (Strube & Hahn, 1999) to the well-known centering model originating from Grosz et al. (1995). The list of discourse entities is accessed to establish proper referential links between an anaphoric expression in the current utterance and the valid antecedent in the preceding one(s). Nominal anaphora (cf. the occurrences of *'the company'* and *'these printers'* in Fig. 10.8) trigger a special searchNomAntecedent message. When it reaches the C_f list, possible antecedents are accessed in the given preference order. If an antecedent and the anaphor fulfil certain grammatical and conceptual compatibility constraints (Strube & Hahn, 1999), an antecedentFound message is issued to the word actor representing the anaphoric expression, and finally, the discourse referent of the antecedent replaces the one in the original anaphoric expression in order to establish local coherence. In case of successful anaphor resolution an anaphorSucceed message is sent from the resolved anaphor to the centering actor in order to remove the determined antecedent from the C_f list (this avoids illegal follow-up references). The effects of these changes at the level of text knowledge structures are depicted in Fig. 10.9, which contains the conceptual representation structures for the sentences in Fig. 10.8.

4 AN EVALUATION EXPERIMENT

Any text understanding system intended to meet the requirements discussed in Section 1 faces severe performance problems. Given a set of strong heuristics, a computationally complete depth-first parsing strategy will usually increase the parsing efficiency in the *average case*, i.e., for input that is in accordance with the parser's preferences. For the rest of the input further processing is necessary. Thus, the *worst case* for a depth-first strategy applies to input which cannot be assigned any analysis at all (i.e., in cases of extra- or ungrammaticality). Such a failure scenario leads to an *exhaustive* search of the parse space. Unfortunately, under realistic conditions of real-world text input this worst-case scenario occurs quite frequently. Hence, by using a computationally complete depth-first strategy one would merely trade space complexity for time complexity.

To maintain the potential for efficiency of depth-first operation it is necessary to prevent the parser from exhaustive backtracking. In our approach this is achieved by two means. First, by restricting memoization of attachment candidates for backtracking (e.g., by retaining only the head portion of a newly built phrase, cf. footnote 5). Second, by restricting the accessibility of attachment candidates for backtracking (e.g., by bounding the forwarding of backtracking messages to linguistically plausible barriers such as punctuation actors). In effect, these restrictions render the parser *computationally incomplete*, since some input, though covered by the grammar specification, will not be correctly analyzed.

4.1   PERFORMANCE CONSIDERATIONS

The stipulated efficiency gain that results from deciding against completeness is empirically substantiated by a comparison of the PARSETALK system, henceforth designated as *PT*, with a standard chart parser,[11] abbreviated as *CP*. As the CP does not employ any robustness mechanisms (one might, e.g., incorporate those proposed by Mellish, 1989) the current comparison had to be restricted to entirely grammatical sentences. We also do not account for prediction mechanisms, the necessity of which we argued for in Section 2 For the time being, an evaluation of the prediction mechanisms is still under way. In fact, the current comparison of the two parsers is based on a set of 41 sentences from our corpus (articles from computer magazines) that do not exhibit the type of structure requiring prediction (cf. Fig. 10.7 and the example therein). For 40 of the test sentences[12] the CP finds all correct analyses but also those overgenerated by the grammar. In combination, this leads to a ratio of 2.3 of found analyses to correct ones. The PT system (overgenerating at a ratio of only 1.6) finds 36 correct analyses, i.e., 90% of the analyses covered by the grammar (cf. the remark on 'near misses' in Section 4.2). Our evaluation study rests on two measurements, *viz.* one considering concrete run-time data, the other comparing the number of method calls.

The loss in completeness is compensated by a reduction in processing costs averaging in the order of one magnitude. Since both systems use the identical dependency grammar and knowledge representation, the implementation of which rests on identical Smalltalk and LOOM/Common Lisp code, a run time

| number of | SPEED-UP FACTOR | | |
samples	minimum	maximum	average
25	1.1	4.2	2.8
10	5.1	8.9	6.9
6	10.9	54.8	45.2

Table 10.1   Ratio of run times of the CP and the PT System, chunked by speed-up

comparison seems reasonable, to some degree at least. For the test set the PT parser turned out to be about 17 times faster than the CP parser (per sentence speed-up averaged at over 10). Table 10.1 gives an overview of the speed-up distribution. 25 short to medium long sentences were processed with a speed-up in a range from 1.1 to 4.2 (average of 2.8) times faster than the chart parser. Another 10 longer and more complex sentences show the effects of complexity reduction even more clearly, averaging at a speed-up of 6.9 (of a range from 5.1 to 8.9). One of the remaining 6 very complex sentences is discussed below.

Accordingly, the PT system spent nearly two hours (on a SPARCstation 10 with 64 MB of main memory) processing the entire test set, while the CP parser took more than 24 hours. The exorbitant run times are largely a result of the (incremental) conceptual interpretation (Romacker et al., 1999), though these computations are carried out by the LOOM system (MacGregor & Bates, 1987), one of the fastest knowledge representation systems currently available (Heinsohn et al., 1994).

While the chart parser is completely coded in Smalltalk, the PT system is implemented in Actalk (Briot, 1989) – an extension of Smalltalk which simulates the asynchronous communication and concurrent execution of actors on sequential architectures. Thus, rather than exploiting parallelism, the PT parser currently suffers from a scheduling overhead. A more thorough comparison abstracting from these implementational considerations can be made at the level of method calls. We here consider the computationally expensive methods SYNTAXCHECK and CONCEPTCHECK (cf. Section 2). Especially the latter consumes large computational resources, as mentioned above, since for each syntactic interpretation variant a context has to be built in the KB system and its conceptual consistency must be checked continuously. The number of calls to these methods is given by the plots in Figs. 10.10 and 10.11. Sentences are ordered by increasing numbers of calls to SYNTAXCHECK as executed by the CP (this correlates fairly well with the syntactic complexity of the input). The values for sentences 39–41 in Fig. 10.10 are left out in order to preserve a proper scaling of the figure for plotting (39: 14389, 40=41: 27089 checks).

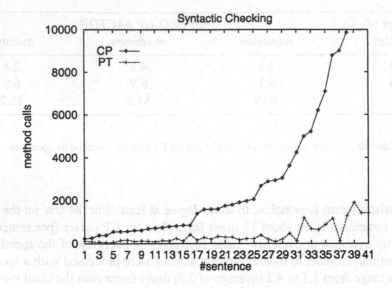

Figure 10.10 Calls to SYNTAXCHECK

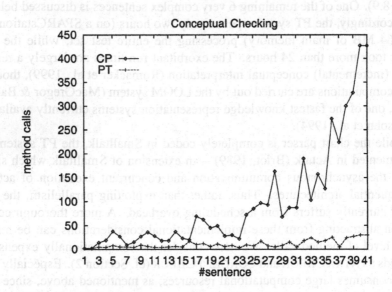

Figure 10.11 Calls to CONCEPTCHECK

A reduction of the total numbers of syntactic as well as semantic checks by a factor of nine to ten can be observed applying the strategies discussed for the PT system, i.e., the basic protocol plus skipping and backtracking.

4.2 LINGUISTIC CONSIDERATIONS

The well-known PP attachment ambiguities pose a high processing burden for any parsing system. At the same time, PP adjuncts often convey crucial information from a conceptual point of view as in sentence 40: *Bei einer Blockgröße, die kleiner als 32 KB ist, erreicht die Quantum-Festplatte beim sequentiellen Lesen einen Datendurchsatz von 1.100 KB/s bis 1.300 KB/s. [For a block size of less than 32 KB, the Quantum hard disk drive reaches a data throughput of 1.100 KB/s to 1.300 KB/s for sequential reading.]*. Here, the chart parser considers all 16 globally ambiguous analyses stemming from ambiguous PP attachments.

Apart from the speed-up discussed above, the PT parser behaves robustly in the sense that it can gracefully handle cases of underspecification or ungrammaticality. For instance, sentence 36 (*Im direkten Vergleich zur Seagate bietet sie für denselben Preis weniger Kapazität. [In direct comparison to the Seagate drive, it (the tested drive) offers less capacity for the same price.]*) contains an unspecified word 'weniger' ('less') such that no complete and correct analysis could be produced. Still, the PT parser was able to find a 'near miss', i.e., a *discontinuous* analysis skipping just that word.

A case where the PT parser failed to find the correct analysis was sentence 39: *Die Geräuschentwicklung der Festplatte ist deutlich höher als die Geräuschentwicklung der Maxtor 7080A. [The drive's noise level is clearly higher than the noise level of the Maxtor 7080A.]*. When the adverb 'deutlich' ('clearly') is processed it is immediately attached to the matrix verb as an adjunct. Actually it should modify 'höher' ('higher'), but as it is not mandatory no backtrack is initiated by the PT parser to find the correct analysis.

5 CONCLUSIONS

The incomplete depth-first nature of our approach leads to a significant speed-up of processing approximately in the order of one magnitude. This result holds at the risk of not finding a correct analysis at all. Our data show that lack of completeness resulted in the loss of about 10% of the parses and correlates with fewer global ambiguities. We expect to find even more favorable results for the PT system when processing the complete corpus, i.e., when processing material that requires prediction mechanisms.

Acknowledgments

We would like to thank our colleagues in the CLIF group for fruitful discussions and instant support. Peter Neuhaus was supported by a grant from the Graduate Program *Menschliche und maschinelle Intelligenz (Human und machine intelligence)* at Freiburg University, while Norbert Bröker was partially supported by grants from DFG (Ha 2097/1-1,1-2,1-3).

Notes

1. This 'reactive' approach is currently complemented by a more 'constructive' approach in which lexical and conceptual specification gaps are incrementally closed by an automatic concept learning procedure (Hahn & Schnattinger, 1998). As part of on-going knowlerning procedure (Hahn & Schnattinger, 1998). As part of on-going knowledge engineering efforts we also aim at the automatic incorporation and semi-automatic refinement of large-scale knowledge repositories such as thesauri and machine-readable dictionaries (Schulz et al., 1999).

2. In the remainder, we will refer to word actors in the figures by objects surrounded by a circle. Embedded in these circles are various geometric objects for referencing specific word actors, if necessary. If no specific reference is necessary, black bullets are used.

3. For brevity, we will base the following explanation on the robustness issue and refer the interested reader to Neuhaus & Bröker (1997), who investigate the theoretical implications (recognition complexity) of dealing with those phenomena within the framework of linguistically adequate dependency grammars.

4. For the provability of partial termination in our parsing model, cf. Schacht & Hahn (1997)

5. Any container which holds the modifying part of the structural analysis of the historical successor (in Fig. 10.4a this relates to 'the' and 'silver') will be deleted. Hence, this decision renders the parser incomplete in spite of backtracking.

6. PARSETALK is, by design, an arc-eager parsing system, a *possible* dependency relation will always be established. Therefore, the adjective reading of *'silver'* will not be considered in the initial analysis.

7. This effect occurs particularly often for verb-final languages such as German.

8. This procedure implements the notion of *mother node constructing categories* proposed by Hawkins (1994), which is a generalization of the notion *head* to all words which unambiguously determine their head. The linguistic puzzle about NP vs. DP is thus solved (cf. Bröker (1999, pp. 70ff and pp. 97ff) for a more elaborate discussion). In contradistinction to Hawkins, we also allow for multiple predictions.

9. We here assume the finite auxiliary to govern the subject (enforcing agreement), while the remaining complements are governed by the nonfinite main verb.

10. Nonprojectivities often arise, e.g., due to the fronting of a nonsubject relative pronoun. As indicated by the dashed line in Figs. 10.7b and 10.7c, we distinguish syntactic (solid line) from linear governors (dashed line), with the former imposing word class, morphosyntactic, and conceptual constraints, while the latter impose ordering constraints. For continuous attachments, the syntactic and the linear governor coincide, while for discontinuous attachments, the linear governor of a word is a (transitive) governor of that word's syntactic governor (Bröker, 1998).

11. The active chart parser by Winograd (1983) was adapted to parsing a dependency grammar. No packing or structure sharing techniques could be used, since the analyses must be continuously interpreted in conceptual terms. We just remark that the cubic time complexity known from chart parsing of context-free grammars does not carry over to linguistically adequate versions of dependency grammars (Neuhaus & Bröker, 1997; Kahane et al., 1998; Lombardo & Lesmo, 1998).

12. The problem caused by the single missing sentence is discussed in Section 4.2.

References

Agha, G. (1990). The structure and semantics of actor language. In J. W. de Bakker, W.-P. de Roever & G. Rozenberg (Eds.), *Foundations of Object-Oriented Languages*, Vol. 489, Lecture Notes in Computer Science, pp. 1–59. Berlin: Springer.

Allen, J. F. (1993). Natural language, knowledge representation, and logical form. In M. Bates & R. M. Weischedel (Eds.), *Challenges in Natural Language Processing*, pp. 146–175. Cambridge: Cambridge University Press.

Briot, J.-P. (1989). Actalk: a testbed for classifying and designing actor languages in the Smalltalk-80 environment. In *ECOOP'89 – Proceedings of* the European Workshop on Object-Based Concurrent Computing, pp. 109–129. Nottingham, U.K., July 10-14, 1989. Cambridge: Cambridge University Press.

Bröker, N. (1998). Separating surface order and syntactic relations in a dependency grammar. In *COLING/ACL'98 – Proceedings of the 36th Annual Meeting of the Association for Computational Linguistics & 17th International Conference on Computational Linguistics*, Vol. 1, pp. 174–180. Montreal, Canada, August 10-14, 1998. San Francisco, CA: Morgan Kaufmann.

Bröker, N. (1999). *Eine Dependenzgrammatik zur Kopplung heterogener Wissensquellen*, Vol. 405. Linguistische Arbeiten. Tübingen: Max Niemeyer Verlag. (Dissertation, Philosophy Department, Universität Freiburg, 1997).

Charniak, E. (1997). Statistical parsing with a context-free grammar and word statistics. In *AAAI'97/IAAI'97 – Proceedings of the 14th National Conference on Artificial Intelligence & 9th Innovative Applications of Artificial Intelligence Conference*, pp. 598–603. Providence, Rhode Island, U.S.A., July 27-31, 1997. Menlo Park, CA & Cambridge, MA: AAAI Press & MIT Press.

Chomsky, N. (1965). *Aspects of the Theory of Syntax*. Cambridge, MA: MIT Press.

Church, K. W. (1980). On parsing strategies and closure. In *Proceedings of the 18th Annual Meeting of the Association for Computational Linguistics and Parasession on Topics in Interactive Discourse*, pp. 107–111. Philadelphia, PA, June 19-22, 1980.

Collins, M. (1997). Three generative, lexicalised models for statistical parsing. In *Proceedings of the 35th Annual Meeting of the Association for Computational Linguistics & 8th Conference of the European Chapter of the Association for Computational Linguistics*, pp. 16–23. Madrid, Spain, July 7-12, 1997. San Francisco, CA: Morgan Kaufmann.

DeJong, G. F. (1979). *Skimming Stories in Real Time: An Experiment in Integrated Understanding*, (Ph.D. thesis). Department of Computer Science, Yale University. Research Report 158.

Earley, J. (1970). An efficient context-free parsing algorithm. *Communications of the ACM*, 13(2):94–102.

Frazier, L. (1987). Theories of sentence processing. In L. Garfield (Ed.), *Modularity in Knowledge Representation and Natural-Language Understanding*, pp. 291–307. Cambridge, MA: MIT Press.

Grosz, B. J., A. K Joshi & S. Weinstein (1995). Centering: a framework for modeling the local coherence of discourse. *Computational Linguistics*, 21(2):203–225.

Hahn, U. & G. Adriaens (1994). Parallel natural language processing: background and overview. In G. Adriaens & U. Hahn (Eds.), *Parallel Natural Language Processing*, pp. 1–134. Norwood, NJ: Ablex.

Hahn, U., K. Markert & M. Strube (1996). A conceptual reasoning approach to textual ellipsis. In W. Wahlster (Ed.), *ECAI'96 – Proceedings of the 12th European Conference on Artifical Intelligence*, pp. 572–576. Budapest, Hungary, August 11-16, 1996. Chichester: John Wiley.

Hahn, U. & M. Romacker (2000). Content Management in SYNDIKATE: How Technical Documents Are Automatically Transformed to Text Knowledge Bases. *Data & Knowledge Engineering*.

Hahn, U., M. Romacker & S. Schulz (1999). Discourse structures in medical reports - Watch out! The generation of referentially coherent and valid text knowledge bases in the MEDSYNDIKATE system. *International Journal of Medical Informatics*, 53(1):1–28.

Hahn, U., S. Schacht & N. Bröker (1994). Concurrent, object-oriented natural language parsing: the PARSETALK model. *International Journal of Human-Computer Studies*, 41(1/2):179–222.

Hahn, U. & K. Schnattinger (1998). Towards text knowledge engineering. In *AAAI'98/IAAI'98 – Proceedings of the 15th National Conference on Artificial Intelligence & 10th Conference on Innovative Applications of Artificial Intelligence*, pp. 524–531. Madison, Wisconsin, July 26-30, 1998. Menlo Park, CA & Cambridge, MA: AAAI Press & MIT Press.

Hawkins, J. A. (1994). *A Performance Theory of Order and Constituency*, Vol. 73. Cambridge Studies in Linguistics. Cambridge, U.K.: Cambridge University Press.

Heinsohn, J., D. Kudenko, B. Nebel & H.-J. Profitlich (1994). An empirical analysis of terminological representation systems. *Artificial Intelligence*, 68(2):367–397.

Hobbs, J. R. & J. Bear (1990). Two principles of parse preference. In *COLING'90 – Papers Presented at the 13th International Conference on Computational Linguistics on the Occasion of the 25th Anniversary of COLING & the 350th Anniversary of Helsinki University*, Vol. 3, pp. 162–167. Helsinki, Finland, 1990.

Huyck, C. R. & S. L. Lytinen (1993). Efficient heuristic natural language parsing. In *AAAI'93 – Proceedings of the 11th National Conference on Artificial Intelligence*, pp. 386–391. Washington, D.C., July 11-15, 1993. Menlo Park, CA & Cambridge, MA: AAAI Press & MIT Press.

Jackendoff, R. (1990). *Semantic Structures*. Cambridge, MA: MIT Press.

Jacobs, P. S. (1990). To parse or not to parse: relation-driven text skimming. In *COLING'90 – Papers Presented at the 13th International Conference on Computational Linguistics on the Occasion of the 25th Anniversary of COLING & the 350th Anniversary of Helsinki University*, Vol. 2, pp. 194–198. Helsinki, Finland, 1990.

Kahane, S., A. Nasr & O. Rambow (1998). Pseudo-projectivity: a polynomially parsable non-projective dependency grammar. In *COLING/ACL'98 – Pro-*

ceedings of the 36th Annual Meeting of the Association for Computational Linguistics & 17th International Conference on Computational Linguistics, Vol. 1, pp. 646–652. Montreal, Canada, August 10-14, 1998. San Francisco, CA: Morgan Kaufmann.

Kaplan, R. M. (1987). Three seductions of computational psycholinguistics. In P. Whitelock, M. Wood, H. Somers, R. Johnson & P. Bennett (Eds.), *Linguistic Theory and Computer Applications*, pp. 149–188. London: Academic Press.

Kay, M. (1982). Algorithm schemata and data structures in syntactic processing. In S. Allen (Ed.), *Text Processing. Text Analysis and Generation. Text Typology and Attribution. Proceedings of the "Nobel Symposium 51"*, Vol. 16, Data Linguistica, pp. 327–358. Stockholm: Almqvist & Wiksell.

Lavie, A. & M. Tomita (1996). GLR*: an efficient noise-skipping parsing algorithm for context-free grammars. In H. Bunt & M. Tomita (Eds.), *Recent Advances in Parsing Technology*, Vol. 1, Text, Speech and Language Technology. Dordrecht, Boston: Kluwer.

Lombardo, V. & L. Lesmo (1998). Formal aspects and parsing issues of dependency theory. In *COLING/ACL'98 – Proceedings of the 36th Annual Meeting of the Association for Computational Linguistics & 17th International Conference on Computational Linguistics*, Vol. 2, pp. 787–793. Montreal, Canada, August 10-14, 1998. San Francisco, CA: Morgan Kaufmann.

MacGregor, R. & R. Bates (1987). *The LOOM Knowledge Representation Language*. Technical Report RS-87-188: Information Sciences Institute, University of Southern California.

Marcus, M. (1980). *A Theory of Syntactic Recognition for Natural Language*. Cambridge, MA: MIT Press.

Markert, K. & U. Hahn (1997). On the interaction of metonymies and anaphora. In *IJCAI'97 – Proceedings of the 15th International Joint Conference on Artificial Intelligence*, Vol. 2, pp. 1010–1015. Nagoya, Japan, August 23-29, 1997. San Francisco, CA: Morgan Kaufmann.

Mellish, C. S. (1989). Some chart-based techniques for parsing ill-formed input. In *Proceedings of the 27th Annual Meeting of the Association for Computational Linguistics*, pp. 102–109. Vancouver, B.C., Canada, 26-29 June 1989.

Menzel, W. (1994). Parsing of spoken language under time constraints. In A. Cohn (Ed.), *ECAI'94 – Proceedings of the 11th European Conference on Artificial Intelligence*, pp. 560–564. Amsterdam, The Netherlands, August 8-12 1994. Chichester: John Wiley.

Neuhaus, P. (1999). *Nebenläufiges Parsing: Ein lexikalisch verteiltes Verfahren zur performanzgrammatischen Analyse beim Textverstehen*, Vol. 194. DISKI. St. Augustin: infix. (Dissertation, Department for Applied Sciences, Universität Freiburg, 1997).

Neuhaus, P. & N. Bröker (1997). The complexity of recognition of linguistically adequate dependency grammars. In *Proceedings of the 35th Annual Meeting of the Association for Computational Linguistics & 8th Conference of the European Chapter of the Association for Computational Linguistics*, pp. 337–343. Madrid, Spain, 7-12 July 1997. San Francisco, CA: Morgan Kaufmann.

Neuhaus, P. & U. Hahn (1996). Restricted parallelism in object-oriented lexical parsing. In *COLING'96 – Proceedings of the 16th International Conference on Computational Linguistics*, Vol. 1, pp. 502–507. Copenhagen, Denmark, August 5-9, 1996.

Robinson, J. J. (1975). Performance grammars. In D. R. Reddy (Ed.), *Speech Recognition. Invited Papers Presented at the 1974 IEEE Symposium*, pp. 401–427. New York: Academic Press.

Romacker, M., K. Markert & U. Hahn (1999). Lean semantic interpretation. In *IJCAI'99 – Proceedings of the 16th International Joint Conference on Artificial Intelligence*, Vol. 2, pp. 868–875. Stockholm, Sweden, July 31 - August 6, 1999. San Francisco, CA: Morgan Kaufmann.

Schacht, S. & U. Hahn (1997). Temporal reasoning about actor programs. In E. Costa & A. Cardoso (Eds.), *Progress in Artificial Intelligence. EPIA'97 – Proceedings of the 8th Portuguese Conference on Artificial Intelligence*, Vol. 1323, Lecture Notes in Artificial Intelligence, pp. 279–290. Coimbra, Portugal, October 6-9, 1997. Berlin: Springer.

Schulz, S., M. Romacker, G. Faggioli & U. Hahn (1999). From knowledge import to knowledge finishing: automatic acquisition and semi-automatic refinement of medical knowledge. In B. Gaines, R. Kremer & M. Musen (Eds.), *KAW'99 – Proceedings of the 12th Workshop on Knowledge Acquisition, Modeling and Management*, pp. 7–8–1–7–8–12. Banff, Alberta, Canada, October 16-21, 1999.

Shieber, S. M. (1986). *An Introduction to Unification-based Approaches to Grammar*, Vol. 4. CSLI Lecture Notes. Stanford, CA: Stanford University, Center for the Study of Language and Information (CSLI).

Strube, M. & U. Hahn (1995). PARSETALK about sentence- and text-level anaphora. In *EACL'95 – Proceedings of the 7th Conference of the European Chapter of the Association for Computational Linguistics*, pp. 237–244. Dublin, Ireland, March 27-31, 1995.

Strube, M. & U. Hahn (1999). Functional centering: Grounding referential coherence in information structure. *Computational Linguistics*, 25(3):309–344.

Thibadeau, R., M. A. Just & P. A. Carpenter (1982). A model of the time course and content of reading. *Cognitive Science*, 6:157–203.

Uszkoreit, H. (1991). Strategies for adding control information to declarative grammars. In *Proceedings of the 29th Annual Meeting of the Association for Computational Linguistics*. Berkeley, Cal., USA, 18-21 June 1991.

Winograd, T. (1983). *Language as a Cognitive Process*, Vol. 1, Syntax. Reading, MA: Addison-Wesley.

Woods, W. A. & J. G. Schmolze (1992). The KL-ONE family. *Computers & Mathematics with Applications*, 23(2/5):133–177.

Chapter 11

PERFORMANCE EVALUATION OF SUPERTAGGING FOR PARTIAL PARSING

Srinivas Bangalore

AT&T Labs – Research, 180 Park Avenue, Florham Park, NJ 07932
srini@research.att.com

Abstract   In previous work we introduced the idea of supertagging as a means of improv-
                ing the efficiency of a lexicalized grammar parser. In this paper, we present
                supertagging in conjunction with a lightweight dependency analyzer as a robust
                and efficient partial parser. The present work is significant for two reasons. First,
                we have vastly improved our results; 92% accurate for supertag disambigua-
                tion using lexical information, larger training corpus and smoothing techniques.
                Second, we show how supertagging can be used for partial parsing and provide
                detailed evaluation results for detecting noun chunks, verb chunks, preposition
                phrase attachment and a variety of other linguistic constructions.

1   INTRODUCTION

A number of grammar formalisms such as HPSG (Pollard and Sag, 1987),
CCG (Steedman, 1987), Lexicon-Grammars (Gross, 1984), LTAG (Schabes
et al., 1988), Link Grammars (Sleator and Temperley, 1991) fall into the class
of lexicalized grammar formalisms. Lexicalized grammar formalisms associate
increasingly rich and complex descriptions with each lexical item. Typically, a
lexical item in these frameworks is associated with more than one description.
The task of a parser for such formalisms can be viewed as first selecting the
appropriate description for individual words given the context of the input and
then combining them to arrive at a description for the entire input.

In Joshi and Srinivas (1994), we introduced the idea of supertagging as a
means of selecting the appropriate descriptions for each word given the context
of a sentence, even before parsing begins, so as to improve the efficiency of a

*This work was done while the author was at the Department of Computer and Information Science,
University of Pennsylvania, Philadelphia, PA 19104

H. Bunt and A. Nijholt (eds.), Advances in Probabilistic and Other Parsing Technologies, 203–220.
© 2000 *Kluwer Academic Publishers.*

lexicalized grammar parser. In this paper, we present supertagging in conjunction with a lightweight dependency analyzer as a robust and efficient partial parser. We provide detailed evaluation results of using supertag representation for detecting noun chunks, verb chunks, preposition phrase attachment, appositives and parenthetical constructions. We also present vastly improved supertag disambiguation results from previously published 68% accurate to 92% accurate, a significant result keeping in mind that the supertags contain richer information than part-of-speech tags.

The outline of this paper is as follows. In Section 2, we present a brief introduction to Lexicalized Tree-Adjoining Grammars. In Section 3, we review the notion of supertags and in Section 4, we discuss the details of the trigram model for disambiguating supertags and the results of evaluation on the Wall Street Journal corpus. In Section 5, we introduce the lightweight dependency analyzer. A detailed evaluation of the supertag and lightweight dependency analyzer system is presented in Section 6. In Section 7, we briefly discuss two new models for supertagging.

2   LEXICALIZED TREE-ADJOINING GRAMMARS

Each elementary tree of Lexicalized Tree-Adjoining Grammar (LTAG, Joshi, 1985; Schabes et al., 1988) is associated with at least one lexical item called the *anchor* of that tree. All the arguments of the anchor are realized as substitution or adjunction slots within an elementary tree. Thus an elementary tree serves as a complex description of the anchor and provides a domain of locality over which the anchor specifies syntactic and semantic (predicate-argument) constraints. Elementary trees are of two types: *initial trees* (α trees in Figure 11.2) that represent non-recursive linguistic structures such as NPs, PPs and *auxiliary trees* (β trees in Figure 11.2) that represent recursive structures which are adjuncts to basic structure (e.g. relative clauses, sentential adjuncts, adverbials).

Elementary trees are combined by two operations, *substitution* and *adjunction*. The result of combining the last row of elementary trees of Figure 11.2 is the *derived tree* (Figure 11.1(a)). But the more important structure in an LTAG parse is the *derivation tree* (Figure 11.1(b)) which represents the process of combining the elementary trees to yield a parse. The derivation tree can also be interpreted as a *dependency tree* (Figure 11.1(c)) with unlabeled arcs between words of the sentence. A wide-coverage English grammar called XTAG has been implemented in the LTAG framework. This grammar has been used to parse sentences from the Wall Street Journal, IBM manual and ATIS domains. A detailed description of this system and its performance results are presented in Doran et al. (1994).

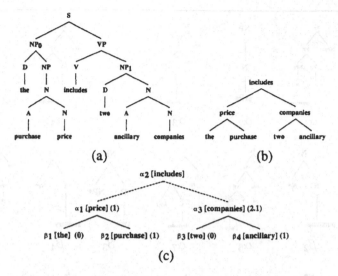

Figure 11.1 (a): Derived tree (b): Dependency tree for the sentence *the purchase price includes two ancillary companies* (c): Derivation structure

3 SUPERTAGS

The elementary trees of LTAG localize dependencies, including long distance dependencies, by requiring that all and only the dependent elements be present within the same tree. As a result of this localization, a lexical item may be (and almost always is) associated with more than one elementary tree. The example in Figure 11.2 illustrates the set of elementary trees assigned to each word of the sentence *the purchase price includes two ancillary companies*. We call these elementary trees *supertags*, since they contain more information (such as subcategorization and agreement information) than standard part-of-speech tags. Supertags for recursive and non-recursive constructs are labeled with βs and αs respectively.

The task of a lexicalized grammar parser can be viewed as a two step process. The first step is to select the appropriate supertags for each word of the input and the second step is to combine the selected supertags with substitution and adjunction operations. We call the first step as *supertagging*. Note that, as in standard part-of-speech disambiguation, supertagging could have been done by a parser. However, just as carrying out part-of-speech disambiguation prior to parsing makes the job of the parser much easier and therefore run faster, supertagging reduces the work of the parser even further. In Bangalore and Joshi (1999), we present a detailed discussion on supertagging, the models of supertag disambiguation and the effect of supertagging in speeding up a lexicalized grammar parser.

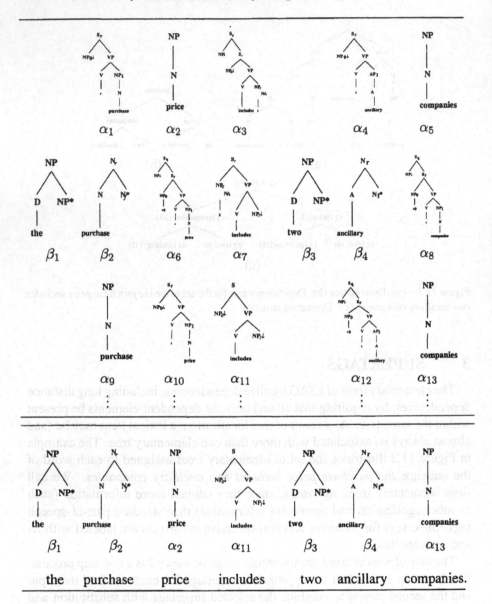

Figure 11.2   A selection of the supertags associated with each word of the sentence *the purchase price includes two ancillary companies*

More interesting is the fact that the result of supertagging is almost a parse in the sense that the parser need 'only' link the individual structures to arrive at a complete parse. We present such a simple linking procedure (*Lightweight*

Dependency Analyzer) in Section 5. This method can also be used to parse sentence fragments where it is not possible to combine the disambiguated supertag sequence into a single structure.

4 TRIGRAM MODEL FOR SUPERTAGGING

The task of supertagging is similar to part-of-speech tagging in that, given a set of tags for each word, the objective is to assign the appropriate tag to each word based on the context of the sentence. Owing to this similarity of supertagging to part-of-speech tagging, we use a trigram model (Church, 1988; Weischedel et al., 1993) to disambiguate supertags. The objective in a trigram model is to assign the most probable supertag sequence for a sentence given the approximation that the supertag for the current word is only influenced by the lexical preference of the current word and the contextual preference based on the supertags of the preceding two words.

Although it is quite evident, owing to the rich information present in supertags, that the dependencies between supertags can easily span beyond the trigram context, one of the goals of this work is to explore the limits of the trigram tagging approach. It appears that a CKY style dynamic programming model that takes advantage of the dependency requirements of each supertag may perform better for supertag disambiguation. However, such an approach is too much like parsing and the objective here is to see how much disambiguation can be done without really parsing.

The lexical and contextual preferences for the trigram model are estimated from a corpus of sentences where the words are tagged with the correct supertag. The estimates for unseen events are arrived at using a smoothing technique. We use the Good-Turing discounting technique (Good, 1953) combined with Katz's back-off model for smoothing. We use word features similar to the ones used in Weischedel et al. (1993), such as capitalization, hyphenation and endings of words, for estimating the unknown word probability. In conjunction with the word features, we exploit the organization of the supertags. The supertags are organized so that transformationally related supertags (indicative, passives, relative clauses, extraction supertags) are grouped into a single 'family'. Using this notion, if a word w_i in the training material appears with a supertag t_i which belongs to a tree family T, then w_i is associated with all the other members of the tree family T.

4.1 EXPERIMENTS AND RESULTS

As reported in Joshi and Srinivas (1994), we experimented with a trigram model for supertagging that was trained on (part-of-speech, supertag) pairs collected from the LTAG derivations of 5000 WSJ sentences and tested on 100 WSJ sentences produced a correct supertag for 68% of the words in the test set. We have since significantly improved the performance of the trigram model by making the model lexically sensitive, using a larger training set and incorporating smoothing techniques.

Table 11.1 shows the performance of the trigram model that was trained on two sets of Wall Street Journal data, 200K words[1] and 1000K words[2] and tested on 50K words[3]. The Treebank parses for the training and test sentences were converted into supertag representation using heuristics specified over parse tree contexts (parent, grandparent, children and sibling information)[4]. A total of 300 different supertags were used in these experiments. Supertag performance is measured as the percentage of words that are correctly supertagged by the model when compared against the supertags for the words in the test corpus.

Size of training set	Training	Size of test set	% Correct
200K	Unigram (Baseline)	50K	75.3%
	Trigram	50K	90.9%
1000K	Unigram (Baseline)	50K	77.2%
	Trigram	50K	92.2%

Table 11.1   Performance of the supertagger on the WSJ corpus

As mentioned earlier, the supertagger can be used as a front-end to a lex-icalized grammar parser so as to prune the search space of the parser even before parsing begins. Alternatively, the dependency information encoded in the supertagger can be used in conjunction with a simple linking procedure as a robust, fast and efficient partial parser. Such an approach can also be used to parse sentence fragments where it is not possible to combine the disambiguated supertag sequence into a single structure.

5   LIGHTWEIGHT DEPENDENCY ANALYZER

Supertagging associates each word with a unique supertag. To establish the dependency links among the words of the sentence, the Lightweight Dependency Analyzer (LDA) exploits the dependency requirements encoded in the supertags. Substitution nodes and foot nodes in supertags serve as slots that must be filled by the arguments of the anchor of the supertag. A substitution slot of a supertag is filled by the complements of the anchor while the foot node of a supertag is filled by a word that is being modified by the supertag. These argument slots have a polarity value reflecting their orientation with respect to the anchor of the supertag. Also associated with a supertag is a list of internal nodes (including the root node) that appear within the supertag. Using the structural information coupled with the argument requirements of a supertag, a simple algorithm such as the one below provides a method for annotating the sentence with dependency links.

> *Lightweight Dependency Analyzer*
> **Begin**
>   *For each* w_i in the sentence
>   *If* supertag s_i is a modifier supertag
>   *Compute Dependencies*(s_i,w_i)
>   Mark the words serving as complements of s_i.
>   *For each* w_i in the sentence
>   *If* supertag s_i is a non-recursive supertag
>   *Compute Dependencies*(s_i,w_i)
> **End**
>
> *Compute Dependencies* (s_i,w_i)
> **Begin**
>   *For each* slot d_{ij} in s_i
>   Link word w_i to the nearest word w_k to the left or right
>   of w_i depending on the direction of d_{ij}, skipping over
>   marked words, if any, such that $d_{ij} \in$ internal nodes(s_k)
> **End**

An example illustrating the output from this algorithm is shown in Table 11.2. The first column lists the word positions in the input, the second column lists the words, the third lists the names of the supertags assigned to each word by a supertagger. The slot requirement of each supertag is shown in column four and the dependency links among the words, computed by the above algorithm, is shown in the fifth column. The * and the . beside a number indicate the type of the dependency relation, * for modifier relation and . for complement relation.

6   EVALUATION OF SUPERTAG AND LDA SYSTEM

Due to the fact that our system produces a dependency annotated sentence as the output of the parsing process, parsing evaluation metrics that measure the performance of constituent bracketing such as Parseval (Harrison et al., 1991) are unsuitable. Although the supertags contain constituent information, and it is possible to convert a dependency linkage into a constituency based parse, the Parseval metric does not have provision for evaluating unrooted parse trees since the output of our system can result in disconnected dependency linkages.

Position	Word	Supertag	Slot requirement	Dependency links
0	The	β_1	+NP*	2*
1	purchase	β_2	+N*	2*
2	price	α_2	–	
3	includes	α_{11}	–NP. +NP.	2. 6.
4	two	β_3	+NP*	6*
5	ancillary	β_4	+N*	6*
6	companies	α_{13}	–	

Table 11.2 An example sentence with the supertags assigned to each word and dependency links among words

By contrast, we evaluate the performance of our system in terms of its ability to identify certain linguistic structures such as noun groups, verb groups, preposition attachments, appositive and parenthetical constructions. We compare the performance of our system to the performance of other systems specifically designed to identify these structures, when available. The results presented in this section are based on a trigram supertagger trained on 200K words of WSJ Sections 15 through 18 and tested on 50K words of Section 20.

6.1   TEXT CHUNKING USING SUPERTAGS

We have applied the supertag and Lightweight Dependency Analyzer system for text chunking. Text chunking, proposed by Abney (1991) involves partitioning a sentence into a set of non-overlapping segments. Text chunking serves as a useful and relatively tractable precursor to full parsing. Text chunks primarily consist of non-recursive noun and verb groups. The chunks are assumed to be minimal and hence non-recursive in structure.

Noun Chunking: Supertag based text chunking is performed by the local application of functor-argument information encoded in supertags. Once the head noun of the noun chunk is identified, the prenominal modifiers that are functors of the head noun or functors of the functors of the noun are included in the noun chunk. The head of a noun phrase is identified as the noun with a particular initial (non recursive) supertag (α) in the grammar. Based on that simple algorithm, we can identify noun chunks, for example, shown in (11.1) and (11.2).

(11.1) its increasingly rebellious citizens

(11.2) two $ 400 million real estate mortgage investment conduits

Ramshaw and Marcus (1995) present a transformation-based noun chunker that uses a learning scheme presented in Brill (1993). The performance of this noun chunker using rules with and without incorporating lexical information is shown in Table 11.3.

System	Training Size	Recall	Precision
Ramshaw & Marcus	Baseline	81.9%	78.2%
Ramshaw & Marcus (with lexical information)	200,000	92.3%	91.8%
Ramshaw & Marcus (with lexical information)	950,000	93.5%	93.1%
Supertags	Baseline	74.0%	58.4%
Supertags	200,000	93.0%	91.8%
Supertags	1,000,000	93.8%	92.5%

Table 11.3 Performance comparison of the transformation based noun chunker and the supertag based noun chunker

Table 11.3 also shows the performance of the supertag based noun chunking, trained and tested on the same texts as the transformation-based noun chunker. The supertag-based noun chunker performed better than the transformation-based noun chunker with lexical templates. Moreover, the supertag-based noun chunking not only identifies the extents of the noun chunks but by virtue of the functor-argument information, provides internal structure to the noun chunks. This internal structure of the noun chunks could be utilized during subsequent linguistic processing.

Verb Chunking: We also performed an experiment similar to noun chunking to identify verb chunks. We treat a sequence of verbs and verbal modifiers, including auxiliaries, adverbs, modals as constituting a verb group (shown in (11.3) and (11.4)).

(11.3) would not have been stymied

(11.4) just beginning to collect

Similar to noun chunking, verb chunking can be performed using local functor-argument information encoded in supertags. However, for verb chunks, the scan is made from left to right starting with a verbal modifier supertag, either an auxiliary verb or an adverbial supertag and including all functors of a verb or a verb modifier. The verb chunker performed at 86.5% recall and 91.4% precision.

Preposition Phrase Attachment: Supertags distinguish a noun-attached preposition from a verb-attached preposition in a sentence, as illustrated by the two different supertags in (11.5) and (11.6). Due to this distinction, the supertagging algorithm can be evaluated based on its ability to select the correct supertag for the prepositions in a text.

(11.5) sell 500 railcar platforms to/B_vxPnx Trailer Train Co. of/B_nxPnx Chicago

(11.6) begin delivery of/B_nxPnx goods in/B_vxPnx the first quarter

The supertagger makes the preposition disambiguation (choosing between B_vxPnx and B_nxPnx) based on a trigram context. It performs at 81.1% accuracy. More often than not the preposition is not within the same trigram window as the noun and the verb due to modifiers of the noun and the verb. Furthermore, the preposition disambiguation is carried out in an on-line fashion as part of the supertag disambiguation process, as opposed to the classifier-based solutions proposed in literature (Hindle and Rooth, 1991; Ratnaparkhi et al., 1994; Brill and Resnik, 1994; Collins and Brook, 1995) where the classifier is trained on at least the verb, noun and preposition triples.

6.1.1   Other Constructions. In this section, we summarize the performance of the supertagger in identifying constructions such as appositives, parentheticals, relative clauses and coordinating conjunctions.

Appositives: In the XTAG grammar, the appositive construction has been analyzed using a Noun Phrase modifying supertag that is anchored by a comma which takes the appositive Noun Phrase as an argument; for example, the comma in (11.7) and the second comma in (11.8) anchor appositive supertags. Thus, a comma in a sentence could either anchor an appositive supertag or a set of coordination supertags, one supertag for each type of coordination. Further, a comma also anchors supertags that mark parentheticals as in (11.9). The task of the supertagger is to disambiguate among the various supertags and assign the appropriate supertag to the comma, in the appositive context. In Table 11.4, we present the performance results of the supertagger on such a task. The baseline of assigning the most likely supertag to a comma results in zero percent recall.

Parentheticals: Propositional attitude verbs such as *say* and *believe* can not only appear in the canonical subject-verb-complement word order, but also at other positions in a sentence, as in (11.8) and (11.9). Also, the relative order of the subject and the verb can also be reversed as in (11.8). The XTAG grammar distinguishes such adverbial constructions from the sentence complement construction by assigning different supertags to the verb. A detailed analysis of this construction is presented in Doran (1996). The task of the supertagger is to disambiguate among the sentence complement supertag and the various adverbial supertags for the verb given the context of the sentence. Table 11.4 presents the performance results of the supertagger on this task. Once again the baseline of selecting the most likely supertag of the verb results in zero percent recall.

(11.7) Van Pell , 44

(11.8) 'The U.S. underestimated Noriega all along,' *says* Ambler Moss , a former Ambassador to Panama

(11.9) Mr. Noriega 's relationship to American intelligence agencies became contractual in either 1966 or 1967, intelligence officials *say*.

Construction	# of present	# identified	# correct	Recall	Precision
Appositive	362	491	306	84.5%	62.3%
Parentheticals	225	200	170	75.5%	85%
Coordination	1886	1750	1329	70.5%	75.9%
Relative Clauses	297	269	116	39.0%	43.2%
Relative Clauses (ignoring valency)	297	269	156	52.5%	58%

Table 11.4 Performance of the trigram supertagger on Appositive, Parenthetical, Coordination and Relative Clause constructions.

Coordination Conjunctions: In Table 11.4, we also present the performance of the supertagger in identifying coordination constructions. Coordination conjunctions anchor a supertag that requires two conjuncts, one on either side of the anchor. There is one supertag for every possible pair of conjunct types. We not only have supertags that coordinate like types, but we also include supertags that coordinate unlike types, amounting to about 30 different supertags for coordination.

Relative Clauses: Due to the extended domain of locality of LTAGs, verbs are associated with one relative clause supertag for each of the arguments of the verb. The task of the supertagger in LTAG is not only to identify that the verb is in a relative clause structure but also to identify the valency of the verb and the argument that is being relativized. The performance of the supertagger with and without the valency information being taken into account is presented in Table 11.4.

We are unaware of any other quantitative results on WSJ data for identifying these constructions, for comparative evaluation. It is interesting to note that the performance of the supertagger in identifying appositives and parenthetical constructions is better than for coordination conjunctions and relative clause constructions. We believe that this might in part be due to the fact that appositives and parentheticals can mostly be disambiguated using relatively local contexts. In contrast, disambiguation of coordinate constructions and relative clauses typically require large contexts that are not available for a trigram supertagger.

6.2   PERFORMANCE OF SUPERTAG AND LDA SYSTEM

In this section, we present results from two experiments using the supertagger in conjunction with the LDA system as a dependency parser. In order to evaluate the performance of this system, we need a dependency annotated corpus. However, the only annotated corpora we are aware of, the Penn Treebank (Marcus et al., 1993) and the SUSANNE corpus (Sampson, 1994), annotate sentences with constituency trees. In the interest of time and the need for a dependency annotated corpus, we decided to transform the constituency trees of the two corpora using some rules and heuristics. It must be noted that the resulting corpora only form an approximation to a manually annotated dependency corpus. However, although the annotation resulting from the transformation does not conform to a standard dependency annotation, it is nevertheless an invaluable resource for performance evaluation of dependency parsers.

To each constituent of a parse a head word is associated using the head percolation table introduced in Jelinek et al. (1994); Magerman (1995). The head percolation table associates with each possible constituent label an ordered list of possible children of the constituent whose head word is passed to the parent. The annotation of a parse tree with head word information proceeds bottom up. At any constituent, the percolation information is consulted to determine which of the constituent's children would pass the head word over to their parent. Once the head words are annotated, the dependency notation is generated by making the head words of non-head constituents to be dependent on the head of the head constituent. We converted in a similar way the subset of the LOB annotation of the SUSANNE corpus into a dependency notation.

In the first experiment, we use the dependency versions of the Penn Treebank annotation of the WSJ corpus and the LOB annotation of the SUSANNE corpus as gold standards. In the second experiment, however, we use derivation structures of WSJ sentences that were parsed using the XTAG system as the gold standard. The derivation structures serve as dependency structures that are closest in conventions to those assumed by the LDA system.

6.2.1   Experiment 1. The trigram supertagger trained on 200,000 words of the WSJ corpus was used in conjunction with the LDA to provide a dependency analysis for 2000 sentences of Section 20 of the WSJ corpus. The Penn Treebank parses for these sentences were converted into dependency notation which was used as the gold standard. A dependency link produced by the LDA was regarded to be correct if the words related by the link were also present in the gold standard. However, to account for the differences in the annotation, the dependency relations among words in a noun group were treated as equivalent to each other, as were the dependency relations among words in a verb group. There were 47,333 dependency links in the gold standard and the LDA produced 38,480 dependency links correctly, resulting in a recall score of 82.3%. Also, a total of 41,009 dependency links were produced by the LDA, resulting in a precision score of 93.8%.

We conducted a similar experiment using the SUSANNE corpus. Using the same trigram supertagger trained on the 200,000 words of the WSJ corpus in conjunction with the LDA, we provided a dependency analysis for the sentences in the SUSANNE corpus (125,000 words). The gold standard was created by converting the phrase structure annotations for these sentences into dependency notation using the procedure described above. As in the case of the WSJ corpus, to account for the differences in the annotation, the dependency relations among words in a noun group were treated as equivalent to each other, as were the dependency relations among words in a verb group. There were a total of 126,493 dependency links in the output of the LDA of which 112,420 were also present in the gold standard, resulting in a precision score of 88.8%. There were a total of 140,280 links in the gold standard, resulting in a recall of 80.1%. It is interesting to note that although the trigram model was trained on the WSJ corpus, the performance of the LDA on SUSANNE is comparable to the performance of the LDA on the WSJ corpus.

On analyzing the errors, we discovered that several of them were due to the approximate nature of the dependency corpus created by the conversion process. A second source of errors was due to the differences in the notion of dependency produced by the LDA system and that resulting from the conversion of the Treebank. This is largely due to a lack of a standard dependency notion.

Corpus	Dependency links	Links produced by LDA	Correct links	Recall	Precision
Brown	140,280	126,493	112,420	80.1%	88.8%
WSJ	47,333	41,009	38,480	82.3%	93.8%

Table 11.5 Comparative evaluation of LDA on Wall Street Journal and Brown Corpus

6.2.2   Experiment 2.   In this experiment we used the correct derivation structure produced by XTAG for 1350 WSJ sentences[5] as the gold standard. These sentences were supertagged using the supertagger trained on 8000 sentences of WSJ and dependency annotated using the LDA system. Table 11.6 shows the performance of the system. Although the derivation trees produced by the XTAG system are closest in terms of conventions used in the dependency output of the LDA system there are a few points of divergence, a major one being the annotation for sentence complement verbs. While in the LDA system the embedded verb depends on the matrix verb, the reverse is the case in an LTAG derivation structure. Also, since the XTAG system as it is implemented does not permit two auxiliary trees to be adjoined at the same node, certain valid derivation structures are not possible in XTAG. A precise formulation of possible derivation structures in the LTAG framework is presented in Schabes and Shieber (1992).

Training Size (words)	Test Size (words)	Recall	Precision
200,000	12,000	83.6%	83.5%

Table 11.6 Performance the of LDA system compared against XTAG derivation structures

% sentences with 0 errors	% sentences with ≤1 error	% sentences with ≤ 2 errors	%sentences with ≤3 errors
35%	60.3%	78%	89.8%

Table 11.7 The percentage of sentences with zero, one, two and three dependency link errors.

Table 11.7 tabulates the percentage of sentences that have zero, one, two and three dependency link errors. In contrast to evaluation against a skeletally bracketed treebank, evaluation against LTAG derivation trees is much more strict. For example, an LTAG derivation contains detailed annotation in terms of the internal structure of the nominal modifiers in noun phrases and verbal modifiers in verb groups. Also, a derivation structure has a stricter imposition of the argument-adjunct distinction and distinguishes readings that have similar phrase structure trees such as predicative and equative readings and idiomatic and non-idiom readings of a sentence. Further, the derivation structure is much closer to the semantic interpretation of a sentence than the phrase structure. Hence the performance figures that are shown in Table 11.6 and Table 11.7 are more strict and hence more significant than the crossing bracket precision and recall figures measured against skeletally bracketed corpora.

7 NEW MODELS FOR SUPERTAG DISAMBIGUATION

In recent work (Chen et al., 1999), a variety of novel models have been explored that improve the performance of supertagging. These models can be categorized as contextual models and class-based models. The contextual models improve supertag performance by combining a variety of features from the context and exploiting the distinction between initial and auxiliary supertags. These contextual models have been combined using voting strategies to provide an error reduction of 9.5% over trigram models. In contrast to contextual models, class-based models improve supertagging performance by assigning words with sets of supertags, thus trading supertag ambiguity for improved accuracy. Different classes of supertags have been derived based on structural properties and also based on an analysis of confusion pairs produced by the trigram model. With a slight increase in supertag ambiguity, 1.3 supertags per word, an error reduction of 45% has been achieved over the trigram model and with 3.8 supertags per word, the error reduction is 65% over a trigram model.

8 SUMMARY

We have presented the trigram model for supertagging in conjunction with a lightweight dependency analyzer as a robust and efficient partial parser. One of the goals of this work is to explore the limits of the trigram tagging approach and to see how much supertag disambiguation can be done without really parsing. A significant result of the current work is that a trigram model can achieve 92% accuracy for supertagging. Second, we have shown how the disambiguated supertags can be used for partial parsing, detecting noun chunks, verb chunks, preposition phrase attachment, appositives and parenthetical constructions. Using supertags, we have achieved a recall rate of 93.0% and a precision rate of 91.8% for noun chunking.

Acknowledgments

We would like to thank Aravind Joshi for the continued support and discussions during the period of this work. We also thank Christine Doran, Raman Chandrasekar and Beth Ann Hockey for help in creating the data used in the experiments.

Notes

1. Sentences in WSJ Sections 15 through 18 of the Penn Treebank.
2. Sentences in WSJ Sections 00 through 24, except Section 20 of the Penn Treebank.
3. Sentences in WSJ Section 20 of the Penn Treebank.
4. An example of the heuristics is given in Srinivas, 1997.
5. Sentences of length less than 16.

References

Abney, S. (1991). Parsing by chunks. In Berwick, R., Abney, S., and Tenny, C., editors, *Principle-based parsing*. Dordrecht: Kluwer Academic Publishers.

Bangalore, S and Joshi, A.K. (1999). SuperTagging - An Approach to Almost Parsing. *Computational Linguistics*, 25:237–265.

Brill, E. (1993). Automatic grammar induction and parsing free text: A transformation based approach. In *Proceedings of the 31st Annual Meeting of the Association for Computational Linguistics*, Columbus, Ohio.

Brill, E. and Resnik, P. (1994). A rule-based approach to prepositional phrase attachment disambiguation. In *Proceedings of the International Conference on Computational Linguistics (COLING '94)*, Kyoto, Japan.

Chen, J and Bangalore, S and Vijay-Shanker, K. (1999). New Models for Improving Supertag Disambiguation. In *Proceedings of 9th Conference of the European Chapter of Association for Computational Linguistics*, Bergen, Norway,1999.

Church, K. W. (1988). A Stochastic Parts Program and Noun Phrase Parser for Unrestricted Text. In *2nd Applied Natural Language Processing Conference*, Austin, Texas.

Collins, M. and Brook, J. (1995). Prepositional phrase attachment through a backed-off model. In *Proceedings of the Third Workshop on Very Large Corpora*, MIT, Cambridge, Boston.

Doran, C. (1996). Punctuation in Quoted Speech. In *Proceedings of the SIG-PARSE 96, workshop on Punctuation*, Santa Cruz, California.

Doran, C., Egedi, D., Hockey, B. A., Srinivas, B., and Zaidel, M. (1994). XTAG System - A Wide Coverage Grammar for English. In *Proceedings of* the 17th *International Conference on Computational Linguistics (COLING '94)*, Kyoto, Japan.

Good, I. (1953). The population frequencies of species and the estimation of population parameters. *Biometrika 40 (3 and 4)*.

Gross, M. (1984). Lexicon-Grammar and the Syntactic Analysis of French. In *Proceedings of the 10th International Conference on Computational Linguistics (COLING'84)*, Stanford, California.

Harrison, P., Abney, S., Flickinger, D., Gdaniec, C., Grishman, R., Hindle, D., Ingria, B., Marcus, M., Santorini, B., and Strzalkowski, T. (1991). Evaluating syntax performance of parser/grammars of English. In *Proceedings of the ACL Workshop on Evaluating Natural Language Processing Systems, ACL.*

Hindle, D. and Rooth, M. (1991). Structural ambiguity and lexical relations. In *29th Meeting of the Association for Computational Linguistics*, Berkeley, CA.

Jelinek, F., Lafferty, J., Magerman, D. M., Mercer, R., Ratnaparkhi, A., and Roukos, S. (1994). Decision Tree Parsing using a Hidden Derivation Model. In *Proceedings of the ARPA Workshop on Human Language Technology*, Plainsborough, NJ.

Joshi, A. K. (1985). Tree Adjoining Grammars: How much context sensitivity is required to provide a reasonable structural description. In Dowty, D., Karttunen, I., and Zwicky, A., editors, *Natural Language Parsing*, pp. 206–250. Cambridge University Press, Cambridge, U.K.

Joshi, A. K. and Srinivas, B. (1994). Disambiguation of Super Parts of Speech (or Supertags): Almost Parsing. In *Proceedings of the 17th International Conference on Computational Linguistics (COLING '94)*, Kyoto, Japan.

Magerman, D. M. (1995). Statistical Decision-Tree Models for Parsing. In *Proceedings of the 33rd Annual Meeting of the Association for Computational Linguistics*.

Marcus, M. M., Santorini, B., and Marcinkiewicz, M. A. (1993). Building a Large Annotated Corpus of English: The Penn Treebank. *Computational Linguistics*, 19.2:313–330.

Pollard, C. and Sag, I. A. (1987). *Information-Based Syntax and Semantics. Vol 1: Fundamentals. CSLI.*

Ramshaw, L. and Marcus, M. P. (1995). Text chunking using transformation-based learning. In *Proceedings of the Third Workshop on Very Large Corpora*, MIT, Cambridge, Boston.

Ratnaparkhi, A., Reynar, J., and Roukos, S. (1994). A maximum entropy model for prepositional phrase attachment. In *Proceedings of ARPA Workshop on Human Language Technology*, Plainsboro, NJ.

Sampson, G. (1994). SUSANNE: a Doomsday book of English Grammar. In *Corpus-based Research into Language*. Rodopi, Amsterdam.

Schabes, Y., Abeillé, A., and Joshi, A. K. (1988). Parsing strategies with 'lexicalized' grammars: Application to Tree Adjoining Grammars. In *Proceedings of the 12th International Conference on Computational Linguistics (COLING'88)*, Budapest, Hungary.

Schabes, Y. and Shieber, S. (1992). An Alternative Conception of Tree-Adjoining Derivation. In *Proceedings of the 20th Meeting of the Association for Computational Linguistics*.

Sleator, D. and Temperley, D. (1991). Parsing English with a Link Grammar. *Technical report CMU-CS-91-196, Department of Computer Science, Carnegie Mellon University*.

Srinivas, B. (1997). Complexity of Lexical Descriptions and its Relevance to Partial Parsing. *PhD Dissertation, University of Pennsylvania*.

Steedman, M. (1987). Combinatory Grammars and Parasitic Gaps. *Natural Language and Linguistic Theory*, 5:403–439.

Weischedel, R., Schwartz, R., Palmucci, J., Meteer, M., and Ramshaw, L. (1993). Coping with ambiguity and unknown words through probabilistic models. *Computational Linguistics*, 19.2:359–382.

Chapter 12

REGULAR APPROXIMATION OF CFLS: A GRAMMATICAL VIEW

Mark-Jan Nederhof
DFKI, Stuhlsatzenhausweg 3, D-66123 Saarbrücken, Germany
nederhof@dfki.de

Abstract   We show that for each context-free grammar a new grammar can be constructed that generates a regular language. This construction differs from some existing methods of approximation in that use of a pushdown automaton is avoided. This allows better insight into how the generated language is affected.

1   INTRODUCTION

In existing literature, a number of methods have been proposed for approximating a context-free language (CFL) by means of a regular language. Some of these methods were expressed in terms of 1) a construction of a pushdown automaton from the grammar, where the language accepted by the automaton is identical to the language generated by the grammar, and 2) an approximation of that pushdown automaton, expressed in terms of a finite automaton.

Pushdown automata manipulate stacks, and the set of different stacks that may need to be considered for processing of different input strings is potentially infinite, and due to this fact, a pushdown automaton may accept a language that is not regular. The approximation process now consists in reducing the infinite set of stacks that are distinguished by the pushdown automaton to a finite set, and thus a finite automaton results. As will be explained later, there are roughly two ways of achieving this, the first leading to regular languages that are subsets of the original context-free languages (Krauwer and des Tombe, 1981; Langendoen and Langsam, 1987; Pulman, 1986; Johnson, 1998), the second leading instead to supersets (Baker, 1981; Bermudez and Schimpf, 1990; Pereira and Wright, 1997).

A disadvantage of this kind of approximation is that it is difficult to understand or to influence how a language is changed in the process. This holds in

221

H. Bunt and A. Nijholt (eds.), Advances in Probabilistic and Other Parsing Technologies, 221–241.

particular for methods of approximation that make use of a nontrivial construction of pushdown automata from grammars. An example is the construction of LR recognizers (Sippu and Soisalon-Soininen, 1990). The structure of a grammar is very different from the structure of the LR automaton constructed from it. How subsequent manipulation of the LR automaton affects the language in terms of the grammar is very difficult to see, and there seems to be no obvious way to make adjustments to the approximation process.

In this chapter we present an approximation that avoids the use of pushdown automata altogether, and which can be summarized as follows. We define a condition on context-free grammars that is a sufficient condition for a grammar to generate a regular language. We then give a transformation that turns an arbitrary grammar into another grammar that satisfies this condition. This transformation is obviously not language-preserving; it adds strings to the language generated by the original grammar, in such a way that the language becomes regular.

The structure of this chapter is as follows. In Section 2 we recall some standard definitions from formal language theory. Section 3 investigates a sufficient condition for a context-free grammar to generate a regular language. An algorithm to transform a grammar such that this condition is satisfied is given in Section 4.

As Section 5 shows, some aspects of our method are undecidable. A refinement for obtaining more precise approximations is presented in Section 6. Section 7 compares our method to other methods. Conclusions are found in Section 8.

2   PRELIMINARIES

A *context-free grammar* G is a 4-tuple (Σ, N, P, S), where Σ and N are two finite disjoint sets of terminals and nonterminals, respectively, $S \in N$ is the start symbol, and P is a finite set of rules. Each rule has the form $A \rightarrow \alpha$ with $A \in N$ and $\alpha \in V^*$, where V denotes $N \cup \Sigma$. The relation $\rightarrow$ on $N \times V^*$ is extended to a relation on $V^* \times V^*$ as usual. The transitive and reflexive closure of $\rightarrow$ is denoted by $\rightarrow^*$.

The language *generated* by G is given by the set $\{w \in \Sigma^* \mid S \rightarrow^* w\}$. By definition, such a set is a *context-free language*. By *reduction* of a grammar we mean the elimination from P of all rules $A \rightarrow \gamma$ such that $S \rightarrow^* \alpha A \beta \rightarrow \alpha \gamma \beta \rightarrow^* w$ does not hold for any $\alpha, \beta \in V^*$ and $w \in \Sigma^*$.

We generally use symbols $A, B, C, \ldots$ to range over N, symbols $a, b, c, \ldots$ to range over Σ, symbols X, Y, Z to range over V, symbols $\alpha, \beta, \gamma, \ldots$ to range over V^*, and symbols $v, w, x, \ldots$ to range over Σ^*. We write ϵ to denote the empty string.

$$S \rightarrow (: S * S :)$$
$$S \rightarrow (: S + S :)$$
$$S \rightarrow 0$$

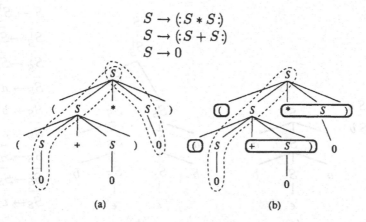

Figure 12.1 (a) two spines in a parse tree, (b) the grammar symbols to the left and right of a spine immediately dominated by nodes on the spine.

A rule of the form $A \rightarrow B$ is called a *unit* rule, a rule of the form $A \rightarrow \epsilon$ is called an *epsilon* rule. A grammar is called *cyclic* if $A \rightarrow^* A$, for some A.

A (nondeterministic) *finite automaton* $\mathcal{F}$ is a 5-tuple $(K, \Sigma, \Delta, s, F)$, where K is a finite set of *states*, of which s is the *initial state* and those in $F \subseteq K$ are the *final states*, Σ is the input alphabet, and the *transition relation* Δ is a finite subset of $K \times \Sigma^* \times K$.

We define a *configuration* to be an element of $K \times \Sigma^*$. We define the binary relation $\vdash$ between configurations as: $(q, vw) \vdash (q', w)$ if and only if $(q, v, q') \in \Delta$. The transitive and reflexive closure of $\vdash$ is denoted by $\vdash^*$.

Some input v is *recognized* if $(s, v) \vdash^* (q, \epsilon)$, for some $q \in F$. The language *accepted* by $\mathcal{F}$ is defined to be the set of all strings v that are recognized. By definition, a language accepted by a finite automaton is called a *regular language*.

3   THE STRUCTURE OF PARSE TREES

We define a *spine* in a parse tree to be a path that runs from the root down to some leaf. Figure 12.1 (a) indicates two spines in a parse tree for the string $((0 + 0) * 0)$, according to a simple grammar.

Our main interest in spines lies in the sequences of grammar symbols at nodes bordering on spines. Figure 12.1 (b) gives an example: to the left of the spine we find the sequence '((' and to the right we find '$+S) * S$)'. The way that such pairs of sequences may relate to each other determines the strength of context-free grammars and, as we will see later, by restricting this relationship we may reduce the generative power of context-free grammars to the regular languages.

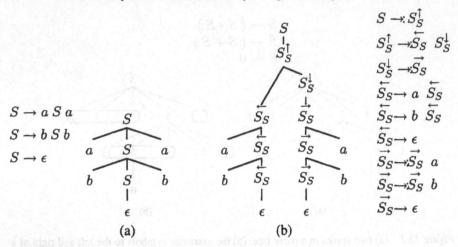

Figure 12.2 Parse trees for a palindrome: (a) original grammar, (b) transformed grammar (Section 4).

A simpler example is the set of parse trees such as the one in Figure 12.2 (a), for a 3-line grammar of palindromes. It is intuitively clear that the language is not regular: The grammar symbols to the left of the spine from the root to ϵ 'communicate' with those to the right of the spine. More precisely, the prefix of the input up to the point where it meets the final node ϵ of the spine determines the suffix after that point, in a way that an unbounded number of symbols from the prefix need to be taken into account.

A formal explanation for why the grammar may not generate a regular language relies on the following definition, due to Chomsky (1959):

Definition 1 *A grammar is* self-embedding *if there is some $A \in N$, such that $A \to^* \alpha A \beta$, for some $\alpha \neq \epsilon$ and $\beta \neq \epsilon$.*

In order to avoid the somewhat unfortunate term *nonself-embedding* (or *non-center-embedding*, as in Langendoen (1975) we define a *strongly regular* grammar to be a grammar that is not self-embedding. Strong regularity informally means that when a section of a spine in a parse tree repeats itself, then either no grammar symbols occur to the left of that section of the spine, or no grammar symbols occur to the right. This prevents the 'unbounded communication' between the two sides of the spine exemplified by the palindrome grammar.

Obviously, right linear and left linear grammars (as known from standard literature such as Hopcroft and Ullman (1979) are strongly regular. That right linear and left linear grammars generate regular languages is easy to show. That strongly regular grammars also generate regular languages will be proved shortly.

First, for an arbitrary grammar, we define the set of *recursive* nonterminals as:

$$\overline{N} = \{A \in N \mid \exists \alpha, \beta [A \to^* \alpha A \beta]\}$$

We determine the partition $\mathcal{N}$ of $\overline{N}$ consisting of subsets $N_1, N_2, \ldots, N_n$, for some $n \geq 0$, of *mutually recursive* nonterminals:

$$\mathcal{N} = \{N_1, N_2, \ldots, N_n\}$$
$$N_1 \cup N_2 \cup \ldots \cup N_n = \overline{N}$$
$$\forall i [N_i \neq \emptyset] \text{ and } \forall i, j [i \neq j \Rightarrow N_i \cap N_j = \emptyset]$$
$$\exists i [A \in N_i \wedge B \in N_i] \iff \exists \alpha_1, \beta_1, \alpha_2, \beta_2 [A \to^* \alpha_1 B \beta_1 \wedge B \to^* \alpha_2 A \beta_2],$$
$$\text{for all } A, B \in \overline{N}$$

We now define the function *recursive* from $\mathcal{N}$ to the set $\{left, right, self, cyclic\}$. For $1 \leq i \leq n$:

$$
\begin{aligned}
recursive(N_i) &= left, &\text{if } &\neg LeftGenerating(N_i) \;\wedge \\
& & &RightGenerating(N_i) \\
&= right, &\text{if } &LeftGenerating(N_i) \;\wedge \\
& & &\neg RightGenerating(N_i) \\
&= self, &\text{if } &LeftGenerating(N_i) \;\wedge \\
& & &RightGenerating(N_i) \\
&= cyclic, &\text{if } &\neg LeftGenerating(N_i) \;\wedge \\
& & &\neg RightGenerating(N_i)
\end{aligned}
$$

where

$$LeftGenerating(N_i) = \exists (A \to \alpha B \beta) \in P [A \in N_i \wedge B \in N_i \wedge \alpha \neq \epsilon]$$
$$RightGenerating(N_i) = \exists (A \to \alpha B \beta) \in P [A \in N_i \wedge B \in N_i \wedge \beta \neq \epsilon]$$

When $recursive(N_i) = left$, N_i consists of only left-recursive nonterminals, which does not mean it cannot also contain right-recursive nonterminals, but in that case right recursion amounts to application of unit rules. When $recursive(N_i) = cyclic$, it is *only* such unit rules that take part in the recursion.

That $recursive(N_i) = self$, for some i, is a sufficient and necessary condition for the grammar to be self-embedding. We only prove this in one direction: Suppose we have two rules $A_1 \to \alpha_1 B_1 \beta_1$, $A_1, B_1 \in N_i$, and $A_2 \to \alpha_2 B_2 \beta_2$, $A_2, B_2 \in N_i$, such that $\alpha_1 \neq \epsilon$ and $\beta_2 \neq \epsilon$. This means that $A_1 \to \alpha_1 B_1 \beta_1 \to^* \alpha_1 \alpha_1' A_2 \beta_1' \beta_1 \to \alpha_1 \alpha_1' \alpha_2 B_2 \beta_2 \beta_1' \beta_1 \to^* \alpha_1 \alpha_1' \alpha_2 \alpha_2' A_1 \beta_2' \beta_2 \beta_1' \beta_1$, for some $\alpha_1', \beta_1', \alpha_2', \beta_2'$, making use of the assumption that B_1 and A_2, and then B_2 and A_1 are in the same subset N_i of mutually recursive nonterminals. In the final sentential form we have $\alpha_1 \alpha_1' \alpha_2 \alpha_2' \neq \epsilon$ and $\beta_2' \beta_2 \beta_1' \beta_1 \neq \epsilon$, and therefore the grammar is self-embedding.

A set N_i such that $recursive(N_i) = self$ thus provides an isolated aspect of the grammar that causes self-embedding, and therefore making the grammar strongly regular will depend on a solution for how to transform the part of the grammar in which nonterminals from N_i occur.

We now prove that a grammar that is strongly regular (or in other words, for all i, $recursive(N_i) \in \{left, right, cyclic\}$) generates a regular language. Our proof differs from a proof of the same fact in Chomsky (1959a) in that it is fully constructive: Figure 12.3 presents an algorithm for creating a finite automaton that accepts the language generated by the grammar.

The process is initiated at the start symbol, and from there the process descends the grammar in all ways until terminals are encountered, and then transitions are created labelled with those terminals. Descending the grammar is straightforward in the case of rules of which the left-hand side is not a recursive nonterminal: the groups of transitions found recursively for members in the right-hand side will be connected. In the case of recursive nonterminals, the process depends on whether the nonterminals in the corresponding set from $\mathcal{N}$ are mutually left-recursive or right-recursive; if they are both, which means they are cyclic, then either subprocess can be applied; in the code in Figure 12.3 cyclic and right-recursive subsets N_i are treated uniformly.

We discuss the case that the nonterminals are left-recursive. (The converse case is left to the imagination of the reader.) One new state is created for each nonterminal in the set. The transitions that are created for terminals and nonterminals not in N_i are connected in a way that is reminiscent of the construction of left-corner parsers (Rosenkrantz and Lewis II, 1970), and specifically of one construction that focuses on groups of mutually recursive nonterminals (Nederhof, 1994a, Section 5.8).

An example is given in Figure 12.4. Four states have been labelled according to the names they are given in procedure *make_fa*. There are two states that are labelled q_B. This can be explained by the fact that nonterminal B can be reached by descending the grammar from S in two essentially distinct ways.

4   APPROXIMATING A CONTEXT-FREE LANGUAGE

Now that we know what makes a context-free grammar violate a sufficient condition for the generated language to be regular, we have a good starting point to investigate how we should change a grammar in order to obtain a regular language. The intuition is that the 'unbounded communication' between the left and right sides of spines is broken.

We concentrate on the sets N_i with $recursive(N_i) = self$. For each set separately, we apply the transformation in Figure 12.5. Thereafter the grammar will be strongly regular. We will explain the transformation by means of two examples.

let $K = \emptyset$, $\Delta = \emptyset$, $s = fresh\_state$, $f = fresh\_state$, $F = \{f\}$;
make fa(s, S, f).
procedure make fa(q_0, α, q_1):
  if $\alpha = \epsilon$
  then let $\Delta = \Delta \cup \{(q_0, \epsilon, q_1)\}$
  elseif $\alpha = a$, *some* $a \in \Sigma$
  then let $\Delta = \Delta \cup \{(q_0, a, q_1)\}$
  elseif $\alpha = X\beta$, *some* $X \in V$, $\beta \in V^*$ *such that* $|\beta| > 0$
  then let $q = fresh\_state$;
    make fa(q_0, X, q);
    make fa(q, β, q_1)
  else let $A = \alpha$;   (* α *must consist of a single nonterminal* *)
    if $A \in N_i$, *some* i
    then for each $B \in N_i$ *do let* $q_B = fresh\_state$ *end*;
      if recursive$(N_i) = left$
      then for each $(C \rightarrow X_1 \ldots X_m) \in P$ *such that*
          $C \in N_i \wedge X_1, \ldots, X_m \notin N_i$
        do make fa$(q_0, X_1 \ldots X_m, q_C)$ *end*;
        for each $(C \rightarrow DX_1 \ldots X_m) \in P$ *such that*
          $C, D \in N_i \wedge X_1, \ldots, X_m \notin N_i$
        do make fa$(q_D, X_1 \ldots X_m, q_C)$ *end*;
        let $\Delta = \Delta \cup \{(q_A, \epsilon, q_1)\}$
      else 'the converse of the then-part'
                  (* *recursive*$(N_i) \in \{right, cyclic\}$ *)
      end
      else for each $(A \rightarrow \beta) \in P$ *do make fa*(q_0, β, q_1) *end*
                  (* A *is not recursive* *)
    end
  end
end.
procedure fresh_state():
  create some fresh object q;
  let $K = K \cup \{q\}$;
  return q
end.

Figure 12.3 Mapping from a strongly regular grammar $G = (\Sigma, N, P, S)$ into an equivalent finite automaton $\mathcal{F} = (K, \Sigma, \Delta, s, F)$.

We first discuss the special case that each nonterminal can lead to at most one recursive call of itself, which holds for *linear* context-free grammars (Hopcroft and Ullman, 1979). Consider the grammar of palindromes in the left

$$S \rightarrow Aa$$
$$A \rightarrow SB \qquad \overline{N} = \{S, A, B\}$$
$$\qquad\qquad\qquad \mathcal{N} = \{N_1, N_2\}$$
$$A \rightarrow Bb \qquad N_1 = \{S, A\}$$
$$B \rightarrow Bc \qquad N_2 = \{B\}$$
$$B \rightarrow d$$

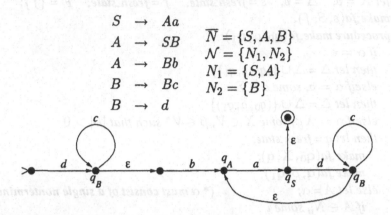

Figure 12.4   Application of the code from Figure 12.3 to a small grammar.

half of Figure 12.2. The approximation algorithm leads to the grammar in the right half. Figure 12.2 (b) shows the effect on the structure of parse trees. Note that the left sides of former spines are treated by the new nonterminal $\overleftarrow{S_S}$ and the right sides by the new nonterminal $\overrightarrow{S_S}$.

The general case is more complicated. A nonterminal A may lead to several recursive occurrences: $A \rightarrow^* \alpha A \beta A \gamma$. As before, our approach is to approximate the language by separating the left and right sides of spines, but in this case, several spines in a single parse tree may need to be taken care of at once.

As a presentation of this case in a pictorial way, Figure 12.6 (a) suggests a part of a parse tree in which all (labels of the) nodes belong to the same set N_i, where *recursive*$(N_i) = self$. Other nodes in the direct vicinity of the depicted part of the parse tree we assume not to be in N_i; the triangles $\triangle$, for example, denote a mother node in N_i and a number of daughter nodes *not* in N_i. The dotted lines labelled $p1, p3, p5, p7$ represent paths along nodes in N_i such that the nodes to the left of the visited nodes are not in N_i. In the case of $p2, p4, p6, p8$ the nodes to the right of the visited nodes are not in N_i.

The effect of our transformation on the structure of the parse tree is suggested in Figure 12.6 (b). We see that the left and right sides of spines (e.g. $p1$ and $p2$) are disconnected, in the same way as 'unbounded communication' between the two sides of spines was broken in our earlier example of the palindrome grammar.

Consider now the following grammar for mathematical expressions:

$$S \rightarrow A * B$$
$$A \rightarrow (A + B)$$
$$A \rightarrow a$$

Assume the grammar is $G = (\Sigma, N, P, S)$. The following is to be performed for some fixed set $N_i \in \mathcal{N}$ such that $recursive(N_i) = self$.

1. Add the following nonterminals to N: $A_B^\uparrow, A_B^\downarrow, \overleftarrow{A_B}$ and $\overrightarrow{A_B}$ for all pairs of $A, B \in N_i$.

2. Add the following rules to P, for all $A, B, C, D, E \in N_i$:

   - $A \to A_A^\uparrow$;

   - $A_B^\uparrow \to \overleftarrow{A_C} X_1 \ldots X_m C_B^\downarrow$, for all $(C \to X_1 \ldots X_m) \in P$, with $X_1, \ldots, X_m \notin N_i$;

   - $A_B^\downarrow \to \overrightarrow{C_A} X_1 \ldots X_m E_B^\uparrow$, for all $(D \to \alpha C X_1 \ldots X_m E \beta) \in P$, with $X_1, \ldots, X_m \notin N_i$;

   - $A_B^\downarrow \to \overrightarrow{B_A}$;

   - $\overleftarrow{A_B} \to X_1 \ldots X_m \overleftarrow{C_B}$, for all $(A \to X_1 \ldots X_m C \beta) \in P$, with $X_1, \ldots, X_m \notin N_i$;

   - $\overleftarrow{A_A} \to \epsilon$;

   - $\overrightarrow{A_B} \to \overrightarrow{C_B} X_1 \ldots X_m$, for all $(A \to \alpha C X_1 \ldots X_m) \in P$, with $X_1, \ldots, X_m \notin N_i$;

   - $\overrightarrow{A_A} \to \epsilon$.

3. Remove from P the old rules of the form $A \to \alpha$, where $A \in N_i$.

4. Reduce the grammar.

Figure 12.5 Approximation by transforming the grammar, given a set N_i.

$$B \to [A]$$
$$B \to b$$

We have $\overline{N} = \{A, B\}$, $\mathcal{N} = \{N_1\}$, $N_1 = \{A, B\}$, and $recursive(N_1) = self$. After applying the approximation algorithm to N_1 we obtain the grammar in Figure 12.7. We emphasize that the transformed grammar in the figure has already been reduced.

Comparing this example to the general picture in Figure 12.6 (b), we conclude that a nonterminal such as $\overleftarrow{B_A}$ derives paths such as $p1, p3, p5$ or $p7$,

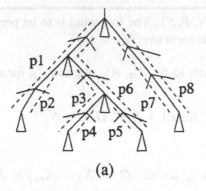

(a)

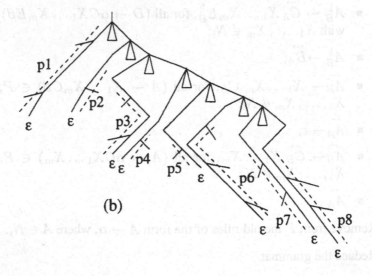

(b)

Figure 12.6   The general effect of the transformation on the structure of parse trees.

where B was the top label at the path in the original parse tree and A occurred at the bottom. A similar fact holds for nonterminals such as $\vec{B}_A$. Nonterminals such as $B_A^\uparrow$ and $B_A^\downarrow$ indicate that the root of the complete subtree was labelled A, and that the last node of the tree that was treated is labelled B; in the case of $B_A^\uparrow$ that node is at the top of a path such as $p1, p3, p5$ or $p7$ in the original tree, in the case of $B_A^\downarrow$ that node is at the bottom of a path such as $p2, p4, p6$ or $p8$.

5   LIMITATIONS

It is undecidable whether the language generated by a context-free grammar is regular (Harrison, 1978). Consequently, the condition of strong regularity, which is decidable and is a sufficient condition for the language to be regular,

$$S \to A * B \qquad A_A^\downarrow \to \overrightarrow{A_A} + B_A^\uparrow \qquad \overleftarrow{A_A} \to (\,\overleftarrow{A_A} \qquad \overrightarrow{A_A} \to \overrightarrow{B_A}\,)$$

$$A \to A_A^\uparrow \qquad B_A^\downarrow \to \overrightarrow{A_B} + B_A^\uparrow \qquad \overleftarrow{B_A} \to [\,\overleftarrow{A_A} \qquad \overrightarrow{A_B} \to \overrightarrow{B_B}\,)$$

$$B \to B_B^\uparrow \qquad A_B^\downarrow \to \overrightarrow{A_A} + B_B^\uparrow \qquad \overleftarrow{A_A} \to \epsilon \qquad \overrightarrow{B_A} \to \overrightarrow{A_A}\,]$$

$$A_A^\uparrow \to \overleftarrow{A_A}\, a\, A_A^\uparrow \qquad B_B^\downarrow \to \overrightarrow{A_B} + B_B^\uparrow \qquad \overleftarrow{B_B} \to \epsilon \qquad \overrightarrow{B_B} \to \overrightarrow{A_B}\,]$$

$$B_A^\uparrow \to \overleftarrow{B_A}\, a\, A_A^\downarrow \qquad A_A^\downarrow \to \overrightarrow{A_A} \qquad\qquad \overrightarrow{A_A} \to \epsilon$$

$$B_B^\uparrow \to \overleftarrow{B_A}\, a\, A_B^\downarrow \qquad B_A^\downarrow \to \overrightarrow{A_B} \qquad\qquad \overrightarrow{B_B} \to \epsilon$$

$$B_A^\uparrow \to \overleftarrow{B_B}\, b\, B_A^\downarrow \qquad A_B^\downarrow \to \overrightarrow{B_A}$$

$$B_B^\uparrow \to \overleftarrow{B_B}\, b\, B_B^\downarrow \qquad B_B^\downarrow \to \overrightarrow{B_B}$$

Figure 12.7 Transformed grammar, resulting from application of Figure 12.5.

cannot also be a necessary condition. This is demonstrated by the following grammar:[1]

$$
\begin{aligned}
S &\to a\,A \mid B\,a \mid C \\
A &\to a\,A \mid C \\
B &\to B\,a \mid C \\
C &\to a\,C\,a \mid c
\end{aligned}
$$

This (non-ambiguous) grammar generates the regular language $a^* c a^*$. Yet it is not strongly regular, due to the cycle pertaining to the rule $C \to a : C : a$. Fortunately, our algorithm transforms this grammar into a strongly regular one which generates the same language $a^* c a^*$.

In some cases, a grammar that is not strongly regular but that generates a regular language is transformed into one that generates a strictly larger language. This cannot be prevented however by any method of superset approximation, since transforming a context-free grammar generating a regular language into a finite automaton accepting the same language is an unsolvable problem (Ullian, 1967).

A simple example where our method has this undesirable behaviour is the following:

$$S \to a S a \mid a S b \mid b S a \mid b S b \mid \epsilon$$

This grammar generates the regular language of all strings over $\{a, b\}$ of even length. Our approximation however results in the exact same grammar as in the example of palindromes. This grammar generates the regular language of *all* strings over $\{a, b\}$ — not only those of even length.[2]

If we represent context-free languages by means of pushdown automata (see also Section 7), we can define a subclass for which regularity is decidable, namely those that allow a deterministic pushdown automaton. If such a deterministic language is regular, we can furthermore construct an equivalent deterministic finite automaton (Stearns, 1967). It turns out that even for this restricted class of context-free languages, the construction of equivalent finite automata is quite complex: The number of states of the (deterministic) finite automata may be a double exponential function in the size of the original deterministic pushdown automata (Meyer and Fischer, 1971; Valiant, 1975).

For arbitrary context-free grammars that generate regular languages, no recursive function in the size of grammars exists that provides an upper bound to the number of states of equivalent finite automata (Meyer and Fischer, 1971).

6   REFINEMENT

Our approximation algorithm is such that the two sides of spines are disconnected for all nonterminals that are involved in self-embedding (i.e. those in some fixed N_i with *recursive*$(N_i) = self$). One can however retain a finite amount of self-embedding in a precise way by unfolding j levels of applications of rules before the approximation algorithm is applied. In the unfolded rules, recursive nonterminals are replaced by new non-recursive nonterminals, so that in those j levels the precision remains unaffected.

One way of achieving this is the following. For each nonterminal $A \in N_i$ we introduce j fresh nonterminals $A[1], \ldots, A[j]$, and for each $A \rightarrow X_1 \cdots X_m$ in P such that $A \in N_i$, and h such that $1 \leq h \leq j$, we add $A[h] \rightarrow X_1' \cdots X_m'$ to P, where

$$X_k' = X_k[h+1], \text{ if } X_k \in N_i \wedge h < j$$
$$= X_k, \text{ otherwise}$$

Further, we replace all rules $A \rightarrow X_1 \cdots X_m$ such that $A \notin N_i$ by $A \rightarrow X_1' \cdots X_m'$, where

$$X_k' = X_k[1], \text{ if } X_k \in N_i$$
$$= X_k, \text{ otherwise}$$

If the start symbol S was in N_i, we let $S[1]$ be the new start symbol. Note that the transformation preserves the language.

If we take $j = 3$, the palindrome grammar becomes:

$$
\begin{aligned}
S[1] &\rightarrow a\, S[2]\, a \mid b\, S[2]\, b \mid \epsilon \\
S[2] &\rightarrow a\, S[3]\, a \mid b\, S[3]\, b \mid \epsilon \\
S[3] &\rightarrow a\, S\, a \mid b\, S\, b \mid \epsilon \\
S &\rightarrow a\, S\, a \mid b\, S\, b \mid \epsilon
\end{aligned}
$$

After applying the approximation algorithm, all generated strings up to length 6 are palindromes. Only generated strings longer than 6 may not be palindromes: these are of the form $wvv'w^R$, for some $w \in \{a, b\}^3$ and $v, v' \in \{a, b\}^*$, where w^R indicates the mirror image of w. Thus the outer 3 symbols left and right do match, but not the innermost symbols in both 'halves'.

In general, by choosing j high enough we can obtain approximations that are language-preserving up to a certain string length, provided however the grammar is not cyclic. Apart from actual cyclic grammars, the above grammar transformation becomes less effective when the original grammar contains many unit rules or epsilon rules, which can be explained by the fact that such rules do not contribute to the length of the generated string. This problem can be overcome by eliminating such rules from the grammar before applying the above transformation.

The transformation above in effect decorates nodes in the parse tree with numbers up to j indicating the distance to the nearest ancestor node not in N_i. The second refinement we discuss has the effect of indicating the distance up to j to the furthest descendent not in N_i.

For this refinement, we again introduce j fresh nonterminals $A[1], \ldots, A[j]$ for each $A \in N_i$. If the start symbol S is in N_i, we first introduce a new nonterminal $S^\dagger$, which is to become the new start symbol and we add the rule $S^\dagger \rightarrow S$. Then, each $A \rightarrow X_1 \cdots X_m$ in P is replaced by a collection of other rules, which are created as follows. We determine the (possibly empty) list $k_1, \ldots, k_p$ of ascending indices of members that are in N_i: $\{k_1, \ldots, k_p\} = \{k \mid 1 \leq k \leq m \land X_k \in N_i\}$ and $k_1 < \ldots < k_p$. For each list of p numbers $n_1, \ldots, n_p \in \{1, \ldots, j, j+1\}$ we create the rule $A' \rightarrow X_1' \cdots X_m'$, where

$$X_k' = X_k[n_k], \text{ if } X_k \in N_i \land n_k \leq j$$
$$= X_k, \text{ otherwise}$$
$$A' = A[h+1], \text{ if } A \in N_i \land h < j, \text{ where } h = \max_{1 \leq k \leq p} n_k$$
$$= A, \text{ otherwise}$$

We assume that h evaluates to 0 if $p = 0$. Note that $j + 1$ is an auxiliary number which does not show up in the transformed grammar; it represents the case that the distance to the furthest descendent not in N_i is more than j. This transformation also preserves the language.

For the running example, with $j = 3$, we obtain:

$$
\begin{aligned}
S^\dagger &\rightarrow S \mid S[3] \mid S[2] \mid S[1] \\
S &\rightarrow a\,S\,a \mid b\,S\,b \mid a\,S[3]\,a \mid b\,S[3]\,b \\
S[3] &\rightarrow a\,S[2]\,a \mid b\,S[2]\,b \\
S[2] &\rightarrow a\,S[1]\,a \mid b\,S[1]\,b \\
S[1] &\rightarrow \epsilon
\end{aligned}
$$

Approximation now results in palindromes up to length 6, but longer strings have the form $vww^R v'$, for some $w \in \{a, b\}^3$ and $v, v' \in \{a, b\}^*$, where it is the innermost, not the outermost, part that still has the characteristics of palindromes.

7   OTHER METHODS OF APPROXIMATION

In existing literature, several methods of regular approximation of context-free languages are described in terms of the approximation of pushdown automata. A *pushdown automaton* $\mathcal{A}$ is a 5-tuple $(Q, \Sigma, \Delta, I, F)$, where Q is a finite set of *stack symbols*, of which I is the *initial* stack symbol and F is the *final* stack symbol, Σ is the input alphabet, and the *transition relation* Δ is a finite subset of $Q^* \times \Sigma^* \times Q^*$.

A configuration here is an element of $Q^* \times \Sigma^*$. The first components of such elements are called *stacks*. We define the binary relation $\vdash$ between configurations as: $(\alpha\beta, vw) \vdash (\alpha\gamma, w)$ if and only if $(\beta, v, \gamma) \in \Delta$. Some input v is *recognized* if $(I, v) \vdash^* (\alpha F, \epsilon)$, for some $\alpha \in Q^*$.

The language *accepted* by $\mathcal{A}$ is defined to be the set of all strings v that are recognized. A language is accepted by a pushdown automaton if and only if it is a context-free language. That every context-free language is accepted by a pushdown automaton is witnessed by a number of constructions of pushdown automata from context-free grammars. Let us call such a construction a *parsing strategy*; see Nederhof (1994b) for a family of parsing strategies.

In general, there is an infinite set of stacks α that satisfy $(I, v) \vdash^* (\alpha, \epsilon)$. Irrespective of the parsing strategy, we can define approximations in terms of operations that in effect reduce the infinite set of stacks that are distinguished by the pushdown automaton to a finite set, and thus lead to a finite automaton.

One such operation is simply a restriction of the relation $\vdash$ to a smaller relation $\vdash_d$ that disallows the stack height to exceed a fixed number $d \geq 1$. Formally, $(\alpha, vw) \vdash_d (\beta, w)$ if and only if $(\alpha, vw) \vdash (\beta, w)$ and $|\alpha| \leq d$ and $|\beta| \leq d$. One can now construct a finite automaton where the set K of states is defined to be the set of stacks α that satisfy $(I, v) \vdash_d^* (\alpha, \epsilon)$. The initial state is I, and the final states are stacks from K of the form αF. The transition relation Δ is defined to be $(\alpha, v, \beta) \in \Delta$ if and only if $(\alpha, v) \vdash_d (\beta, \epsilon)$.

This kind of subset approximation is proposed in Krauwer and des Tombe (1981); Langendoen and Langsam (1987); Pulman (1986); Johnson (1998) in combination with the (slightly modified) left-corner parsing strategy. The motivation for this strategy is that the approximation is then exact when the grammar is strongly regular, provided that d is chosen high enough. However, any other parsing strategy can be used as well, which may lead to different approximating languages.

Some theoretical limitations of subset approximation have been investigated by Ullian (1967): Given a context-free language, it is undecidable whether an infinite regular subset exists; yet, given that it exists, it can be computed. Note that for practical purposes one is interested in determining a 'large' regular subset, not just any infinite subset of a context-free language as in the theorem from Ullian (1967). Experiments reported in Nederhof (2000) show that computing subset approximations may be very expensive for practical grammars.

Superset approximations result if we define a mapping f from the infinite set of stacks to a finite domain. We then construct a finite automaton of which K, the set of states, consists of the elements from that finite domain of the form $f(\alpha)$ such that α satisfies $(I, v) \vdash^* (\alpha, \epsilon)$, for some v. The initial state is defined to be $f(I)$ and the final states are the elements from K of the form $f(\alpha F)$, for stacks αF satisfying $(I, v) \vdash^* (\alpha F, \epsilon)$, for some v. The transition relation Δ of the finite automaton is defined to be the least relation such that $(I, w) \vdash^* (\alpha, \epsilon)$ and $(\alpha, v) \vdash (\beta, \epsilon)$ implies $(f(\alpha), v, f(\beta)) \in \Delta$.

As an example, let us consider a top-down parsing strategy, described as follows. We define Q to be the set of 'dotted' rules of the form $[A \to \alpha \bullet \beta]$, where $(A \to \alpha\beta)$ in P. Let us further assume, without loss of generality, that there is only one occurrence of start symbol S, which is found in the (unique) rule of the form $S \to \sigma$. We then choose $I = [S \to \bullet \sigma]$ and $F = [S \to \sigma \bullet]$. The transition relation Δ is defined by the following:

- $([A \to \alpha \bullet B\beta], \epsilon, [A \to \alpha \bullet B\beta][B \to \bullet \gamma]) \in \Delta$, for all $(A \to \alpha B\beta), (B \to \gamma) \in P$;

- $([A \to \alpha \bullet a\beta], a, [A \to \alpha a \bullet \beta]) \in \Delta$, for all $(A \to \alpha a\beta) \in P$;

- $([A \to \alpha \bullet B\beta][B \to \gamma \bullet], \epsilon, [A \to \alpha B \bullet \beta]) \in \Delta$, for all $(A \to \alpha B\beta), (B \to \gamma) \in P$.

If we define f to map each stack to its top element (i.e. $f(\alpha q) = q$, for all $\alpha \in Q^*$ and $q \in Q$), then we obtain an approximation that is very close to our approximation from Section 4; in fact, the two approximations are identical if all nonterminals belong to a single N_1 such that $recursive(N_1) = self$. This becomes even more clear if the approximation from Section 4 is expressed in a form inspired by recursive transition networks, as in Nederhof (2000). The approximation above also concurs with the simplified approximation from Grimley Evans (1997) (omitting conditions 7 and 8 therein).

The same mapping f, but in combination with a different parsing strategy, viz. LR parsing, underlies an approximation in Baker (1981). By generalizing f to yield the top-most t elements of the stack (or the entire stack if it is less than t elements high), given some fixed parameter t, the approximation in Bermudez and Schimpf (1990) is obtained, also in combination with LR parsing.

Another approximation based on LR parsing is given in Pereira and Wright (1997), and is obtained by defining f to map each stack to another stack in which no stack symbol occurs more than once. Given a stack α, the stack $f(\alpha)$ is reached by iteratively replacing substacks of the form $q\beta q$ by q; in case there are several such substacks, one chooses one among them in a canonical way to ensure f is uniquely defined.

The main purpose of this chapter is to clarify what happens during regular approximation of context-free languages. Our grammar-based method represented by Figure 12.5 can be seen as the simplest approach to remove self-embedding leaving other parts of the grammar unaffected, and as we have shown, removing self-embedding is sufficient for obtaining a regular language.

Given its simplicity, it is not surprising that more sophisticated methods, such as those based on the LR parsing strategy, produce strictly more precise approximations, i.e. regular languages that are smaller, in terms of language inclusion $\subseteq$. However, our experiments have shown that such sophistication sometimes deteriorates rather than improves practical usefulness.

For example, the method from Baker (1981) in many cases yields the same regular language as our method, yet the intermediate results in the approximation are much larger, which can be argued theoretically but is also confirmed by experiments reported in Nederhof (2000). The 'sophistication' of LR parsing is here merely a source of needless inefficiency.

The high costs involved in applying the LR parsing strategy are even more apparent in the case of the method from Pereira and Wright (1997): First, the construction of an LR automaton, of which the size is exponential in the size of the grammar, may be a very expensive task in practice (Nederhof and Satta, 1996). This is however only a fraction of the effort needed for considering all stacks in which stack symbols occur at most once, i.e. the stacks obtained by applying f, which is in turn exponential in the size of the LR automaton.[3]

By contrast, the complexity of our approximation algorithm (Figure 12.5) is polynomial. The only exponential behaviour may come from the subsequent construction of the finite automaton (Figure 12.3), when the grammar is descended in all ways, a source of exponential behaviour which is also part of the methods based on LR parsing. There is a representation of the automata however that also avoids this exponential behaviour (Nederhof, 2000; Mohri and Pereira, 1998).

That the grammar-based method in general produces less precise approximations may seem a weakness: *ad hoc* refinements such as those discussed in Section 6 may be needed to increase precision. For example, consider the grammar in Section 9 of Church and Patil (1982) and the 4-line grammar of noun phrases from Pereira and Wright (1997). Neither of these grammars are strongly regular, yet they generate regular languages. For the first grammar, the method from Pereira and Wright (1997) and the grammar-based method give the same result. But for the second grammar, the two methods give the same result only provided the second refinement from Section 6 is incorporated into our grammar-based method, with $j = 1$.

Our viewpoint is however that the methods relying on LR parsing also incorporate ad hoc mechanisms of obtaining approximations that are more precise than what is minimally needed to obtain a regular language, and that these are outside of the control of the user.

A case in point is the grammar of palindromes. In Section 6 we demonstrated how precision for our method can be improved in a controlled manner. However, the method from Pereira and Wright (1997) forces a result upon us which is given by $\epsilon \cup (a\{a, b\}^*a - a(ba)^*) \cup (b\{a, b\}^*b - b(ab)^*)$; in other words, just the left-most and right-most symbols are matched, but alternating series of a's and b's are excluded. This strange approximation is reached due to some intricate aspect of the structure of the LR automaton, and there is no reason to consider it as more natural or desirable than any other approximation, and although this method allows additional refinement as well, as shown by Rood (1996), the nature of such refinement may be that even more of the same kind of idiosyncrasies is introduced.

We now consider the method of approximation from Grimley Evans (1997), which is rephrased as follows. For each rule $A \rightarrow X_1 \cdots X_m$ we make a finite automaton with states $q_0, \ldots, q_m$ and transitions (q_{i-1}, X_i, q_i), where $1 \leq i \leq m$. These automata are then joined: Each transition (q_{i-1}, B, q_i), where B is a nonterminal, is replaced by a set of ϵ-transitions from q_{i-1} to the 'left-most' states for rules with left-hand side B, and conversely, a set of ϵ-transitions from the 'right-most' states for those rules to q_i.

This essentially replaces recursion by ϵ-transitions, which leads to a crude approximation (which is identical to the method above based on the top-down parsing strategy). An additional mechanism is now introduced that ensures that the list of visits to the states $q_0, \ldots, q_m$ belonging to a certain rule satisfies some reasonable criteria: a visit to q_i, with $0 \leq i < m$, should be followed by a visit to q_{i+1} or q_0. The latter option amounts to a nested incarnation of the rule. Similarly there is a condition for what should precede a visit to q_i, with $0 < i \leq m$. Since only pairs of consecutive visits to states from the set $\{q_0, \ldots, q_m\}$ are considered, finite-state techniques suffice to implement such conditions.

The emphasis on treating rules individually has the consequence that the order of terminals in a string can become scrambled even when the approximation is still exact with respect to the *number* of occurrences of terminals. As in the case of the method from Pereira and Wright (1997), the resulting approximations are often surprising. E.g. for the palindrome grammar, the language we obtain is $\epsilon \cup a^2a^* \cup b^2b^* \cup (\Sigma^*a\Sigma^*b\Sigma^* \cup \Sigma^*b\Sigma^*a\Sigma^*)^2$, where $\Sigma = \{a, b\}$.

As reported in Grimley Evans (1997) and confirmed by the empirical data in Nederhof (2000), the resulting finite automata may be quite large, even for small grammars. The explanation is that conceptually a state of the finite automaton indicates for each grammar rule individually how far recognition of the right-hand side has progressed, which leads to exponential behaviour in the size of the grammar. It seems however that the method always results in approximations that are more precise than our grammar-based method without the refinements from Section 6.

Another way of obtaining a regular approximation of a grammar is to retain only the information about allowable pairs (or triples, etc.) of adjacent parts of speech (cf. bigrams, trigrams, etc.). This simple approach is proposed in Herz and Rimon (1991); Rimon and Herz (1991), and is reported to be effective for the purpose of word tagging in Hebrew. (For extension to probabilistic formalisms see Stolcke and Segal, 1994.)

8   CONCLUSIONS

Comparing the respective superset approximations discussed above, we see that an important distinguishing property of our grammar-based method is that the structure of the context-free grammar is retained as long as possible as much as possible. This has two advantages. First, the remnants of the original structure present in the transformed grammar can be incorporated into the construction of the automaton, in such a way that the automaton (a finite transducer) produces output that can be used to build parse trees according to the original grammar. This has been shown in Nederhof (1998).

Secondly, the approximation process itself can be monitored: The author of a grammar can still see the structure of the old grammar in the new strongly regular grammar, and can in this way observe what kind of consequences the approximation has on the generated language.

Further comparison of different methods of approximation is provided in Nederhof (2000), which concentrates on two questions. First, what happens when a context-free grammar grows in size? What is then the increase of the size of the obtained minimal deterministic automaton? Second, how 'precise' are the approximations? That is, how much larger than the original context-free language is the language obtained by a superset approximation, and how much smaller is the language obtained by a subset approximation? An attempt is made to answer these questions by making measurements on a practical grammar for German and a corpus of spoken language.

Acknowledgments

The main part of this research was carried out within the framework of the Priority Programme Language and Speech Technology (TST), while the author was employed at the University of Groningen; the TST-Programme is sponsored by NWO (Dutch Organization for Scientific Research). Further support was obtained from the German Research Foundation (DFG), under grant Be1953/1-1, and from AT&T Labs.

Notes

1. We use an abbreviated notation for sets of context-free rules. Vertical lines separate respective right-hand sides of rules with identical left-hand sides.

2. The method from Pereira and Wright (1997) does a little better: of the strings of odd length it excludes those of length 1; yet it does allow all strings of length 3, 5, ... The alternative method from Grimley Evans (1997) excludes a, b, aba and bab, but allows all other strings of odd length. The methods are compared more closely in Section 7.

3. A suggestive example of the difficulty of applying the approximation from Pereira and Wright (1997) is provided by a grammar describing part of the Java programming language. Although two independent implementations we made have crashed before finishing the task, we can make a reasonable estimate of the costs that would be involved in constructing the (nondeterministic) finite automaton. The grammar has 28 nonterminals and 57 rules. The LR(0) characteristic machine has 120 states and 490 transitions. The number of stacks without multiple occurrences of states can be estimated as follows. We order the states as $q_0, \ldots, q_{119}$, and assume that from each q_k, with $0 \le k \le 115$, there are transitions to $q_{k+1}, q_{k+2}, q_{k+3}$ and q_{k+4}; note that $4 * 116 = 464$, which is not far from 490, and therefore this scenario may be similar to the actual situation. One stack that can be constructed is $q_0 q_4 q_8 \cdots q_{116}$, but at least 29 times, another choice can be made which of 4 elements to push, starting from stack q_0, which results in different stacks. Thus there may be more than $4^{29} \approx 2.9 * 10^{17}$ different stacks and as many states in the finite automaton!

References

Baker, T. (1981). Extending lookahead for LR parsers. *Journal of Computer and System Sciences*, 22:243–259.

Bermudez, M. and Schimpf, K. (1990). Practical arbitrary lookahead LR parsing. *Journal of Computer and System Sciences*, 41:230–250.

Chomsky, N. (1959a). A note on phrase structure grammars. *Information and Control*, 2:393–395.

Chomsky, N. (1959b). On certain formal properties of grammars. *Information and Control*, 2:137–167.

Church, K. and Patil, R. (1982). Coping with syntactic ambiguity or how to put the block in the box on the table. *American Journal of Computational Linguistics*, 8:139–149.

Grimley Evans, E. (1997). Approximating context-free grammars with a finite-state calculus. In *35th Annual Meeting of the Association for Computational Linguistics, Proceedings of the Conference*, pp. 452–459, Madrid, Spain.

Harrison, M. (1978). *Introduction to Formal Language Theory*. Reading, MA: Addison-Wesley.

Herz, J. and Rimon, M. (1991). Local syntactic constraints. In *Proc. of the Second International Workshop on Parsing Technologies*, pp. 200–209, Cancun, Mexico.

Hopcroft, J. and Ullman, J. (1979). *Introduction to Automata Theory, Languages, and Computation*. Reading, MA: Addison-Wesley.

Johnson, M. (1998). Finite-state approximation of constraint-based grammars using left-corner grammar transforms. In *36th Annual Meeting of the Association for Computational Linguistics and 17th International Conference on Computational Linguistics*, volume 1, pp. 619–623, Montreal, Quebec, Canada.

Krauwer, S. and des Tombe, L. (1981). Transducers and grammars as theories of language. *Theoretical Linguistics*, 8:173–202.

Langendoen, D. (1975). Finite-state parsing of phrase-structure languages and the status of readjustment rules in grammar. *Linguistic Inquiry*, 6(4):533–554.

Langendoen, D. and Langsam, Y. (1987). On the design of finite transducers for parsing phrase-structure languages. In Manaster-Ramer, A., ed., *Mathematics of Language*, pp 191–235. Amsterdam: Benjamins.

Meyer, A. and Fischer, M. (1971). Economy of description by automata, grammars, and formal systems. In *IEEE Conference Record of the 12th Annual Symposium on Switching and Automata Theory*, pp. 188–191.

Mohri, M. and Pereira, F. (1998). Dynamic compilation of weighted context-free grammars. In *36th Annual Meeting of the Association for Computational Linguistics and 17th International Conference on Computational Linguistics*, volume 2, pp. 891–897, Montreal, Quebec, Canada.

Nederhof, M.J. (1994a). *Linguistic Parsing and Program Transformations*. PhD thesis, University of Nijmegen.

Nederhof, M.-J. (1994b). An optimal tabular parsing algorithm. In *32nd Annual Meeting of the Association for Computational Linguistics, Proceedings of the Conference*, pp. 117–124, Las Cruces, New Mexico, USA.

Nederhof, M.-J. (1998). Context-free parsing through regular approximation. In *Proceedings of the International Workshop on Finite State Methods in Natural Language Processing*, pp. 13–24, Ankara, Turkey.

Nederhof, M.-J. (2000). Practical experiments with regular approximation of context-free languages. *Computational Linguistics*, 26(1). In press.

Nederhof, M.-J. and Satta, G. (1996). Efficient tabular LR parsing. In *34th Annual Meeting of the Association for Computational Linguistics, Proceedings of the Conference*, pp. 239–246, Santa Cruz, California, USA.

Pereira, F. and Wright, R. (1997). Finite-state approximation of phrase-structure grammars. In Roche, E. and Schabes, Y. (eds.), *Finite-State Language Processing*, pp. 149–173. MIT Press.

Pulman, S. (1986). Grammars, parsers, and memory limitations. *Language and Cognitive Processes*, 1(3):197–225.

Rimon, M. and Herz, J. (1991). The recognition capacity of local syntactic constraints. In *Fifth Conference of the European Chapter of the Association for Computational Linguistics, Proceedings of the Conference*, pp 155–160, Berlin, Germany.

Rood, C. (1996). Efficient finite-state approximation of context free grammars. In Kornai, A., editor, *Extended Finite State Models of Language, Proceedings* of the *ECAI'96 workshop*, pp. 58–64, Budapest University of Economic Sciences.

Rosenkrantz, D. and Lewis II, P. (1970). Deterministic left corner parsing. In *IEEE Conference Record of the 11th Annual Symposium on Switching and Automata Theory*, pp. 139–152.

Sippu, S. and Soisalon-Soininen, E. (1990). *Parsing Theory, Vol. II: LR(k) and LL(k) Parsing*, volume 20 of *EATCS Monographs on Theoretical Computer Science*. Berlin: Springer.

Stearns, R. (1967). A regularity test for pushdown machines. *Information and Control*, 11:323–340.

Stolcke, A. and Segal, J. (1994). Precise N-gram probabilities from stochastic context-free grammars. In *32nd Annual Meeting of the Association for Computational Linguistics, Proceedings of the Conference*, pp. 74–79, Las Cruces, New Mexico, USA.

Ullian, J. (1967). Partial algorithm problems for context free languages. *Information and Control*, 11:80–101.

Valiant, L. (1975). Regularity and related problems for deterministic pushdown automata. *Journal of the ACM*, 22(1):1–10.

Chapter 13

PARSING BY SUCCESSIVE APPROXIMATION

Helmut Schmid
IMS-CL, University of Stuttgart, Azenbergstr. 12, D-70174 Stuttgart, Germany
schmid@ims.uni-stuttgart.de

Abstract   A parsing method for unification-based grammars with a context-free backbone is proposed which processes the input in three steps. The first step is context-free parsing. The second step evaluates syntactic feature constraints and the third step builds a semantic representation. It is argued that for each of these steps a different processing strategy is optimal. A novel iterative processing strategy for syntactic feature constraints is presented which computes the feature structures in multiple passes through the parse forest and represents the feature structures as trees rather than graphs. Experimental results are presented which indicate that the time complexity of this parser is close to cubic in the length of the input for a large English grammar. Finally, a compilation technique is presented which automatically compiles a set of finitely valued features into the context-free backbone grammar.

1   INTRODUCTION

The efficiency of context-free parsing is well known (see e.g. Younger, 1967). Since many feature structure-based grammars either have a context-free backbone or can be transformed into a grammar with a context-free backbone, it is possible to take advantage of the efficiency of context free parsing if the parser proceeds in two steps: First a context-free parser builds the context-free part of the syntactic analysis which is then extended by the computation of feature structures. Maxwell III and Kaplan (1994) experimented with variants of this strategy in their LFG parser. One result of their experiments was that their grammar is processed more efficiently by their parser if the rather broad context-free categories chosen by the grammar writers are replaced with more specific categories. To this end some relevant features have been compiled manually into the context-free grammar. Of course one would prefer to have a compiler perform this task automatically. This would enable the grammar

243

H. Bunt and A. Nijholt (eds.), Advances in Probabilistic and Other Parsing Technologies, 243–261.

writer to use the categories which he considers appropriate, without loosing efficiency. How this can be done is shown in section 3.

It is often useful to split the second part of processing, the evaluation of feature constraints, into two steps as well. Feature constraints which are likely to eliminate analyses (filtering constraints) are evaluated first whereas the evaluation of other constraints (structure-building constraints) which mainly serve to build some (e.g. semantic) representation is delayed. The ALEP system (Advanced Language Engineering Platform (Simpkins, 1994) allows the user to explicitly specify features whose constraints are to be delayed. Kasper and Krieger (1996) present a similar idea for HPSG parsing.

Separating filtering constraints and structure-building constraints has two advantages: Since many or even most analyses are eliminated by the filtering constraints, the parser will not waste time on the – usually expensive – evaluation of structure-building constraints for analyses which will fail anyway. Another advantage is that the most efficient processing strategy can be chosen for each of the two constraint types independently.

Structure-building features reflect to a large extent the syntactic structure of a constituent. The semantic feature of a VP node e.g. would encode the attachment side of an embedded PP if it is ambiguous. In order to avoid that such local ambiguities multiply in the semantic representation, it is necessary to have means to represent ambiguity locally; i.e. the feature structure representation must allow for embedded disjunctions. A representation in disjunctive normal form (i.e. as a set of alternative non-disjunctive feature structures) is inefficient because the number of feature structures can grow exponentially with the number of local ambiguities. Algorithms for processing disjunctive feature constraints have been presented e.g. by Kasper (1987), Dörre and Eisele (1990), Maxwell III and Kaplan (1996), and Emele (1991). Schiehlen (1996) and Dörre (1997) presented algorithms for semantic construction.

It will be shown that filtering constraints, on the other hand, can be processed efficiently with standard unification algorithms and a disjunctive normal form representation for feature structures if the feature values restricted by these constraints have limited depth and therefore limited complexity. The SUBCAT and SLASH features in HPSG e.g. have this property whereas e.g. the SUBJ and OBJ features in LFG do not. Even if the depth of a feature value is unbounded, it is still possible to limit the complexity of the feature structures artificially by pruning feature structures below some level of embedding. Little of the restrictive power of the constraints is lost thereby because constraints seldom refer to deeply embedded information. In this case, however, the filtering constraints have to be evaluated again in the next step together with the structure-building constraints in order to ensure the correctness of the final result.

The parser presented here implements the first two steps of the parsing strategy outlined above. It is assumed that the grammar contains no structure-building constraints which the parser cannot handle efficiently (see also section 4.3). A method which isolates the structure-building constraints automatically, has not been implemented, yet. Section 2 provides a short overview of the grammar formalism which the parser uses. Section 3 describes the compilation of the grammar. Details of the parsing strategy are given in section 4. Section 5 presents results from experiments with the parser and section 6 closes with a summary.

2   THE GRAMMAR FORMALISM

The parser uses a rule-based grammar formalism. A simple toy grammar written in this formalism is shown in the appendix. Each grammar rule has a context-free backbone. One of the daughter nodes is marked as the head with a preceding backquote. Trace nodes are marked with an asterisk after the category name. At least one daughter node has to be non-empty because rules which generate empty strings are not allowed. For each node, there is a set of feature constraint equations. Two features are unified by assigning the value of the same variable to both of them (e.g. $f1 = v; f2 = v;$). Feature structures are totally well-typed, i.e. they are typed and each feature which is appropriate for some type is present and has a value of an appropriate type.

The feature structures are represented by trees. Because there is no finite feature tree which models cyclic feature constraints like e.g. $f1=v; f1.f2=v;$ (see Shieber, 1992), cyclic constraints are not allowed. Equality of features is interpreted extensionally (i.e. two feature structures are considered equal if and only if they have the same type and all of their feature values are equal) because feature trees fail to represent equality constraints. Type hierarchies are not supported by the formalism.

There are two predefined feature types and three classes of user-defined types. Features of the predefined type STRING accept any character string as value. Features of the predefined type FS_LIST take a list of feature structures of the class *category* (see below) as value. This feature type is needed for Subcat and Slash features. The grammar writer defines a new feature type of the class *enumeration type* by listing the corresponding set of possible values (see e.g. the NUMBER feature type of the grammar in the appendix). Another class of user-defined feature types are the *structured types* which are defined by listing the set of attributes appropriate for this type with the types of their values (see the AGR feature type in the appendix). *Categories* are the last class of user-defined feature types. Their definition is analogous to that of a structured type. Each node of category X has an associated feature structure of type X.

To simplify the task of the grammar writer, the grammar formalism supports templates, default inheritance between the mother node and the head daughter of a rule, automatic handling of the two features *Phon* and *HeadLex* (lexical head), and special variable types called 'restrictor' types which define a subset of features which are to be unified when two *category* feature structures are (partially) unified by assigning the same variable to both of them. The last feature is needed e.g. to exclude e.g. the *Phon* feature from unification when the feature structure of a trace node is unified with the feature structure of a filler node.

The grammar formalism allows disjunctive value specifications in the case of features of an *enumeration type*. Such disjunctions are efficiently stored and processed with a bit vector representation.

3   COMPILATION

A compiler transforms the textual representation of the grammar into the format which is read by the parser and detects and reports errors. The compiler expands the templates, adds constraint equations for the automatic features and for inherited features, flattens the feature structures by replacing structured features with a set of new features which correspond to the subfeatures of the structured feature, and infers additional implicit constraints. To exemplify these inferences, consider the following rule:

$$VP \{Subcat=[*];Subcat=r;\} \rightarrow {}'V \{Subcat=[NP\{\}=np|r];\}$$
$$NP \{\}=np;$$

The notation $NP\{\}=np$ here means '*unify the feature structure of the node NP with the feature structure denoted by the variable np according to the definition of the restrictor type of the variable np*,' i.e. unify the subset of features listed in the restrictor definition. '*' is a dummy value and [*] is a list with a single element.

The compiler extracts the following feature constraints from this rule:

$$r = 0.VP.Subcat \qquad x = 0.VP.Subcat.cdr(1)$$
$$r = 1.VP.Subcat.cdr(1) \quad x = [] \quad ...$$

The lefthand side of each constraint is a variable, the righthand side is either a feature path or a constant. [] is the empty list. The number in front of a path expression refers to the position of the node in the rule. The expression $cdr(1)$ refers to the rest list at position 1 of a list, i.e. the list minus its first element.

From these constraints the compiler infers the additional constraint:

$$x = 1.VP.Subcat.cdr(2)$$

These inferences are required by the constraint evaluation algorithm presented in section 4.1.

Finally, the compiler replaces unified variables with a single variable, merges equations of the form $x=constant1;$ $x=constant2$ into some new equation $x=constant3$, eliminates redundant equations and generates *fixed assignments* for equations with a feature path expression on the right hand side if the variable on the left hand side is unified with an unambiguous constant in some other equation. This is e.g. the case for the third equation and the inferred equation above. The fixed assignments derived from these equations are:

$$0.VP.Subcat.cdr(1) := []   1.VP.Subcat.cdr(2) := []$$

The three equations involved are removed at this point. For each of the remaining equations with a path expression on the right hand side, the compiler generates a *variable assignment*:

$$0.VP.Subcat := r   1.VP.Subcat.cdr(1) := r$$

Equations with the same variable on the left hand side are then grouped together:

$$r: r = 0.VP.Subcat   r = 1.VP.Subcat.cdr(1)$$

The variables representing these groups are sorted so that each variable follows all the variables which it depends on. A variable s depends on variables r and t if there is a constraint $s := \mathtt{cat(r,t)}$ or if two variable assignments constraints $s := p$ and $r := q$ exist such that p is a subfeature of q (i.e. q is a prefix of p). The ordering is required by the constraint evaluation algorithm presented in section 4.1. If no ordering exists which is compatible with all dependencies, then some feature definition is cyclic and the compiler reports an error. Remember that cyclic feature definitions have been excluded.

3.1   GENERATION OF CONTEXT-FREE RULES

The compiler supports the compilation of feature constraints into the context-free backbone of the grammar, but only for features of the class *enumeration type*. Features of other types like STRING and FS_LIST can not be compiled because the number of possible values is infinite. The user specifies which features are to be *incorporated* – i.e. compiled – for each category, and the compiler automatically generates all valid context-free rules with the refined categories.

The following algorithm is used for the generation of the refined context-free rules: First the compiler orders the incorporated features of all nodes of a given grammar rule. A sequence $f_1, f_2, \ldots, f_n$ is obtained. Then the set of permitted values for the first feature f_1 is determined. To this end, the compiler checks whether there is a fixed assignment for this feature. If one exists, the corresponding value is the only permitted value. Otherwise, the compiler checks whether there are two constraint equations of the form $v = f_1$ and $v = (c_1; c_2; \ldots; c_m)$ where $(c_1; c_2; \ldots; c_m)$ is a disjunction of constant values. In this case, the set of permitted values is $\{c_1, c_2, \ldots, c_m\}$. Otherwise all values appropriate for feature f_1 are permitted features. The compiler chooses one of the permitted values and switches to the next feature.

While assigning a value to feature f_i, the compiler first checks whether f_i is unified with some feature f_k where $k < i$. This is the case if there are two equations $y = f_i$ and $y = f_k$. If there is such a feature f_k (which already has a value because it has a smaller index) then its value is assigned to feature f_i. Otherwise the set of permitted values is computed as described above and the first value is selected. After the value of the last feature has been fixed in this way, the corresponding context-free rule is printed to the output. The other context-free rules are obtained by backtracking.

Assuming that the feature *Number* is to be incorporated into the categories *NP*, *DT*, and *N*, the parser will generate in case of the rules:

$$NP \; Number=n; \; -> DT \; Number=n; \; `N \; Number=n;;$$

the following two context-free rules:

$$NP\_sg \; -> DT\_sg \; N\_sg$$
$$NP\_pl \; -> DT\_pl \; N\_pl$$

3.2   LEXICON COMPRESSION

A parser for unrestricted input requires a large lexicon to obtain high coverage. In order to reduce the space requirements of such a large lexicon, the compiler checks for redundancies. Most information is stored in the form of linked lists and if two lists are identical from some position up to the end, the common tail of the lists is stored only once. Also if two list elements (not necessarily of the same list) are identical, only one copy is stored. With this technique it was possible to compress a lexicon with 300,000 entries to about 18 MBytes, which is about 63 Bytes per entry.

4   PARSING

The parser itself consists of two components. The first component is a context-free parser which generates a parse forest, i.e. a compact representation of a set of parse trees which stores common parts of the parse trees only once. The BCKY parser developed by Andreas Eisele[1] is used for this purpose. It is a fast bit-vector implementation of the Cocke-Kasami-Younger algorithm. The second component of the parser reads the context-free parse forest and computes the feature structures in several steps. In each step, the parse forest is traversed and a new parse forest with more informative feature structures is generated. Parsing terminates when the feature structures do not change anymore. The first iteration is computationally the most expensive one because most analyses are typically eliminated in this iteration. Therefore it is more important to make the first step as efficient as possible than to minimize the number of iterations.

The recomputation of the parse forest proceeds bottom-up and top-down in turn. During bottom-up processing, the parser first recomputes the feature structures of terminal nodes by evaluating the constraints associated with the lexical rules. Since the number of lexical rules for a terminal node can be larger than one, there may be more than one resulting feature structure. The new nodes with their feature structures are inserted into a new chart. If a node with the same category and feature structure already exists in the new chart, the parser just adds the new analysis (i.e. the rule number and pointers to the daughter nodes) to the list of analyses at this node. Otherwise, a new node is generated. In both cases, the parser stores a link from the old node to the new one.

When the feature structure of a nonterminal node is recomputed, the parser checks all analyses of this node if it has more than one. For each analysis it tries all combinations of new nodes which are linked to its daughter nodes (Figure 13.1). For each consistent combination, the parser builds an updated feature structure for the mother node which satisfies the local rule constraints and stores it in the new chart as described for terminal nodes.

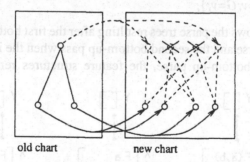

old chart   new chart

Figure 13.1 Bottom-up recomputation of the parse forest

During top-down processing, the parser first copies the top-level nodes which cover the whole input string to the new chart and inserts them into a queue for further processing. Then the first node is retrieved from the queue and its daughter nodes are recomputed for each analysis. The recomputed daughter nodes are inserted into the new chart and – if new – also inserted into the queue for recursive processing. After each traversal of the parse forest, the parser checks whether the feature structure of some node has changed in the last two iterations. If not, parsing is finished. Otherwise the old chart is cleared, the charts are switched and the next iteration begins.

Why is it necessary to traverse the parse forest more than once? In contrast to formalisms like LFG and HPSG it is not assumed that the feature structure of the root node of a parse tree contains all relevant information. It is even assumed that this is *not* the case (see section 4.3). Hence it is necessary to compute the feature structures of all nodes in the parse forest. In case of a single unambiguous parse tree, it is sufficient to traverse the parse tree once. By means of value sharing it is possible to update the values of unified features of different nodes in the parse tree synchronously. This is not possible with parse forests, however, because cross-talk would result whenever two different analyses have a common node, unless such a shared node is always copied before it is modified which is expensive and in vain if the analysis later fails. The alternative is to traverse the parse forest again in top-down direction to update the feature structures of the non-root nodes.

The presented parser has to traverse the parse forest even more than twice. Consider the following grammar:

> *enum T {a,b};*
> *category Y {};*
> *category X { T F,G; };*
> *T v;*
> *Y {} -> 'X {F=a;};*
> *"a" : X {F=v;G=v;};*

Figure 13.2 shows the parse trees resulting after the first bottom-up parse, the first top-down parse and the second bottom-up pass when the input a is parsed. During the first bottom-up parse, the feature structures remain unchanged.

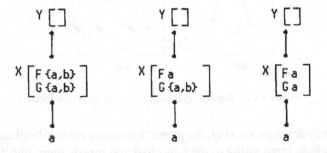

Figure 13.2 Intermediate results of the feature computation

The Y node has no features anyway and the X node is unchanged because the constraints of the lexical entry are already satisfied by the initialisation values of the features, and because daughter node feature structures are not modified during bottom-up parsing, so that the constraint F=a; has no effect in the bottom-up pass. In the first top-down pass, the value a is assigned to the F feature. In the second bottom-up pass finally the lexical constraints are evaluated again and the features get their final values.

The repeated computation of the feature structures ensures that information is propagated in the parse forest until all constraints are satisfied. This iterative strategy might seem inefficient at first, but it turns out that the first two passes typically account for about three quarters of the total processing time and the number of passes rarely exceeds five. As mentioned earlier, it seems more important to speed up the first pass than to reduce the number of passes.

4.1 CONSTRAINT EVALUATION

The recomputation of feature structures is carried out in four steps. First the input feature structures are selected. During top-down processing, the mother node is a node in the new chart and the daughter nodes are from the old chart. During bottom-up processing the mother node is in the old chart and the daughter nodes are from the new chart.

The parser then checks whether the fixed assignments (see section 3) are compatible with the input feature structures. If this is the case, the parser computes the values of the variables used in this rule by non-destructively unifying the values specified in the constraint equations for this variable. The values to be unified are either values of feature paths, or constants[2], or results of string concatenation operations.

Once the values of the variables have been computed, the new feature structures are built by modifying the old feature structures according to the set of fixed assignments and variable assignments. The assignments have been sorted by the compiler so that assignments to less deeply embedded features are carried out first. A lazy copying strategy is used: Before the value of a feature is changed, all levels of the feature structure above this feature are copied unless they have been copied before.

After all assignments have been made, the resulting feature structure is inserted into a hash table. If an identical feature structure is already contained in the hash table, a pointer to this feature structure is returned. Otherwise, the new feature structure is inserted. The hashing is done recursively: All embedded feature structures (i.e. elements of feature structure lists), are hashed before an embedding feature structure is hashed. Hashing simplifies the comparison of feature structures to a mere comparison of pointers.

4.2   OPTIMIZATION

The parsing scheme presented so far has been modified in several ways in order to improve the speed of the parser.

1. The compatibility check for fixed assignments can be done for each node independently of all the other nodes. It is not necessary to repeat it for all combinations of daughter nodes. If a feature structure turns out to be incompatible, the number of combinations is reduced.

2. The probability that a constraint is violated is not identical for all constraints in a rule. Therefore the constraints are sorted so that those constraints which are more likely to fail will be checked first. Inconsistent analyses are therefore eliminated earlier on average. The required statistics are collected during parsing.

3. Sometimes it is known in advance that a recomputation of a feature structure will not change it. This is the case if all input feature structures remained unchanged when they were recomputed the last time. In this case it is sufficient to copy the feature structures to the new chart without recomputing them.

4. Expensive computations are sometimes done repeatedly during parsing, e.g. feature structure unifications. In order to avoid this redundancy, the parser stores each unification operation with pointers to the argument feature structures and the resulting feature structure in a hash table. Before a unification of two feature structures is carried out it is checked whether the result is already in the hash table. Other expensive operations like string concatenations are stored as well.

The parser and the compiler have been implemented in the C programming language.

4.3   LIMITATIONS

The presented parser will be rather slow if the grammar contains the sort of structure-building features discussed in section 1. Explicit links to the daughter nodes of a constituent (like the DAUGHTERS feature in HPSG theory) are a good example of the type of features that a grammar writer has to avoid. Semantic representations have to be built with different methods like those described in Schiehlen (1996) and Dörre (1997).

The presented parsing method cannot immediately be used to process other grammar formalisms like LFG or HPSG. LFG has no feature typing which is essential for the compilation of the context-free grammar. A separation of filtering constraints and structure-building constraints is difficult in LFG because the SUBJ and OBJ features are used to check subcategorization and to build a simple semantic representation at the same time. The pruning strategy outlined in section 1 might help, but an additional module for the processing of structure-building constraints would still be needed. Of course, many other modifications would also be necessary.

HPSGs cannot be directly parsed with the presented method because HPSGs lack the context-free backbone required by the first parsing step. The feature type system is also more expressive than that of the grammar formalism just described.

5   EXPERIMENTAL RESULTS

An English grammar with 290 phrase structure rules has been written for the parser. More emphasis was put on coverage than on accuracy and the grammar often produces a large number of analyses for a sentence. A lexicon of about 300,000 entries with subcategorization information was extracted from the COMLEX lexical database (Grishman et al., 1994). The parser has been used to parse 30,000 sentences from the Penn Treebank corpus (Marcus et al., 1993). Missing lexical entries were automatically generated from the part-of-speech tags in the tagged version of the corpus. However, the part-of-speech tags were not used for parsing itself. Quotation marks were ignored during parsing. More than 7 words per second could be parsed on average with a Sun Ultra-2 workstation. Three times the parser stopped prematurely due to memory exhaustion. The calculation of the feature structures was the most time-consuming part of parsing.

For 80 percent of the sentences the parser produced at least one analysis. For 54 percent of the sentences there was at least one analysis which was compatible with the Penn Treebank analysis. An analysis was considered compatible if there were no crossing brackets. However, analyses without crossing brackets are not necessarily acceptable analyses. 100 sentences have been parsed and inspected manually to estimate how often there was an acceptable analysis. For 57 of these sentences the parser had produced a Treebank-compatible analysis, but for only 48 an acceptable one. Interpolating these results, the portion of sentences with an acceptable analysis is probably around 45 percent in the larger corpus.

Figure 13.3 shows the empirical runtime complexity which was determined by parsing randomly selected sentences of length 10 to 55. The complexity is close to n^3 (the dashed line in the diagram) where n is the sentence length. There is an outlier at (48, 36.7) which is not shown in the diagram.

Another experiment was carried out to check the influence of some of the optimization strategies described in section 4.2 on parsing time. A randomly selected set of 25 sentences was parsed with different variants of the parser in

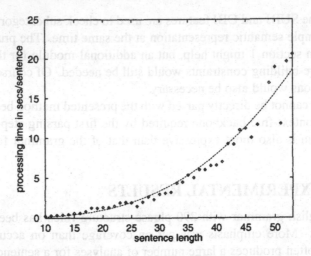

Figure 13.3 Empirical parsing complexity

strategy	25 sentences	1 complex sent.
all optimizations	65.9	180
no hashing of unifications	67.4	193
no hashing of string concatenations	79.3	244
recomputing always	67.3	236

Table 13.1 Parse times for 25 randomly selected sentences and a single complex sentence

the first part of the experiment. In the second part a single complex sentence
was parsed. In each variant of the parser one optimization was switched off.
Table 13.1 shows the results. Hashing of unifications only showed minor effects on parsing speed. Hashing of string concatenation operations was more
effective. Presumably string concatenation operations are more likely to be
repeated than feature structure unifications. Avoiding unnecessary recomputation of feature structures had a bigger influence on the parsing of the complex
sentence than on the parsing of the simpler sentences.

The impact of the incorporation of features into the context-free grammar
has also been examined. We observed in contrast to Maxwell III and Kaplan
(1994), only a marginal speedup of about 3 percent from feature incorporation.
The incorporation of some features to very bad results because the parse forest
generated by the context-free parser became very big, slowing down both
context-free parsing and the calculation of the feature structures. A close

relationship between the number of nodes in the context-free parse forest and parsing time has been observed.

The parser was also compared to a state-of-the-art parser, the XLE system developed at Rank Xerox which was available for the experiments. A corpus of 700 words which both parsers have been able to parse completely was used in this experiment. The XLE system parsed this corpus in 110 seconds whereas our parser needed 123 seconds. Of course it is very difficult to compare these figures since the parsers are too different wrt. the grammar formalisms used, the information contained in the analyses, the degree of ambiguity and other criteria.

In another experiment[3], a simple German subordinate clause grammar with extraposition of relative clauses was written in LFG and the grammar formalism of the presented parser. Sample sentences of different length and degree of ambiguity have been parsed with these grammars. All of these sentences had an extraposed relative clauses with one or more possible attachment positions. Due to PP attachment ambiguities the number of readings of the sentences (and also the number of attachment sites of the extraposed relative clause) grew exponentially with the length of the input. The presented parser was much faster on this task. Again its empirical complexity was close to $O(n^3)$ whereas the XLE system showed exponential complexity with a standard LFG grammar for the given task. For all input lengths, the XLE system was at least an order of magnitude slower. The result of this experiment is displayed in Fig. 13.4. Both axes have logarithmic scale.

The LFG grammar was then modified in order to find out whether an LFG grammar which was similar to the grammar of the presented parser would be faster and in fact, this was the case. The second LFG grammar used *slash* feature percolation rather than the *functional uncertainty* mechanism for the attachment of the extraposed clause. Furthermore the f-structure contained no information about adjuncts and only agreement information was percolated in the *slash* feature. The empirical complexity of this simplified LFG grammar was still $O(n^4)$. Finally, we also checked a version of the LFG grammar which left the relative clause unattached. The run time of this grammar was close to cubic.

So this experiment indicates that it is indeed a good idea to avoid structure-building constraints in parsing. The fact that the presented parser was at least an order of magnitude faster for all input lengths than a state-of-the-art system further indicates that – at least in this task – the presented feature computation method is very efficient.

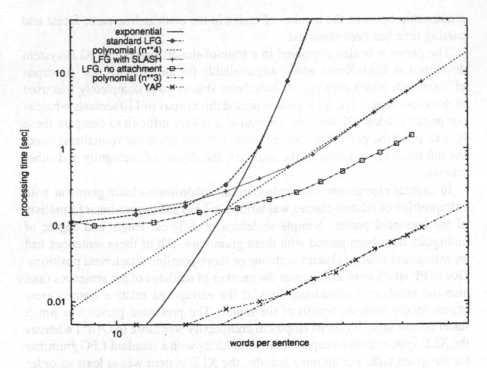

Figure 13.4   Comparison with the XLE system on a simple extraposition grammar

6   SUMMARY

A parsing strategy has been outlined which splits parsing into three steps: context-free parsing, the evaluation of filtering constraints and evaluation of structure-building constraints. A parser has been presented which implements the first two steps. A compiler transforms the grammar description into a form which the parser is able to process efficiently. The compiler automatically refines the context-free backbone of the grammar by compiling a user-defined set of feature constraints into the context-free backbone. An iterative procedure is used to compute the feature structures after a context-free parse forest has been built. This method repeatedly solves local constraints which apply to a single node and its daughter nodes. The computation of the feature structures is finished when all local constraints are satisfied. As long as the feature structures are not used to build representations which encode the structure of constituents, this parsing strategy works very well: Wall Street Journal data has been parsed at a speed of 7 words per second. A comparison with a state-of-the-art system showed that it is indeed important to avoid structure-building constraint in parsing and that the presented feature computation method is very efficient for such grammars.

Notes

1. Andreas Eisele, IMS-CL, University of Stuttgart, andreas@ims.uni-stuttgart.de
2. Such constants are necessarily disjunctive values because otherwise a set of fixed assignments would have been generated.
3. I would like to thank Jonas Kuhn for his collaboration on this experiment.

References

Dörre, J. (1997). Efficient construction of underspecified semantics under massive ambiguity. In *Proceedings of the 35th Annual Meeting of the ACL*, Madrid, Spain.

Dörre, J. and Eisele, A. (1990). Feature logic with disjunctive unification. In *Proceedings of the 13th International Conference on Computational Linguistics*, pp. 100–105, Helsinki, Finland.

Emele, M. (1991). Unification with lazy non-redundant copying. In *Proceedings of the 29th Annual Meeting of the Association for Computational Linguistics*, pp. 323–330, Berkeley.

Grishman, R., Macleod, C., and Meyers, A. (1994). Comlex syntax: Building a computational lexicon. In *Proceedings of the 15th International Conference on Computational Linguistics*, Kyoto, Japan.

Kasper, R. T. (1987). A unification method for disjunctive feature descriptions. In *Proceedings of the 25th Annual Meeting of the ACL*, pp 235–242, Stanford, CA.

Kasper, W. and Krieger, H.-U. (1996). Modularizing codescriptive grammars for efficient parsing. In *Proceedings of the 16th International Conference on Computational Linguistics*, pp. 628–633, Copenhagen, Denmark.

Marcus, M. P., Santorini, B., and Marcinkiewicz, M. A. (1993). Building a large annotated corpus of English: the Penn Treebank. *Computational Linguistics*, 19(2):313–330.

Maxwell III, J. T. and Kaplan, R. M. (1994). The interface between phrasal and functional constraints. *Computational Linguistics*, 19(4): 571–589.

Maxwell III, J. T. and Kaplan, R. M. (1996). Unification-based parsers that automatically take advantage of context freeness. Draft.

Schiehlen, M. (1996). Semantic construction from parse forests. In *Proceedings of the 16th International Conference on Computational Linguistics*, Copenhagen, Denmark.

Shieber, S. M. (1992). *Constraint-Based Grammar Formalisms: Parsing and Type Inference for Natural and Computer Language*. The MIT Press, Cambridge, Ma.

Simpkins, N. K. (1994). *ALEP-2 User Guide*. CEU, Luxembourg. online available at http://www.anite-systems.lu/alep/doc/index.html.

258   *Advances in probabilistic and other parsing technologies*

Younger, D. H. (1967). Recognition and parsing of context-free languages in time n^3. *Information and Control*, 10:189–208.

Appendix: A Toy Grammar

```
% comments start with a percent sign

%%%%%% declarations %%%%%%%%%%%%%%%%

% definition of the automatic
% feature 'Phon'
auto Phon;

% enumeration type features
enum PERSON   {1st,2nd,3rd};
enum NUMBER   {sg,pl};
enum CASE     {nom,acc};
enum VFORM    {fin,inf,bse,prp,pap,pas};
enum BOOLEAN {yes,no};

% definition of a structured feature
struct AGR {
  NUMBER  Number;
  PERSON  Person;
  CASE    Case;
};

% category definitions
category TOP {
};

category COMP {
};

category SBAR {
  BOOLEAN Wh;
};

category S {
  FS_LIST Slash;
};

category VP {
  VFORM    VForm;
  BOOLEAN  Aux;
  FS_LIST  Subcat;
  FS_LIST  Slash;
};

% Definition of the features which
% are to be compiled into the context
% free grammar.

VP incorporates {VForm, Aux};
```

```
category VBAR {
  VFORM    VForm;
  FS_LIST Subcat;
  FS_LIST Slash;
};

VP incorporates {VForm};

category V {
  VFORM    VForm;
  BOOLEAN Aux;
  FS_LIST Subcat;
};

VP incorporates {VForm,Aux};

category NP {
  BOOLEAN Wh;
  AGR      Agr;
};

NP incorporates {Wh};

category N {
  AGR      Agr;
};

category DT {
  BOOLEAN Wh;
  AGR      Agr;
};

DT incorporates {Wh};

category PP {
};

category P {
};

% definition of restrictor types
restrictor+ NP_R(NP) {Phon, Wh, Agr};

% In the next definition, the Phon
% feature is exempted from unification.
restrictor+ NP2_R(NP) {Wh, Agr};
restrictor+ SBAR_R(SBAR) {Phon, Wh};

% variable declarations
BOOLEAN wh;
AGR agr;
NP_R np;
NP2_R np2;
SBAR_R sbar;
FS_LIST r, r2;

%%%%%%% grammar rules %%%%%%%%%%%%%%%%%
```

```
TOP {} ->
    'S {Slash=[];};

S {} ->
    NP {Agr.Case=nom;}=np
    'VP {Subcat=[NP{}=np];};
% The subject-NP is unified with the
% single element of the Subcat list.

VP {} ->      % All features of the two
    'VP {}     % VP nodes are unified due
    PP {};     % to feature inheritance.

VP {} ->
    'VBAR {};

VBAR {} ->
    'VBAR {}
    PP   {};

VBAR {Subcat=r;} ->
    'VBAR {Subcat=[NP{}=np|r];}
    NP    {Agr.Case=acc;}=np;
% All features of the VBAR nodes are
% unified by default feature inheritance
% excepted the Subcat features.

VBAR {Subcat=r;} ->
    'VBAR {Subcat=[SBAR{}=sbar|r];}
    SBAR {}=sbar;

VBAR {Slash=[];} ->
    'V {};

PP {} ->
    'P   {}
    NP {Agr.Case=acc;};

NP {Wh=wh;} ->
    DT {Wh=wh;Agr=agr;}
    'N {Agr=agr;};

SBAR {Wh=no;} ->
    COMP {}
        'S {Slash=[];};

SBAR {Wh=yes;} ->
    NP {Wh=yes;}=np2
    'S {Slash=[NP{}=np2];};
% All features of the NP node and the
% element on the Slash list are unified
% excepted the Phon feature.
% See the definition of NP2_R.

VBAR {Subcat=r;Slash=[np|r2];} ->
    'VBAR {Subcat=[NP{}=np|r];Slash=r2;}
    NP* {Agr.Case=acc;}=np;
```

```
% An NP trace is generated. Information
% from the filler node is threaded via
% the Slash feature.


%%%%%% template definitions %%%%%%%%%%

N_sg    : N {Agr.Number=sg;};
PRO     : NP {Agr.Number=sg;
              Agr.Person=3rd;};
NPRO    : PRO {Wh=no;};
WHPRO   : PRO {Wh=yes;};

%%%%%% lexical entries %%%%%%%%%%%%%%%%

"the"   : DT {Wh=no;Agr.Person=3rd;};
"a"     : DT {Wh=no;Agr.Number=sg;
                    Agr.Person=3rd;};
"which": DT {Wh=yes;Agr.Person=3rd;};
"man"   : N_sg {};
"pizza": N_sg {};
"restaurant": N_sg {};
"he"    : NPRO {Agr.Case=nom;};
"him"   : NPRO {Agr.Case=acc;};
"it"    : NPRO {};
"what"  : WHPRO {};
"eats"  : V {Subcat=[
              NP{},
              NP{Agr.Number=sg;
                 Agr.Person=3rd;}];};
"at"    : P {};
"that"  : COMP {};
```

Index

Accepting path, 49
Acoustic model, 48
Accuracy
  of parsing, 24, 32, 76, 114–117, 128, 140, 163, 255
  of parse selection, 172–176
  of supertagging, 214, 219
Actor
  centering, 193
  container, 184–186, 188
  phrase, 183–184, 188
  word, 183–184, 188, 193, 198
Affix hopping, 48
Agglutinative language, 128
Alternating Probabilistic Feature Grammar, 71
Ambiguity, 1, 3–4, 13, 22, 179, 184
  handling, 3, 5, 13, 22, 179, 184
  lexical, 34, 40
    See also polysemy
  semantic, 5, 10
  syntactic, 3–6
Analysis
  optimal, 45–46
Anaphor resolution, 193
Approximation, of grammar, 4, 223–243
Approximative parsing, 5, 245–263
ATIS
  corpus, 22
  system, 22
Automaton, 43
  deterministic finite state, 34, 44, 53, 58
  finite-state, 49
  pushdown, 224, 234, 236
  weighted, 244, 254, 257

Backtracking, 179, 186, 188, 194, 196–198
Backward-looking center, 193
BCKY parser, 250
Bigram, 36, 47–48, 94, 102, 240
  lexical dependency parsing, 74

model, 94
  context-sensitive, 94
Bilexical
  Dependency Grammar, 54–55
  Grammar, 32–62
    Probabilistic, 54
    Weighted, 32–62
  models
    probabilistic, 54–55
  Phrase Structure Grammar, 55–56
  recognition, 40–43
Binarization, 73, 76, 115–118
Binary
  branching, 55, 66, 71, 76, 78
  event, 70–71
  grammar, 117, 129
  left-corner projection, 119
  parse tree, 138
  phrase structure tree, 129, 138
  relation, 183, 225
  rule, 116, 119
  tree, 129
Brackets
  crossing, 114, 117, 121–122, 171–174
    See also Accuracy
Branching
  binary, 55, 66, 71, 76, 78

Capitalization, 49
CARAMEL system, 6
Center, 193
  embedding, 57
  backward-looking, 193
  forward-looking, 193
Centering, 193
  actor, 193
CFG (Context-Free Grammar), 4, 31, 88, 90, 224ff
Chart parsing, 35, 37, 127, 138, 195, 197–198, 256

263

Text, Speech and Language Technology

1. H. Bunt and M. Tomita (eds.): *Recent Advances in Parsing Technology.* 1996
    ISBN 0-7923-4152-X
2. S. Young and G. Bloothooft (eds.): *Corpus-Based Methods in Language and Speech Processing.* 1997   ISBN 0-7923-4463-4
3. T. Dutoit: *An Introduction to Text-to-Speech Synthesis.* 1997   ISBN 0-7923-4498-7
4. L. Lebart, A. Salem and L. Berry: *Exploring Textual Data.* 1998
    ISBN 0-7923-4840-0
5. J. Carson-Berndsen, *Time Map Phonology.* 1998   ISBN 0-7923-4883-4
6. P. Saint-Dizier (ed.): *Predicative Forms in Natural Language and in Lexical Knowledge Bases.* 1999   ISBN 0-7923-5499-0
7. T. Strzalkowski (ed.): *Natural Language Information Retrieval.* 1999
    ISBN 0-7923-5685-3
8. J. Harrington and S. Cassiday: *Techniques in Speech Acoustics.* 1999
    ISBN 0-7923-5731-0
9. H. van Halteren (ed.): *Syntactic Wordclass Tagging.* 1999   ISBN 0-7923-5896-1
10. E. Viegas (ed.): *Breadth and Depth of Semantic Lexicons.* 1999 ISBN 0-7923-6039-7
11. S. Armstrong, K. Church, P. Isabelle, S. Nanzi, E. Tzoukermann and D. Yarowsky (eds.): *Natural Language Processing Using Very Large Corpora.* 1999
    ISBN 0-7923-6055-9
12. F. Van Eynde and D. Gibbon (eds.): *Lexicon Development for Speech and Language Processing.* 2000   ISBN 0-7923-6368-X; Pb: 07923-6369-8
13. J. Véronis (ed.): *Parallel Text Processing.* Alignment and Use of Translation Corpora. 2000   ISBN 0-7923-6546-1
14. M. Horne (ed.): *Prosody: Theory and Experiment.* Studies Presented to Gösta Bruce. 2000   ISBN 0-7923-6579-8
15. A. Botinis (ed.): *Intonation.* Analysis, Modelling and Technology. 2000
    ISBN 0-7923-6605-0
16. H. Bunt and A. Nijholt (eds.): *Advances in Probabilistic and Other Parsing Technologies.* 2000   ISBN 0-7923-6616-6

KLUWER ACADEMIC PUBLISHERS – DORDRECHT / BOSTON / LONDON